Forty Years Catching Smugglers

Malcolm G Nelson

Dedication

"Forty Years Catching Smugglers" is dedicated to my lovely wife, Carol. Without her support and drive it may never have been written.

About the Author

Malcolm Nelson was born on the 7th of August 1946 in Hackney, London, and he was brought up in Loughton, Essex. His career in HM Customs and Excise was unique, in that he rose from the lowest rank Assistant Preventive Officer to Assistant Collector (almost the highest), without ever moving away from the operational arm of the Department. In HM Customs and Excise promotion was invariably accompanied with or obtained by a move to Headquarters or VAT. Somehow he avoided this. He has been married to Carol for 40 years and he has three children, Mark, James, and Claire. He has one grandchild, Neoma Mary, and he now lives near Reading with his wife Carol, and their border collie, Daisy. He supports Spurs and Essex County Cricket Club, and drinks rum. This is his first book.

Contents

1. Introduction

It was my dad's fault. As an ex Royal Navy Petty Officer of Signals Walter George Nelson was absolutely certain that the job of the Customs Officer was the best and most prestigious job on the dockside and was the career he had always wanted for himself. And as he was the person I respected more than anyone else in the world, except maybe Spurs manager Bill Nicholson, he had planted a seed that was to grow and grow until it reached fruition. Also, at a more down to earth level, he was the person who saw the recruitment advert in the Daily Telegraph, which is probably more relevant.

I duly sent in my application, I was fed up with Westminster Bank and their computers, so a change was on the horizon anyway. Of course I heard nothing. Not even an acknowledgement. Then one day, just when I had come to the conclusion that I never would hear anything, I received a terse letter informing me that I had to attend an office in Saville Row in three days time for an interview. It seemed very strange, I hear nothing for three months, then I'm given three days notice to attend an interview at an address world famous for high quality mens suits.

However I duly attended, answered a whole series of seemingly meaningless questions such as:-

"Which newspaper do you read?"

"Why do you want to be a Waterguard Officer?"

I had by this time established that the Waterguard was the uniform Branch of HM Customs and Excise.

To the second question I replied,

"To catch smugglers"

It seemed that, to quote Basil Fawlty, I was stating the bleeding obvious. But I really couldn't think why else a person would want to be a Customs Officer.

I came away convinced I had got the job and was therefore a bit disappointed when I received a letter saying that I was borderline case and I would hear more in due course. I put it all down to the fact that I had dropped egg yolk all down my dark red waistcoat before the interview, and as I had the habit of walking in such a way that I could show off the waistcoat, which I considered to be the height of fashion, they couldn't have failed to see it.

However they did eventually see sense and decided that even if all I wanted to do was catch smugglers and even if couldn't eat a fried egg without getting it all down myself, I was worth a place in Her Majesty's Customs and Excise Waterguard, I would be based in London Port and I would start on Monday the 3rd of March 1966

So just in case I never said it before. Thanks dad for nudging me into a career which, although not well paid, was full of interest and excitement, was never dull, brought me into contact with all types of interesting people, and gave me a sense of purpose.

**

Perhaps a little bit about me might be appropriate here. I was born on the 7th of August 1946, in Hackney, London. My dad, Walter George mentioned above, my mum Marjorie Alice, the brains of the family, and my sister Valerie Jennifer. I was brought up in Loughton, Essex; the family moved there in 1948 and were still there when my career began, although Valerie was by then Valerie Morgan, having married Tommy in

1964. That's it really. I spent two years at a mixed sex Boarding School in Sonning Common, Berkshire, and five years at William Morris, Technical High School, in Walthamstow. I passed three A levels and eight O levels. I am now married with three children, more of them later, and a dog called Daisy. I am a Spurs and Essex County Cricket supporter, and I love dogs.

**

2. Welcome to the Waterguard

On Monday the 3rd of March 1966 I Malcolm George Nelson, son of the aforementioned Walter George, and Marjorie Alice, and younger brother of Valerie Jennifer Nelson, walked down the gangway on to the Harpy Waterguard Station in the Pool of London. The Harpy was a floating office at the end of a pontoon in the River Thames just east of London Bridge and directly in front of the Custom House on the north bank. The lovely smell of old fish greeted me wafting across from the old Billingsgate fish market. It was grey, it was cold and windy, it was an inauspicious beginning to 40 years of excitement, comedy, tragedy, of unusual happenings, of working with and meeting amazing people, and despite of everything a sense of achievement. Actually it was 39 years and 7 months but that didn't have quite the same ring to it.

As I walked into the downstairs office I was surrounded by men in dark blue uniforms with gold braid, I was greeted, sat down, and given a mug of tea by the Harpy "Watcher". Now once upon a time the "Watcher" had a role that actually helped to protect the Revenue. However, by the time I arrived their main role was to keep morale high by providing copious amounts of tea and advice. The advice normally sounded something like,

"I fink you've probably ad enough son don't you" And they were usually right.

I then spotted another chap in civvies who looked about as lost I did. I soon established that this was Francis Alan Kiy, better known as Alby, and that this was his first day as well. Alby and I were to become lifelong friends. There were lots of handshakes, lots of introductions, lots of old timers shaking their heads in a very knowing way, and lots and lots of warm welcomes. Then as if by magic suddenly Alby and I were alone. One minute we were in the middle of a scene that resembled a Royal Navy reunion the next we were sitting there totally alone, even the Watcher had disappeared. We had just witnessed the tidal effect and it was something that would dominate our working lives until we moved away from the Thames. Ships were arriving, departing, or needing Customs attendance. And when they could move, or we could get alongside was dictated by the tides. Ergo the working lives and sometimes the social lives of the Waterguard Officers were dictated to by the tides.

Anyway, there was Alby and I, alone. We then did just what any young men would do when left to their own devices. No not that. There were no young women around. There was nothing to eat or drink, so we talked about football. And miracle of miracles discovered we were, and sadly still are, Spurs supporters. Having made this most important discovery we were about to explore it further when something happened that was to have a profound effect on the rest of my career. As we sat there an oldish chap; probably my age as I write, so not too old; dressed in civvies came half way down the stairs and barked:-

"Where's the thermometer"

No introduction, no hello who are you etc. Just,

"Where's the thermometer?"

To which we both just looked up and said

"Don't know".

A few moments later the same oldish chap reappeared, came all the way down the stairs stamped across the floor of the office and consulted the thermometer, which was on the wall opposite us. He then turned round, looked at us, and barked at us again. I later found out barking was his only means of communication. It was said, although not to his face, that as a child he lived next door to Battersea Dogs Home.

"Fine f****** Customs Officers you're going to make .Can't even see the f****** thermometer on the f******* wall"!

We discovered later that we had just met Pat Kiley, Chief Preventive Officer, Lord and master of the Harpy, and later to become OBE, and I had just learnt several important lessons. Firstly, it was never good enough to simply not know. Customs Officers especially those in the Waterguard are expected to have enquiring minds and if they don't know then they should do their utmost to find out, or at least pretend they are. Secondly I would have to cope with a range of communication techniques far beyond those that I had previously encountered at Westminster Bank and before that at school. Lastly never trust someone in a suit but also never underestimate them. I had arrived in a Service that was still based very much on how the armed forces operated.

Years later I would spend a whole week on Induction courses, as a trainer, trying to get these messages across to my trainees. Pat Kiley was obviously a man ahead of his time. I also wondered if he actually did this on purpose or was he just a naturally bad tempered forerunner to Victor Meldew, who enjoyed chewing up and spitting out new entrants.

Hallo Malcolm wake up, smell the coffee, and welcome to the Waterguard section of Her Majesty's Customs and Excise.

After this began a period of furious activity because we were off to the Waterguard Training Centre at Southend on March the 24th, only three weeks away. First we, me and Alby, were off to Woolwich Arsenal where we were issued with a hairy uniform which we were reliably informed were surplus Midshipman uniforms left over from World War Two. They were without doubt the most uncomfortable items of clothing I have ever had the misfortune to wear. It was then off to the Appointers Office to get my staff number, 45279, a number that would stay with me for forty years. Explanations about shift pay, overtime, rosters, fixed stations; when you were senior enough you actually got to stay in the same place for a whole year; training programmes , arranging digs in Southend. What I could claim and what I couldn't claim, just like MP's, but without their discretion. It really was information overload. But no doubt it meant someone could tick various boxes and show it had all been done, should they ever be asked. Throughout all of this Alby and I were joined at the hip it really was a case of the blind leading the blind. We found that we lived relatively close to each other me in Loughton, Essex and him just up the road in Harlow.

Then later on, on the 18th of March I was issued with my Commission. This quaintly worded document issued to me by one of the Board of Commissioners, Dorothy Johnstone, was to give me almost unlimited powers in certain situations. It's a document of about 350 words without a full stop or a comma. In one sentence it allowed me to look anywhere, go anywhere, open anything, search anyone, and remove anything, by force if necessary. All this power and not a single means of being able to prove that I really was the person referred to on the Commission, no picture, address, fingerprint, nothing. Amazingly these documents were treated with the utmost reverence by all and sundry within Ports, Airports, and their surrounding areas. Even the London dockers who had almost no respect for anyone, not even the people who paid their wages, bowed to the power of the Commission.

Amidst this blur of activity one morning stands out amongst the rest. This was the first time I stepped on board a ship. The M/V Jaroslav Dubrowski was moored alongside Butlers Wharf south of the river adjacent to Tower Bridge. A PO (Preventive Officer) Bob Curtis without his usual APO was brave enough to take me on for the day. This for me was a marvellous experience but sadly it stands out for one reason and one reason only. Now in most stories it would be that the hero, that's me, did something fantastic and revealed all sorts of innate skills that showed the whole world that HM Customs had acquired its latest super hero. However the one thing I took away from that experience was, never to ask for a ham sandwich on a Polish ship that has a Chief Steward with a complete set of steel teeth. I was offered a beer, which was nice; I was then asked if I would like a ham sandwich. Being nineteen years old, and permanently hungry I ignored the look of horror on Bobs face and accepted. I was then presented with the most delicious looking sandwich, freshly baked crusty bread absolutely brimming with carved gammon. Half an hour later I still had at least three quarters of the sandwich on my plate plus a mouthful of barely cooked meat that simply refused to go away no matter how much I chewed. Now the one thing that Bob had impressed on me before we boarded the ship was that in no circumstances do we ever upset the Chief Steward. Without him on our side getting our job done is almost impossible, plus we rely on them to provide refreshments when necessary. So I was left to chew and chew. Every now and then I stopped to give the impression that I had swallowed what was in my mouth. Then I took another minute mouthful of sandwich and carried on chewing again. My jaws were aching, I was sweating and I was desperately wondering just how I could get out of my predicament. It was like a celebrity game show except that I wasn't a celebrity and it wasn't a show. Eventually, after looking like he was going to burst with suppressed laughter, Bob took pity on me and found an excuse to get the Chief Steward out of the cabin and I promptly hid the remains of my sandwich in my boarding case.

Lesson learnt; beware of Poles, with steel teeth, bearing gifts; especially ham sandwiches.

I also realised that I had moved into a community that believed in learning by your mistakes, it was a theme that was to repeat itself again and again. Or was it that there was a sadistic pleasure in seeing people like me squirm! Mmmm well its forty years later and the jury's still out on that one.

**

So off to Southend and the Waterguard Training Centre. The next eight weeks were yet another blur although to be fair a lot of this was self inflicted. Forty young men, there were no women officers in those days, money on the hip and no responsibilities.

I took possession of my first car the day I drove down to Southend. An Austin A40, light grey with a black roof, GOO 300, with no synchromesh when you changed down into second gear. Not a lot of fun driving down the Southend arterial road in the middle of the rush hour with driving snow, yes snow on the 24th of March, coming straight at me, no global warming in those days. It was two days after I had passed my test and the first time I had driven on my own. Looking back I never thought about it at the time but my mum must have been so worried, especially with me being the first person in the family to own a car.

To all to whom these Presents shall come
Greeting.

We the Commissioners of Her Majesty's Customs and Excise pursuant to the powers in that behalf vested in us *Do Hereby* appoint

———— Malcolm George NELSON ————

to be an *Officer* of Customs and Excise and to be employed on any Duty or Service which We may from time to time direct and approve at any Port or Place within the United Kingdom with full power and authority to do and perform all such matters and things as are by any Act of Parliament in force relating to the Revenues of Customs or Excise or any other matter assigned to the Commissioners of Customs and Excise directed or authorised to be done and performed by an Officer of Customs and Excise and to enforce all laws, regulations, penalties and forfeitures as directed by the Commissioners of Her Majesty's Customs and Excise by virtue whereof he hath power to board any ship, aircraft or vehicle and remain therein and rummage and search any part thereof and also with a Writ of Assistance to enter any building or place where there are reasonable grounds to suspect that anything liable to forfeiture under the Customs or Excise Acts is kept or concealed at any time and if at night in the company of a constable and to search for seize and detain or remove any such thing and so far as is reasonably necessary for the purpose of such entry search seizure detention or removal to break upon any door, window or container and force and remove any other impediment or obstruction in all which premises he is to proceed in such manner as the law directs hereby praying and requiring all and every Constable and member of Her Majesty's armed forces or coastguard and all others whom it may concern to be aiding and assisting to him in all things as becometh the said ———— Malcolm George NELSON ———— to observe and obey all such orders instructions and directions as he hath received and shall from time to time receive from the said Commissioners and to hold the office to which he is hereby appointed during the pleasure of the said Commissioners.

In Witness whereof I the undersigned being one of the Commissioners of Her Majesty's Customs and Excise have hereunto set my Hand and Seal at King's Beam House, London, this ——— eighteenth day of March in the year of

The Royal Commission issued to Malcolm George Nelson in March 1966. Not a single full stop or comma.

Anyway back to Southend. Alby and I were in the same digs with Mr and Mrs Thompson and their daughter Carol and their son. There was one other trainee Stevie Goodrich, all 6 foot 11 inches of him from somewhere west, probably Plymouth. Mrs T was smashing; her one aim in life seemed to be to see just how much we could eat. Unfortunately Mr T was the other side of the coin; he always looked like he had the cares of the world on his shoulders. I suppose in hindsight it can't have been a lot of fun for him, a pretty young daughter rapidly approaching the wrong age and three young men in the house who had already reached it.

Looking back the most significant events during the two months at Southend didn't actually involve anything I actually learnt about how to be a Waterguard Officer. Although Bill Waddington, the man in charge, Jack Jolly, his sidekick and Ted Young my trainer, did their best to instil the technicalities of "timber deck cargoes", "oil in double bottom tanks", and how to fill out the "Blue Book" of the good ship" Halizones". No trainee at the Waterguard Training Centre will ever forget the SS Halizones, I still have her Blue Book as proof that I was actually listening at some point during the two months. I wasn't the most brilliant student as I wasn't really interested in what I saw as the boring part of the job.

The "events" I mentioned earlier were actually two people I met there, who along with Alby were to stay with me all through my career and as I say, beyond. Sadly one of them, Bob, was to have his career cut tragically short, but more of that later. And the other Joe, ended up at Heathrow with me, revolutionising the way we trained new entrants.

Bob was Bob Highstead, six foot three inches tall, all the way from East Ham, and looking like a blond Viking. He, Alby and I hit it off straightaway. We were three Londoners who basically spoke the same language and had the same sense of humour. Bob was a West Ham supporter but apart from that he was a top guy. The three of us would go to Dover together, live in a caravan, play football together, work on rummage crews together and drink together. We were all promoted on the same list. At different times our lives, working and private went in different directions but we always knew what one another were doing. Like elephants in the jungle we couldn't always see each other but we knew what the others were up to.

Joe was Joe Baird, a Scot from a small village somewhere north of Edinburgh; he was based at that time in Hull, and had the driest sense of humour I ever came up against. When people describe Scots, if they, the Scots that is, are at all intelligent, they always seem tempted to describe them as "canny". Now I'm not sure if Joe was canny, but he certainly had the ability to retain an amazing amount of minutia. Years later this skill was to prove invaluable when we teamed up as trainers at Heathrow.

**

The one thing I did learn was courtesy of the top entrant of our intake. Jim Herculeson from Boston, Lincolnshire, was undoubtedly bright, and he was as I have said the top man on the course. He was a really good bloke with a great sense of humour. Sadly Jim's common sense didn't match his ability.

One night at the Penny Farthing Club in Leigh-on- Sea Jim nearly succeeded in getting a real beating, and what made it worse he nearly took a few of us down with him.

Jim had decided that he fancied a particular girl and was having a good drink to summon up the courage to ask her to dance. Those of us from bigger towns than Boston had looked at the situation and decided it wasn't a good idea. The girl was with a big mixed crowd and one of the blokes was almost certainly with her. As I say those of us from bigger towns, and who knew the protocol from places like the Tottenham Royal and the Ilford Palais, knew that Jim going up and asking this girl to dance was going to go down like a lead balloon. If you did something like that at the Tottenham Royal it would probably precipitate a riot, and you'd end up learning to dance on one leg with one arm. Now although Southend wasn't Tottenham, the culture was much the same.

We tried to explain to Jim that the only girls that were available were those on their own or in twos. Any more than that and they were likely to be part of a "crowd". But he wasn't having it, he knew best. But to be fair to him he was cute enough to let us believe we had persuaded him. Then when our backs were turned he was off.

"Oh no, look at Jim" someone says.

There's Jim leaning towards the girl and gesticulating towards the dance floor.

The girl is shaking her head.

Jim doesn't give up. He asks again.

Three or four of us are half way across the floor by then.

A Neanderthal then gets between Jim and the girl and raises his fist in a gesture that obviously means, get lost. This would be a good point for Jim to take the hint, unfortunately the bravado that beers can bring is in control. Next thing Jim is raising his fist at the Neanderthal, this is not a good idea, whereupon about a dozen Neanderthal lookalikes are all shaking their fists at Jim.

Jim is unperturbed and turns towards them. At the same moment we reach Jim and get between him and the Iron Age group and we drag him off. The crowd are still looking ugly Bob manages to persuade the cavemen that Jim is a bit simple and isn't accountable for his actions. They still look quite threatening but Bob is tall and talks their language.

"He's from the country" he explains.

"He doesn't understand". I add.

Years later when a famous hotelier had made the saying famous we might have said.

"He's from Barcelona"

Eventually the grunts emanating from the cavemen subside and we retain our dignity, back away, and leave. Next day Jim is still blaming us for ruining his life by stopping him dancing with the girl of his dreams. But we're just happy to be all in one piece.

Confucius says.

"Intelligence is fine, but common sense and local knowledge count for a lot more when you're in the real world."

**

3. The Formative Years

DOVER

Nearing the end of the training course we were asked to volunteer to go to Dover for the summer. Now although we had been warned about the dangers of volunteering for places like Dover and Heathrow, Alby, Bob, and I decided to go.

"Never volunteer son" the old timers would mutter.

Firstly we had been told we would probably end up there anyway, and we reasoned that if we got there first we would have the pick of the accommodation, and we would know our way around before things became too hectic. We certainly hit the nail on the head as far as the accommodation was concerned and we settled into a large caravan next to the Plough Inn at Capel Le Ferne on the Folkestone Road. I'm not sure if we ever really managed to know our way around as Dover was like a madhouse from day one, right up until I finally left some time in November. But sure enough the vast majority of our course gradually trickled into town. Joe appeared sometime in June along with the rest of the Hull contingent; Dave Watson, who was a lovely footballer and was on Hull City's books at the time, and who I later had the pleasure of playing football with at Heathrow; Alan Ward, Martin Arnold, Andy Dinsdale, with Mike Teale in tow. Mike was famous for being able to drink more than anyone else on the course, but then as he trained so hard at it, it wasn't really surprising. Then the Welsh contingent arrived among them Gary Davis the Cardiff Town hooker, then the lads from Liverpool, quickly followed by the Scots. By the end of June we had almost a full compliment.

Now you will probably have gathered by now that nineteen years old Malcolm Nelson, previously a Westminster Bank employee, was on a pretty sharp learning curve. And the curve was about to become even sharper. Work wise Dover had everything, foot passengers at the Western Docks, car ferries at the Eastern Docks and Merchant ships in the harbour. Dover was where I learnt to climb a Jacob's ladder; you know the rope ladder with wooden rungs in between. It was always easier getting off than getting on, something to do with the refreshment we received on board. Also passenger carrying trains, the night train, where the passenger were segregated in a sealed off carriage, and we APO's stood guard making sure the cleared passengers didn't mix with the uncleared passengers while it was on its way to or from Victoria Station. This was always popular with the APO's because we were based in the Dining Car and we were fed for free. It remained popular even after we discovered that one of the chefs was the brother of Harry Roberts the Shepherds Bush murderer. The man who killed three policemen outside of Wormwood Scrubs.

As stated previously Dover was a madhouse even when we arrived in May, and the blur that seemed to have surrounded me ever since the 3rd of March continued. It has been suggested that some of this might have been alcohol induced, but I think most of it was due to the frenetic pace of life. Aged nineteen there just wasn't time to stand still and take a breather. Anyway I'll let you make your own mind on that one.

Despite the blur some incidents do stand out. On my very first day in the Eastern Docks, which was the end where the car ferries berthed, I was amazed to see the skeleton of a caravan in one of the inspection bays. There was the base on wheels, four perpendicular struts, and four connecting struts on top of them. On one side was the rest of the caravan in bits and on the other side there was about 50,000 cigars. Not only was this a most amazing sight to a mere rookie, when I spoke to the crew responsible it taught me a lesson that was to stay with me throughout my career and helped answer that often asked question.

"What makes a good Customs Officer"?

What had happened was that one of the crew went inside the caravan whilst one was doing the car and one was searching the baggage. The lad (APO) who went into the caravan found nothing, but he noticed that for the time of year it was remarkably hot in the caravan. He also noticed that there was no heating and the cooker hadn't been used. He had a quick word with the driver but that fine fellow quite naturally couldn't shed any light on the matter. The lad then had a word with his "guv", who agreed that the interior was unusually warm. This caused a further search of the caravan and during this second search it was noticed that some of the screws attaching the caravan lining to the frame were ever so slightly marked. They had obviously been unscrewed recently. On removing one of the panels cigars were found in the lining and the crew then systematically dismembered the caravan. The cause of the extra heat was thermal insulation using cigars instead of polystyrene. The cigars had acted as a form of insulation between the lining and the exterior of the caravan.

The lesson learnt was to always question the unusual. If something doesn't seem quite right check it out, it probably isn't.

The answer to the question "What makes a good Customs Officer"?

An enquiring mind! If something looks, or as in this case feels, a bit odd then don't be satisfied until you know why.

That APO who went into the caravan didn't think for a moment that his observation about the heat would lead to 50,000 cigars. But something in him wanted to know why it was so bloody hot!

**

One Saturday in the middle of that July I was working in the Baggage Hall at the Western Docks. This was the foot passenger end and Saturday afternoons looked like a re-inaction of the battle of the Little Bighorn. There were three enclaves of Customs Officers surrounded by a vast sea of passengers who were fighting their way towards the Customs Officers. Remember this was before Red and Green Channels were introduced and every passenger had to be spoken to by an Officer and asked if they had read the notice that informed them of their allowances. In the middle of this seething mass of humanity were the DSO, the Duty Senior Officer, who on this occasion was one Ossie Jones, and his runner, who on this occasion was one Malcolm Nelson, APO, that's me. It was the DSO's job to assess where the pressure was the greatest and to deploy his troops accordingly. And it was the job of the runner to tell the Officers in the enclaves just what the DSO wanted. Now as I say it was a hectic Saturday afternoon and Ossie was under pressure and he wasn't a happy man. One end of the Baggage Hall was completely gridlocked. Ossie was trying to figure how many Officers to move and from where to where, and every time he moved people the gridlock moved to another part of the hall. I know a moving gridlock is a contradiction in terms but I think you'll understand what I mean. He was glaring at his clipboard and at me with a ferocity that was making me remember those people who said never volunteer for anything.

Just when I thought it couldn't get any worse. It did.

An unsuspecting passenger, who had been seen by an Officer and had the chalk marks on his suitcase to prove it, was trying to find his way out.

He tugged Ossie's sleeve. Ossie froze and glared at the passenger;

"Which way to the trains?" asked the passenger?

"Just follow the arrows" said Ossie.

The passenger wasn't satisfied." Which way to the trains?" he asked again.

"Just follow the arrows", repeated an obviously exasperated Ossie.

"Well there aren't many arrows are there" commented the passenger.

Now the real issue with the Western End Baggage Hall was that there were too many arrows.

To the toilets.

To London.

To Canterbury.

To the Car Park.

To the Trains.

To the coach station.

To the Exit.

To the A2 or A20. No Motorways in 1966.

And so on and so on. Arrows everywhere.

Ossie stopped dead in his tracks. He's going to hit him I thought. He pulled himself up to his full height, and gave me his badge of office, that is, his beloved clipboard. I am now convinced he's going to hit him.

"Sir" he spat through clenched teeth."

The only place there were more f****** arrows, was the f****** Battle of Hastings"

He snatched his clipboard back from me giving me an extra glare as if to insinuate that I'd been somehow responsible for the whole affair and imperiously disappeared into the crowd, leaving behind an astonished passenger who was none the wiser and still didn't know which way to the trains.

Lesson learnt; The F word is normally inappropriate, even more so back in 1966, but when it is used with a Welsh accent and is delivered with such aplomb, it can be extremely funny to those looking on, and it does make one's point perfectly.

**

Now in Dover in those days the biggest source of seizures, a seizure being a smuggling offence where the goods are actually taken away from the offender, were Italians coming here to visit relatives who were resident in this country, or Italians who lived here and were returning from a short trip back to the homeland. It was easy enough to find the goods, normally spirits and wine, but getting them to admit why they hadn't declared them was an entirely different matter. No matter how detailed the questioning on the baggage bench had been.

The answer to the question; "So can you tell me why you didn't declare the brandy, grappa, wine "

Was invariably: "Mumma packa da bag".

It didn't matter how old the passenger was, what sex, how many times they'd travelled, how good or bad their English was, whether or not

"The only place there was more *!*!*** arrows was the *!*!*** Battle of Hastings"

they'd told you that they had packed the bag themselves, whether or not they knew their allowances and that goods like brandy were liable to duty. None of this mattered when the crunch question was put to them, it was always:

"Mumma packa da bag".

Now back in 1966 the Senior Officers were the adjudicating Officers and they decided if a case had been proven. That is, could it be proven that the passenger had failed to declare in order to evade the duty that was liable? If they did so decide then the choice of paying a Compromise Penalty or going before a Magistrate could be offered.

This changed three years later when the 1969 Finance Act introduced the Red/Green system of control. At the same time Section 6 of that Act introduced "Failure to declare in the proper manner" as an offence, albeit a lesser offence than the intent to defraud. So to put it in layman's terms before 1969 you had to get a smuggler to admit that they had done it to avoid paying the duty. Post 1969 you only had to prove that the goods had not been declared. So in 1966 we had the position where most of these cases were deemed not proven because the offender had not uttered those immortal words.

"It's a fair cop guv "

The rule was simple no cough (admission of guilt), no job (offence).

To put it mildly it was frustrating, to open a person's baggage and find up to 50 bottles of cheap Italian brandy. Then have to take the duty because all you could get him or her to say was:-

"Mumma packa da bag."

"Mumma packa da dormobile"

When I say 50 bottles this is a slight exaggeration. The most I ever seized was 46. I was working alongside one of the most famous of all seizing PO's at Dover, Gerry Vaughan. Gerry liked to present himself as someone who was a sandwich short of a picnic. He would wear his cap a slight angle and he always had a slightly soppy grin on his face. But once the passenger had made the mistake of thinking he would believe anything he was told, then his whole demeanour would change and he would pounce like a cat in uniform.

On this particular day I was approached by a family of six or seven coming from Italy by train. They were resident in this country and they actually lived in Waltham Abbey, which was quite close to my home in Loughton. In all they had about ten pieces of baggage. Gerry was hovering as I questioned them.

"Ask them again who packed the bags", he muttered. This I did, and various members of the group put their hands up.

"Ask them one by one if they know what's in the bags", he whispered out of the side of his mouth. Whilst smiling at the group with a sort of inane grin on his face. I had already asked, but I repeated my question. I was answered with a whole chorus of "si" and "yes", and lots of nods. I then searched the bags and on top of what they declared I found forty six bottles of brandy and grappa. I had them all lined up on the floor, and Gerry went through a very elaborate counting procedure. He then looked at the man who was obviously the leader of the group, and who spoke very good English. The expression on his face had completely changed; he now looked every inch the efficient Customs Officer

"Forty six bottles", he said.

"Si" said the Italian, then in the same breath started to say "Mumma.....", but Gerry cut him off mid sentence.

"Not on this occasion she didn't. She'd have to be Charles Atlas to lift this bloody lot".

None of the Italians admitted to anything. But because Gerry was involved the CPO, Freddy Smallwood, offered the leading Italian the option. He was only too pleased to pay a fine rather than go to court, even though it was three times the duty and he lost all the undeclared bottles.

My frustration was complete when one day working in the Car Hall in the Eastern Docks I pulled over a Dormobile with four young lads, even younger than I was at the time, travelling in it. The interior of the Dormobile had been gutted and the floor was covered with the mattresses that they were sleeping on. On removing these mattresses I found a total of 36 bottles of Champagne. On retrieving the bottles and lining them up on the baggage bench I looked at the driver and said:-

"Don't tell me, mumma packa da bag"

The driver shrugged looked me square in the eye and said:-

"No, mumma packa da Dormobile"

I had spent six months trying to get my questioning so tight that even "mumma packa da bag" wouldn't work" but on this occasion I had to admit defeat. Despite this I took away a realisation that only by being precise with my questioning and by giving the person I was dealing with every opportunity to declare would I be successful as a Waterguard Officer. It was a lesson that would result in me being one of the top two seizing officers in the country during the late seventies when I was working at Heathrow.

**

My time at Dover was drawing to a close, Bob had already returned to London; after doing his best to nip my less than promising career in the bud; so Alby and I moved into a flat in Castle Street. It was getting too cold.

How did Bob nearly get me sacked? Well I was the train APO one evening and Bob decided he would come along for the ride. He did this mainly because it meant a free meal and we APO's were always hungry and skint. When we arrived at Victoria the cleared passengers were put in their segregated carriage. I was put in charge; with strict instructions not to let out of my sight; of a San Raphael original painting. Valued at about £75,000, it had been on loan to the Tate and was on its way back to the Louvre. It was to be cleared by the agent in Dover. Bob and I took up residence in the restaurant car, leaving the painting in our carriage.

Eventually we were the only two people left in the carriage except for two young attractive American girls. We got chatting, as you do, and Bob, never one to take no for an answer, eventually persuaded them that we should all have a dance, yes a dance. So there we were as we pulled into Dover me and Bob dancing with two Americans, Bob singing because we didn't have any music, all thoughts of a San Raphael original completely out of my head. When as the train slowed, I spotted two Chief Preventive Officers, two not one, marching down the platform with a gentleman, who I later found out was the agent, and two representatives from the Louvre. Fortunately I could move pretty quickly in those days and I reached the compartment with the painting in it seconds before the Senior Officers. Even more fortunately the painting was still there and intact. Apart from some funny looks from the CPO's, probably wondering why I was out of breath after sitting still for an hour and a half, nothing was said. I was thanked by the men from the Louvre my diligence.

And Bob's response to my remonstrations later in the bar?

"You'd have thought of something to say. You always do".

**

When it became too cold Alby and I decided that home seemed like a good bet. We had a tremendous first floor flat in the centre of town, no heating bills, and no washing up , because if we left our door open one of the two old ladies who owned and lived in the house, would pop in and do it for us. Amazing how easy it is to forget to close your front door. But still, after six months, it was time to head back to the Smoke.

**

SHADWELL Station in London Docks

Back in London I was supernumerary, basically nowhere to call my base. So they did just what they always did with APO's with no home to call their own. They made them fourth hand on a three man Rummage Crew. A Rummage Crew being a team consisting of one Officer, and either two or three Assistant Preventive Officers. These crews or teams spent their time searching ships and were known by a variety of different names around the docks and wharves. The politest of which was the "Blackgang", this name coming from the fact that we spent most of our time in overalls, and we were normally extremely dirty.

The crew that were blessed with my presence was the one at the old "London Docks, based at Shadwell, and run by Eric Emblin, or Guvvie as he was affectionately known. The other two members of the crew were John Salter and Steve Currie and although we didn't set the world alight, at least not while I was there, we jogged along quite nicely. I learnt how to drink Crème de Menthe out of a half pint glass, thanks for that Guvvie. Also, thanks to the Cook/Steward on the M/V Avocet I learnt that stuffed hearts are a gastronomic delight not to be missed if the opportunity arises.

As I was really surplus to requirements I was often moved to work with one of the Preventive Officers to cover if another Officer was on holiday or sick. And strangely enough it was during one of these very brief spells that I made my first seizure on a ship. A bottle of Four Bells rum, concealed within a coiled rope. What made it even better was that my PO, Tony Grow, took charge of it and told me not to worry about the paper work, he would sort it out for me. I had already learnt by then that there were times when you just shut your mouth and accepted what your PO said. But strangely enough I never did see that seizure entered in the Station Record.

At this time I also had the great pleasure of working with, and playing football alongside, a PO by the name of Ken Hencher. Ken at the time was the captain of the London Port football team and had previously captained Millwall Athletic in the old Division Three (South) of the Football League. Although now in his late forties he was still a formidable player, he was a stopper centre half in the true meaning of the word. And if he couldn't stop them, then for sure he would see how fast they could limp. But Ken was a gentleman and he would sit at the back and direct our efforts. Then when necessary, at corners, free kicks, penalties, we would roll him forward like a great gun in the Spanish Civil War. He could despatch a penalty with a calm ferocity that England could well have used in several World Cup campaigns. Kens great claim to fame, or maybe notoriety, was that in the early fifties he was once caught on camera leading Millwall out at Fratton Park, Portsmouth, at 3 o'clock on a Saturday afternoon. The problem was that he should have been on an 8 to 4 shift somewhere in the Port of London. And unluckily for Ken the picture was splashed all over the Sunday newspapers. He was apparently called before the Higher Waterguard Superintendent and asked to explain, I've no idea what his explanation was but it didn't seem to affect his career at all.

I also had the pleasure of knowing one of the genuine reasons why Concord was delayed by more than six months. At the time you couldn't open a newspaper without reading about this fantastic new supersonic jet that we were manufacturing along with our French brothers. The Russians had dropped out of the race and so had the Americans. The superstructure was being assembled near Bristol and the engines were being put together in Bordeaux and then shipped over here to be put together with the body of the aircraft. Then calamity; the inaugural test flight was put back six months. Rumour was rife. The engine was too big; it wasn't powerful enough, the Trade Unions were demanding more money; it was a health hazard that couldn't be accepted. The truth was a lot closer to home. The first prototype engine was shipped from Bordeaux to London on the M/V Heron, of the General Steam Navigation line. It arrived safely enough. But nobody had informed the dockers in London Docks that the chocks that were holding it in place had to be removed in a specific sequence. They simply knocked them away starting at one end and working their way down the hold, continued knocking them out until they reached the point where it was completely unbalanced. At this point the engine simply toppled over and fell into the bottom of the hold. It's a wonder it didn't go straight through the hull and into the dock. The fine upstanding British dockers of course blamed the French dockers for loading it incorrectly. The French blamed the British. The British threatened to go on strike if they didn't get their bonus even though they had just set the whole project back six months. And in the end it was all hushed up and blamed on a design fault. It was a bad day for the Shadwell dockers, especially as I rounded it off by seizing six cases of wine that they had stolen from the cargo and re-located into the forepeak. Guvvie decided not to make matters worse by interviewing the gang that were working in that part of the hold. He felt that one potential strike was enough for one day. So we just seized the goods. Still everyone was happy; the rewards on wine were particularly high despite the low duty on it. It was at the time my biggest seizure off of a ship.

My short time at Shadwell was brought to a close after a few months but on my last day on duty, we had the pleasure of a visit by a full blown member of the Board of Customs and Excise. Fireman Billy Blunt; so called because he was a part time Fireman and he kept his fireman's helmet on his desk; the Chief Preventive Officer (CPO), was in a flap because he knew he had a few old timers who might say anything if given the right provocation, and how right he was. There we were all lined up in our number ones (smartest uniforms). The Member of the Board was making his way along the line making polite conversation with each member of the staff.

He spoke to the grizzly old PO who was stood next to me, Bob Greenman, exchanged a few pleasantries, then made his one big mistake. He shook Bob's hand and said.

"So everything's fine is it?"

He had just turned away and was looking directly at me when Bob said;

"No it's not. Every time I want a p*** I get my f****** b****s frozen off".

The Member of the Board had this fixed grin frozen on his face, he was still staring straight at me, Fireman Bill had gone puce, and I would have liked to have been swallowed up.

Fireman Bill interceded:-

"We've got an outside toilet". In later years a certain Sybil Fawlty with her "He's from Barcelona" reminded me very much of Bill Blunt on that day.

The Member of the Board, it sounds like a pop group doesn't it, regained his composure, thanked Bob for his comments, instructed one of his sidekicks to make a note, and walked straight passed me. But Bob Greenman knew what he was doing. Six months later when I was visiting Shadwell I noticed a nice new inside toilet had been constructed, which showed the power of going straight to the men at the top. Sadly it also meant the men at the top didn't have a clue what was going on, because six months later Shadwell was closed ,as the London Docks no longer had enough ships to warrant a separate Customs Station of its' own.

**

WEST INDIA DOCK

Next stop the Isle of Dogs, West India Docks. This is where I arrived in what I always felt was my spiritual home while I worked in London Port. Almost from day one West India Dock suited me and for some reason I suited West India dock. The PO's and APO's were senior enough to know their job without being so senior that they had lost all interest, or so senior they couldn't be bothered with junior APOs. The ships were big enough but not so big that you felt intimidated by them, like the ships in King George the 5th and Victoria Docks, the Royals as they were known colloquially. Bigger than the little toshers at Dagenham and at the Harpy but not too big. The only other place there was left to go now that Shadwell was gone was Surrey Docks, but they were South of the river and being a North Londoner they never really appealed. North Londoners just don't do South London.

And it was busy, Ben Line boats, Harrison Line ships, City boats, Strick and Ellerman Line, the Monte boats from the Canaries, Fred Olsen cruisers, and various other miscellaneous ships from all over the world. The dockers hadn't managed to get their stranglehold on the West in 1967, but sadly by the time I left the Port in 1971, their restrictive practices had. It was amazing how a ship would have discharged 90% if it's cargo by the Wednesday. Yet somehow come Friday evening there would be just enough left in the hold to mean the dockers had to return on the Saturday. On double time of course.

Perhaps at this point I should explain what the work in London Port consisted of for an APO. In the main, no pun intended, there was rummage, and I have already explained this in my paragraph about London Docks. Secondly there were Boarding duties. This referred to the job of going on board ships and dealing with all the control procedures. The cargo, the duty free stores, clearing the crew, the health procedures, deck cargoes, making sure they had health clearance making sure their papers were in order, and anything else that needed an official seal of approval. When I say seal of approval I mean it. Every PO, not APOs we were far too low for that, had his own seal. I still have mine that received after I was promoted. Seal number 1398. Now on the Stations where there were only larger ships these control procedures were managed by two PO's. But on the smaller ships that tended to moor on wharves which were sited actually on the Thames, or up one of the many creeks, they were managed by a PO and an APO. West India Dock Station also included the East India Dock car patrol and this was a PO/APO team, normally with the APO as the driver. And we covered the all of the wharves on the Isle of Dogs and down river as far Tate and Lyles at Silvertown, including the old East India Dock and Bow

Creek. If an APO didn't want to do rummage year in year out, West India was one of the best Stations in the Port because of the variety of work, on many of the Stations there was no Boarding work for APOs.

When I arrived at the West the CPO was one Vic Roberts ex captain of the British Lions Rugby team, he was larger than life, and twice as interesting. He set the tone for West India Dock. He worked hard and played hard. He had the ability to be drinking with you one minute in "The Gun", and buying his round, and then giving you the most almighty dressing down the next. It's a great skill, and one that I tried desperately hard to emulate later on my career. Vic and I would end up together at Heathrow where we worked very closely together for a time, negotiating a lost baggage warehouse for British Airways. It was a different world, a million miles away from our time at the West.

When I first arrived I was put straight on the car patrol with a PO called Dennis Fowler. Dennis was a gentleman and a very modern thinker. I was allowed to call him Mr Fowler in public instead of the more formal "Sir", that most of the PO's insisted on. And I was allowed to call him Dennis in private instead of Mr Fowler as with the others. Now Dennis took my education very seriously, and he was determined that I would become the complete APO. However he had grave misgivings about my dislike of gin, and he set about changing that dislike with the same fervour that he went about the rest of my education. To the reader it may seem strange that my likes or dislikes would worry my revered PO, but Dennis couldn't see me as the finished article unless I was able to say yes to whatever was offered when we went on board ship.

"No real Customs Officer would decline a drink just because he didn't like it" he said. We were scheduled for a week of nights, that's six nights, and Dennis drew up his cunning plan. On the first night Dennis arrived fully laden with several bottles of gin and several more bottles of bitter lemon. It was bitter lemon or lime in those days, gin and tonic was yet to be seen. On the first night after we had finished our patrols he plied me with a large glass of bitter lemon with a very small shot of gin. Then throughout the week he gradually upped the amount of gin and reduced the amount of bitter lemon. By the end of the week not only did I like it, but I could match my mum glass for glass. And she was able to drink her "special water in the fridge"; as the grandchildren were told when they came along; until she was eighty eight.

However not only did Dennis teach me to drink gin, he taught me something of much greater import, although I'm not sure he would see it this way round. Whenever we boarded a vessel, as soon as we had finished the paperwork, which mainly consisted of preparing the "Blue Book" with all the ships relevant details, and we had cleared the crew, he would encourage me to do some "surface" rummage. By surface rummage, we meant rummaging without getting your hands dirty, not like the blackgang style of rummage. Now on one occasion I was doing this when I came upon 3,000 Marlboro cigarettes, under the bottom drawer in what appeared to be an admin office. The ships duty free stores were under seal and the C142 (Crew Declaration) showed no amount of 3,000 cigarettes. Dennis was delighted but not half as much as I was. It quickly transpired that the cabin I had found the ciggies in was the Captains day office and he alone had free access to it. Now the ship was moored at Tate and Lyles, Silvertown, and had just traversed the Atlantic bringing sugar from the Caribbean. So although the captain wouldn't have been seen as demi-god, as he would if on board ships like the Titanic, he would have been held in some esteem, and he had to be handled accordingly. On the other hand he might not have been a demi-god but he was obviously a lot better at missing icebergs.

Anyway back to the plot. The captain's attitude was. "Surely you must realise that as the captain of a vessel this size I wouldn't lower myself to smuggling cigarettes"

And this would have been accepted by the vast majority of PO's, especially the ex servicemen, but not by Dennis. The captain was very vague and evasive but eventually Dennis decided he had enough evidence and offered the choice of going before a Magistrate or paying a Compromise Penalty. I was amazed, he immediately agreed to pay the fine, and I could tell by the relief on his face that the whole charade had been a bluff. His guilt was confirmed by the Chief Steward who told us he was the only person on board who smoked that particular type of Marlboro. I think they were menthol tipped, which were quite unusual back then.

From this incident I realised that rank and position meant nothing when it came to smuggling. It was an important lesson, not only on board ship, but when I reached Heathrow. I learnt not to be intimidated by whoever I was dealing with. I was lucky later on to work for eighteen months with Danny Buckle , PO, who not only wasn't intimidated, he loved the cut and thrust with people who thought they could pull rank. I treated Captains, Chief Stewards, Members of Parliament, famous comedians, even men of the cloth, with the same amount of suspicion. I was dealing with a "Lady" later on in my career. She was trying to persuade me the fur coat she was wearing was bought in this country, when she used the captain's words almost exactly, she said:-

"Surely you must realise that I am a lady (this was obviously the inspiration for Little Britain), I wouldn't lower myself to smuggling" Actually she might have said lying rather than smuggling. But John Liggett the Senior Officer, we'd lost CPO's by then, hardly paused for breath when he offered her the same option as Dennis had all those years before. And she accepted with the same alacrity as the captain had. I can still hear John muttering in his Scouse accent:-

"Just because they live in a bloody castle they think they can do what they like". And she did, live in a castle that is.

**

Then a few weeks later just as I was getting really comfortable, and thinking that perhaps I would stay at the West. The Office PO, Bob Maddox called me into his office and told me I was on the road again off to Dagenham Dock, Sammy Williams Wharf.

**

DAGENHAM DOCK/SAMMY WILLIAMS WHARF

Now Dagenham was good in many ways. I could drive there from home in Loughton where I still lived with my mum and dad, plus Bob and Alby were there. When I had returned to London it had seemed very strange not working with the two of them, especially Alby as we'd been together in our working life and socially, virtually every day since our arrival on March 3.

Dagenham was also good as I met a chap by the name of Keith Warner, Whirly, to his friends. Keith and I were to become very close friends and indeed despite not seeing one another for a number of years we still are. Keith lived in Ilford so he was on the route home for Alby and me. Because of this happy coincidence we not only worked together, we socialised and travelled together.

However I wasn't there long before I was sent off to Southend Airport for a month. This wasn't a happy time. There were too many people with their fingers in too many pies. It was all a bit dark for me. Then back to Dagenham. Sometimes on Boarding sometimes on rummage with Bob and Alby, or Bob and Keith. The PO in charge of the Rummage Crew was Eric Leeks; an interesting sort of chap known as "Lucky Leeky" because he had once fallen between the ship he was stepping off of, and the wharf. And instead of killing himself like most people do, he went straight down, didn't touch the sides, came up again, right next to a ladder and he still had his boarding case in his hand. The only thing he had to report himself for was losing his cap.

Eric loved nicknames. Bob became "Shirley shoe trees", because he once brought in some shoe supports. Alby was Alby, because he was Alby. Keith became "Whirly", and this is where I acquired the undeserved "Alky" label. The reader will understand that this was purely and simply because it rhymed with Malky. He was a great joker and loved a laugh, unless the laugh was against Eric. On one occasion we were on our way to the Isle of Grain to rummage a tanker. Bob was driving the Zephyr, Eric was next to him and Alby and I were in the back. As you approached the Isle of Grain there was a long straight road with a hump back bridge at the end of it and Eric always had a moan about how fast we went over this bridge. So we decided to wind him up. The Zephyr had adjustable steering so you could change the angle of the steering wheel. Eric, who never drove, wasn't aware of this. So we agreed that Bob would go as fast as he could without Eric telling him to slow down. Then when we bumped over the bridge Bob would flick the switch that released the steering column and pretend the steering had failed. At the same time Alby and I in the back would throw ourselves about and cause a general furore to make it seem more real. So plan A was put into action, we hit the bridge, the Zephyr bounced, Eric was just about to remonstrate with Bob when Bob hit the switch. Whereupon the steering column became loose and Bob shook it as much as he could without losing control.

"The steerings' gone, the steerings' gone." He was very convincing.

Alby and I were throwing ourselves like demented dervishes in the back.

Eric went white as a sheet and swore at the top of his voice, he obviously thought the steering had failed and we were about to crash. Bob promptly put the steering back to normal and the three of us fell about laughing.

Now this had seemed like a really good scheme when we planned it, a chance to put one over on Lucky Leeky. What we hadn't allowed for was Eric's total lack of a sense of humour when he was the target of the joke. For the next week he worked us and worked us and worked us. No drinks on board, no early aways, no extended lunches, no late starts.

As usual Leeky had the last laugh.

**

LUTON AIRPORT

Then it was to Luton Airport for another months Detached Duty. For a young single bloke living away from home Luton was paradise. The work was pretty mundane, and it was my first experience of air passengers, but the social life was magnificent. For a start 90% of the people who worked at Luton were young and female, and mostly attractive.

For the first time since I'd been old enough to be interested the odds were in my favour. Added to that I was only there for four weeks and I was on the high rate Detached Duty allowance for those four weeks. So I had plenty of money in my pocket.

What little I did learn about air passenger work was around profiles, even in those days we had profiles, we might not have called them that but that's what they were. For instance it was a recognised fact that a man in his twenties or thirties coming through the controls wearing a sombrero would be carrying extra bottles of spirits in his baggage. This profile turned out to be true on nine out of ten occasions. Consequently every sombrero wearer was stopped. As you can imagine there was pandemonium the day a man came through wearing an enormous sombrero with a small sombrero perched on top of it.

As I say the social life was hectic and often very complicated. At one time I was dating a girl, let's call her Annie, whose regular boyfriend was the captain of Luton Town FC, let's call him Jimmie. One Saturday all three of us ended up at a party together and I, realising that my evening wasn't going to be everything I would have wished, decided to have a good drink instead of doing the sensible thing and going up the pub. After a few hours the alcohol took effect and I decided I had to lie down. I found an empty bed, crawled under the eiderdown, and quickly became unconscious. The next thing I knew there was Jimmie jumping up and down in front of me doing a highland fling on his bonnet, he was very Scottish, he was also absolutely speechless with rage. I looked at him for a few moments decided it was nothing to do with me, rolled over and went back to sleep. When I woke up the next morning I thought it must have been a dream until I looked on the floor and saw Jimmie's bonnet, that's his hat, lying on the floor all trampled upon where he had jumped up and down.

Later that day Annie called me to explain and apologise. Apparently she had decided at some point that she also needed to sleep so she had managed to get under the covers on the same bed as I was on, which probably wasn't a good idea. Jimmie had walked in and found us apparently in bed together. Fortunately Annie was sober enough to point out to him that she was in the bed and I was under the eiderdown, and we were both fully dressed. Jimmie calmed down and

The author with Davey Jug, alias Dave Hewer, in the Luton Airport Boarding Office.

Dave went on the head up the Section that controlled the Cutters.

decided not to remove my head from my body, for which I am eternally grateful. He never actually spoke to me again so I'm not sure if he really believed Annie, but they eventually got married so I suppose he must have.

Then the month was up and it was back to Dagenham Dock. Then it was off to the West and so on and so on.

**

DAGENHAM DOCK

That Christmas I was at Dagenham and somehow or other I ended up doing Christmas Day. It was the only Christmas Day I ever worked in my whole time with H M Customs. The one I did work was only remarkable in that it ended with me having my PO's front door slammed in my face by his wife.

I picked up Vic Ward, who was the Office PO but who had volunteered for Christmas Day, from his house in Upminster at about seven thirty. It wasn't far out of my way and Vic didn't drive. His wife was pleased to see me and thanked me for giving Vic a lift, and reminded me that his dinner was planned for three o'clock. So far so good. When we reached the office it went downhill rapidly. We had three ships that had just arrived on the tide. Now Vic was a smashing bloke and he was a real gent. But he didn't get to go on ships very often and when he did he liked to make the most of the opportunity. Three fresh ships meant we were going to receive a lot of Christmas Day hospitality. By the time we had finished the second ship Vic was feeling so unwell that he felt the need to sit where he was and continue with his course of "medicine"! So I went and boarded the third ship on my own. When I returned to pick up Vic he was feeling so unwell; probably all that "medicine"; that he wanted to stay on board and have dinner with the captain and his wife. I managed to persuade him otherwise got him off the ship, back in the car, and back to the office. It wasn't easy because the "medicine" obviously hadn't worked and his legs had gone all floppy. This had taken a lot longer than it should have and by the time we left the office we were already running late for his three o'clock dinner. However as we neared the outskirts of Upminster Vic insisted on getting out of the car and popping into his local to wish the landlord a happy Christmas. As a result by the time I finally escorted Vic to his front door, he was about an hour and a half late, and he was so unwell he was incoherent, hence the door being slammed in my face. I think it probably scarred me mentally which is why; as I said previously; I never did any more Christmas Days throughout my entire career.

My last memory of Dagenham involves a PO by the name of Arthur, "Boots", Rubython. He was known as Boots because of the great big boots he always wore. Not very original but everybody knew who you meant if you mentioned, "Boots".

Well Boots was a nice bloke; in fact he was too nice to have to put up with us lot. If it wasn't Bob describing bath night and what he did in the bath before he handed the water over to his sister Sue, which was enough to make anyone feel sick. It was the team providing a bottle of gin, which was really an empty bottle, filled with water. Then asking him if he wanted water to go with it. This was supposed to be a great practical joke. But it actually backfired on us because Boots became quite emotional at the thought that we had gone out and bought a bottle of gin to mark his term in charge of the team. Compared to Boots we really were a load of Barbarians.

Anyway nice or too nice Boots did actually know what he was doing and one Sunday evening in the summer he put us all to shame. There was information that a converted fishing smack was going out on weekend trips to the continent and coming back to its mooring in Barking Creek laden to the gunnels with contraband ciggies and bottles of spirits. So into action went the Dagenham Dock rummage crew, which on this occasion was, Boots, Alby, Keith, and yours truly. We received news over the radio from the Gravesend health launch that it was on its way up river. We were in position to stop any sudden dashes for the gates once they knew they'd been rumbled. The boat eventually came alongside. From the noise on board they'd obviously had a really good time. Then we swooped. Boots went straight to the bridge to talk to the skipper and secure the crew/passenger declaration, and the three of us proceeded to run around like headless chickens. After about an hour we had found absolutely nothing. There were about sixteen people on board, eight couples, and when we did the cabins they told us their allowances were on the bridge. This wasn't unusual and we knew it was all quite safe because Boots was up there with the skipper. We did absolutely everything on that little ship, we even undid the hard shell lifeboats, the type that fold away and are encased in a fibre glass shell. Nothing. Eventually we made our way back to the bridge, we weren't expecting any refreshments because we had obviously just ruined what had been a very convivial weekend. And there was Boots with something close to a smug look on his face. It wasn't actually smug because he was too genuine to be smug.

"What's up then Mr Rubython" We were in public, no nicknames or first names, very formal.

What was up was that Boots had secured the C142; that is the crew declaration, and the C142A, the passenger declaration. He had asked the skipper where all the declared goods were, and the skipper had vaguely gesticulated around the bridge. There were a lot of bottles and cartons all over the place. But there were sixteen people on board, so they were entitled to sixteen bottles of spirits and sixteen cartons of cigarettes. Boots was making general conversation and the skipper appeared to be tidying up the bridge. Now at first sight Boots didn't come across as the fizziest drink in the fridge, but in fact he missed very little. And although he had accepted the skippers vague declaration at first it wasn't long before he realised two things. Firstly the skipper wasn't actually tidying anything. He was simply moving the ciggies and the spirits around. He was putting some in cupboards then he was getting some out. He was moving some of it from one side of the wheel, then moving some of the others back to the spot he'd just vacated. Secondly even though it was all moving around there was obviously a lot more than the Duty Free Allowances for sixteen people. So he stopped the skipper and made him stand by the wheel. He removed everything from the cupboards and counted it all properly. There was approximately four times as much as there should have been.

Two hours later sixteen people had admitted to trying to evade the revenue, sixteen Compromise Penalties had been paid in lieu of going before a Magistrate, and sixteen R & R's had been issued. An R&R was the form issued to an offender if they elected to pay a Compromise Penalty, rather than go before a Magistrate. The offender was issued the pink copy of the R&R, consequently they were often referred to as the pink raffle tickets. However I must say I never heard of anyone actually winning anything.

Boots had put us to shame; although small quantities, Boots had sixteen seizures to his name, all off of one ship. Nice work if you can get it. We surmised after the event, that the information was probably malicious, and whoever had passed it over had a strange idea of what full to the gunwales actually meant. Some Officers would have received a commendation for 16 seizures on one ship. Sadly all Boots got was a Complaint File. The Captain alleged that one of us had undone a lifeboat, taken it out of its' hard shell and not put it back again properly.

On this occasion the Higher Waterguard Superintendent; the Capo de Tutti Capi, or the boss of all the bosses; decided it was sour grapes and told the Captain that he was lucky to still have a boat on which to have a lifeboat. So whether one was done up or not was irrelevant.

**

BACK TO LUTON

By the following summer I had had enough of not having a base and along with Alby and Whirly volunteered for long term Detached Duty at Luton. By doing this we were sure of being in the same place for about 6 months. And it had serious attractions that I have mentioned previously. Alby and I shared a massive house in Harpenden, with Wacky Jack Dawson a PO from Glasgow, and Dave Rockman an APO from London Port. Whirly was in digs in Luton at the home of a Mrs Dransfield. He shared his digs with Tim Connolly from London Port. It was a great summer. The social life was just as good as previously, weather wise it was superb and we had a magnificent garden which was a great attraction as most of the stewardesses lived in flats and didn't have access to a garden. We played football, played cricket, drank too much. Whirly met his bride to be, Brenda, and in so doing set an unfortunate precedent as both Alby and I would meet our prospective "other halves" at Luton.

I met a newly promoted PO there by the name of George Atkinson. George was from Preston Dock and later on we played football together for Heathrow. I only mention this because George was responsible for my only serious injury whilst playing football. And he was on my side. He was as tough as old boots and ended up as a DLO in Kingston, Jamaica. Not a place for the fainthearted.

I have to say work wise it was probably lost time. But it served as a prelude before we all reached enough seniority to get permanent Stations back in the Port. The flights were all Charter flights, "bucket and spaders". The passengers were 90% holiday makers and 10% troops. A lot of petty smuggling but not much serious stuff.

There were some amusing cameos to lighten the mood. A PO by the name of Pete Phillips was holding the Notice Number 2, upside down. He then asked his passenger if he had read the notice, the passenger pointed out that it was upside down. Pete suggested that if that was so the passenger should stand on his f****** head. Only he did use slightly more colourful language. Sadly Pete later left Customs under a cloud when some detained goods went missing from the lock-up. He was a London Port PO, he was a lovely footballer and the London Port team really missed him.

Then there was Larry Burford and the incontinent passenger. It's often said that so and so scared the s*** out of someone. Well Larry actually achieved when questioning a couple one day in the Baggage Hall. The lady passenger was transfixed with embarrassment and Larry was never allowed to forget it.

**

WEST INDIA DOCK RUMMAGE CREW

And so to West India Dock Rummage. Our PO was Danny Buckle. The crew was Whirly a lad called Austin Down, and myself, Austin was the senior hand. Danny Buckle was sharp, straight, rarely drank alcohol, and he had a wicked sense of humour, which is probably why we got on so well. He also just loved knocking off; the phrase used when bringing home an offence; Captains, Officers and Chief Stewards. Which is another reason we got on so well?

As far as I remember we had a steady year, not fantastic, but it must have been pretty good, because Danny was given the Harpy Mobile the following year; the Mobiles being the crème de la crème; and he took me with him. I'm jumping ahead a bit but just to explain the Mobiles were allowed to go anywhere in the Port whereas the Station crews were, for the most part, expected to stay on their own patch.

It was around this time that the nickname Alky Malky stuck. As I said before, it wasn't that I drank any more than anyone else, that would have been nigh impossible, it was just that Alky rhymed with Malky. I do remember I had a lot of trouble convincing my mum that this was the reason when she saw it inscribed on my overalls. But then mums always are suspicious aren't they? In that respect they'd all make very good Customs Officers.

It was also about this time that I picked up a tag for being a "lucky" rummager. It was Danny who first picked up on it. It came about because of my ability to walk into the right cabin. When we first went on a ship we would decide what we were going to do on that particular ship. Because of the size of the ships in the West you couldn't do it all. So we would get on board, Danny would obtain the Crew declaration, that is the C142, and some coffee, we'd all have a look at the C142, and make up our minds what we were going to do. For instance we might ignore the crew's cabins and do the decks or the engine room, or the holds. Or we might decide to do the crews cabins. When we did this we would do the cabins entirely at random, and this is where the luck came in. If you search a cabin, ninety nine times out of a hundred you will find what's hidden, if it's there. It's just a matter of picking the right cabin. And I went through a spell when no matter how we picked the cabins we were going to search, I was the one who ended up with a seizure, hence the lucky so and so tag.

**

The biggest job we had that year was one Austin found in keel duct of a Danish ship in South West India Dock. It was good job, partly because of the quantity involved, about 20,000 cigarettes, but also because of where he found it. The keel duct is a pipe about two feet six inches in diameter that runs the length of the ship and enables the engineers to keep the prop shaft lubricated. To get along it you lie on your back on a trolley and use a series of pulleys to move along it. Just like in the Great Escape when they were building the tunnels. It is dangerous and dirty, and when you get to the end there is normally a little space for storing the grease needed for the lubrication. Only on this occasion there were 20,000 cigarettes as well as the grease. It was extremely dangerous getting in and out of it, which is precisely why it was used for hiding smuggled goods. It was also a good job because it gave us an insight into how Police interrogation methods were applied. The ship was a DFDS Line ship, the translation for DFDS being Don't F*** Danish Stewardesses .It was out of Amsterdam, via Greenock, on its way to New York. And it was full of Danish cigarettes and Scottish spirits for the USA, some of which had been stolen and hidden in the keel duct; hence the presence of the Police. Anyway, as the boatswain had control of the keel duct he was a pretty good bet to be the embryonic smuggler, and when Danny interviewed him he invited the Police; in the form of a very large Detective Constable; to sit in because of the theft angle. So there was Danny trying his hardest to get a cough out of the boatswain. And there was the boatswain, who had been round the block a few times, batting away the questions with all the panache of a Roger Federer. When suddenly the constable stood up displaying his full height and breadth and said;

"So what would your reply be if I punched you on the nose?" At which point the boatswain, who had been seated when we entered the lounge where the interview was taking place, also stood up, looked down at the constable, who was still standing. And said."Then my reply would be to punch you back" It was bizarre.

The constable looked up at this man mountain standing in front of him. To continue the Federer analogy, it was game, set, and match to the boatswain. The constable sat down and didn't utter another word. Danny later spoke to the captain. He intimated to him that unless he could find the owner there might be a ships fine to pay because of the quantity involved. The captain had a private word with the boatswain. And amazingly the boatswain, who couldn't remember a thing up until then, was blessed with total recall, and admitted the offence.

Not only was it amazing. It was also a much more civilised way of doing things.

The other seizure of note that we had was Keith's. We were rummaging a Ben boat one day in West India, when Keith found some Chinese heroin in a drawer in a crewman's cabin. It was the first heroin we had found and it resulted in the crewman appearing before Magistrates at Arbour Square and being sentenced to fourteen days for possession of a controlled substance. In these days drugs were still very rare and any seizure was a seizure of note. This wasn't long before Keith married Brenda and disappeared up north to Hull. And very sad to say that was last we all saw of him for many a long year. His career took him into VAT and from there into an Accountancy career with a company in the City. He is now back down south, and living at Dunbar Wharf, on the river, about half a mile from the West India Dock office. It's a funny old world isn't it?

As ever the year was full of incident, some funny, some not so funny. For instance: getting up at four o'clock so that we could be in position at six am to stag the Monte Ulia on its arrival, shows commendable dedication and determination. We were convinced there was large scale cigarette smuggling going on. It came in once a fortnight from Vigo in Spain where ciggies were very cheap. Yet we and all the other crews never had a sniff. However it doesn't matter how dedicated and determined you are using the back of a borrowed Post Office van to stag a ship is not such a good idea when the ship itself is carrying Royal Mail. There we were parked along the dock well away from the ship, looking out from the back of the van, watching the usual gang of seaman and agents at the bottom of the gangway, when suddenly they all turned and looked at us, and started pointing. It was obvious our cover was blown, but we sat tight. Eventually a large Spanish looking seaman walked over to the van:

"You pickin up", he asked in a pure East London accent.

"No we're not" I said.

"You sure you're not pickin up"

"No we're not" said I as the senior hand. "Now f*** off"

And I banged the door shut. Amazingly he did just that. We realised what we had done. Never having been on board a Monte boat so early in the morning none of us had realised we were using as a disguise the one type of vehicle that everybody was actually waiting for. As we left we saw the real Royal Mail van coming in the opposite direction. Obviously on their way to do the "pickin up"

**

Then there was the time we decided to board a small German ship that was sitting on the knuckle just outside the West India Dock lock. Danny was safely aboard, and as the senior hand, by then Austin had emigrated to Canada, it was my job to come aboard last. The means of access was a ladder placed precariously on deck and leaning on the knuckle, not tied to anything just leaning there. Having made sure the other two were safely aboard I started my descent. The ladder was moving around a fair bit because of the motion of the water, and then when I was about half way down it started to lurch sideways. I looked round to see what was happening. Danny and the other two were shouting at me to jump. The Chief Mate was leaning out of the wheelhouse looking very unconcerned. The rest of the crew were all yelling and shouting at me, but it might as well have been in German for all I could understand. I realised in that instant that reason for the ladders unusual movement was that the Chief Mate had chosen the precise moment I was half way down the ladder to move the ship into the lock. I went down that ladder like a fireman goes down a pole, and the ladder clattered onto the deck behind me. I wasn't happy, especially as at that time I was still a non swimmer, and by the time we'd finished the First Mate wasn't very happy either. Needless to say we were quite a long time on that ship, sadly without success. He wasn't doing it because he had something to hide; he just had a strange sense of humour. Or maybe he was still peeved about the World Cup.

**

We were constantly being made aware that we would encounter diversion techniques to try and put us off of the scent. And just as we were warned, it manifested in a variety of ways.

My first encounter was on a Polish ship. On entering the cabin of one of the engineers, the gentleman in question promptly threw himself on the floor and proceeded to hug me round the knees crying something incomprehensible in Polish. I backed away. He shuffled after me still hanging on to my knees. I backed away a bit more but he continued to hold my knees in a vice like grip and he kept shuffling to keep up with me. At this point, when we just about on lap three of his cabin, Austin appeared at the doorway, he said he wasn't sure if he was watching a strange type of dance or if we were practicing a weird sexual act. I assured him it was neither. And this seemed to have the desired affect and the engineer climbed to his feet and shook hands with the two of us.

Now this was a strange sort of diversion bearing in mind that not only had I not actually found anything at this point, I hadn't even started looking. If it was meant to put me off it didn't, in fact, quite the opposite. I decided he was worth spending some time over and eventually found a dozen bottles of Polish vodka under his bunk.

On the second occasion, we were on a Finnish timber ship in Surrey Docks, and on this occasion the seaman let me get into the cabin. He was obviously slightly inebriated, in fact he was p*****. However he appeared to be quite docile so I decided to carry on. Then just as I was approaching the drawer that contained his extra carton of cigarettes he pulled a cut throat razor out of his toilet bag and proceeded to cut his wrists. Not very deeply I later found out, but deep enough to produce a lot of blood. Not quite knowing what to do, in fact not having a clue what to do, I put my head out of the cabin door and shouted for help. By this time he was smearing the blood all over the cabin walls. A couple of the ship's crew poked their heads in the cabin and said;

"Oh he does this all the time"

"Does this all the time", what did they mean. How many times can you cut your wrists and get away with it.

The crew then promptly disappeared.

I was now really in a quandary. I couldn't leave him because I was pretty sure he must have something significant hidden in the cabin. On the other hand it looked a bit callous to carry on searching his cabin while he appeared to be bleeding to death. So I stood in the doorway and alternated between shouting for help and watching the seaman to make sure he didn't either expire or try to retrieve his stash and do a runner. I also tried the rummagers whistle; this is two long notes whistled as tunelessly as is possible. This in my case was extremely tuneless. But all to no avail.

Eventually the First Officer turned up looked at the seaman, and guess what he said. Yes that's right;

"Oh he does this all the time".

But he did get him to sit down and he called for the ship's doctor on the radio. I carried on my search. The ship's doctor arrived and stopped the bleeding, the cuts were only superficial. I completed my search of the cabin and imagine my chagrin when I found out that the whole episode had been because of an extra carton of cigarettes. It taught me something about Finnish sailors and vodka. But I'm not sure what.

Lastly and perhaps most obviously, were the diversions provided by the Norwegian Stewardesses on the Fred Olsen ships. These ships were cruise liners, the Black Watch and the Black Prince; they plied their trade between Millwall Dock, now Canary Wharf, and the Canaries. Obviously as they were cruise liners they carried a lot of crew, and unlike most ships a good percentage of the crew were female, and young.

What always struck me as strange was that these young women when they were in their cabins, only ever wore underwear. No skirts, jeans, jumpers, blouses, tops, not even dressing gowns; nothing but bras and pants. Now you may call me an old cynic. But was this just for our benefit? Was it to take our minds off of what we were supposed to be doing? I can only say that if it was. Well! It was 100% effective. I don't ever remember anyone actually making a seizure in female stewardess's accommodation on a Fred Olsen boat. Or maybe it was just to embarrass us. If this is so then it was 100% ineffective. We were too busy looking to be embarrassed. We were instructed by Danny to work in pairs, no APO was allowed to be in a cabin on his own with a stewardess. He was careful to explain that this was for our protection and to make sure we weren't falsely accused of something. I think it was for his protection, he was more worried that the accusation wouldn't be false.

**

The more perceptive amongst you will probably have gathered by now that there was quite a drinking culture in London Port Waterguard during this era, and one short cameo really epitomised this. We were on board a large German registered cargo ship in the West one morning. Austin, Keith, and I were getting changed in the lounge while Danny tried to find us some accommodation where we could stow our gear. It was about 8.30 and as we were getting changed the boarding crew, Bill Plumb PO and his APO, Duggie Fraser, came into the lounge with the Chief Steward. The ship was a fresh arrival so they had a lot of paper work to do. The Chief Steward offered them a coffee, and Plumbo, as he was affectionately known, accepted for both of them. As the Chief went to move away Plumbo said to himself, but loud enough for the Chief to hear:-

"I always think a drop of Charlotteberg goes down well with a coffee" Charlotteberg being a particularly nice German brandy. The Chief turned round came back to the two of them and said.

"You vud like some Charlotteberg, ja?" (Apologies to any German readers for the terrible accent.)

The questioning tone in his voice suggested that either he thought it was a bit early for brandy, or he just couldn't believe his ears.

"That would be very nice Chief", said Plumbo. With just a hint of surprise in his voice as if he hadn't realised his previous remark could be overheard.

The Chief went to move away but he wasn't quite quick enough.

"Tell you what", said Plumbo.

"Let's forget about the coffee just bring the Charlotteberg, eh"

Objective achieved, Plumbo had his early morning waxer, a waxer being Waterguard slang for an alcoholic drink. I'm not sure where it comes from or why it means a drink. My only thoughts are around the theory that wax was used to line vessels in previous centuries, and the early morning waxer was drunk to give the stomach a lining to prepare it for the rest of the day; hence waxer.

"Nice one Plumbo" murmured Austin. It had been a master class in how to get a drink from a Chief Steward, when a drink wasn't really on offer.

**

THE HARPY MOBILE

It's 1970 and it's the Harpy Mobile. For Alby and I its like two salmon coming home to spawn as neither of us have worked on the Harpy since 1966 when we joined, or was that enlisted. Danny Buckle in charge again. He brings me with him from the West India crew, mainly as his "cabins man" and because of my previously mentioned good luck. He recruits Bob from Dagenham where he has gained a reputation as a good "deep" rummager, and has had some excellent seizures. On one occasion finding over 100 litres of spirits cemented under the floor of the ships hold. Lastly he recruits Alby who he knows will fit in well, and has a reputation for knowing his way around a ship. This was a general term for someone who was a good all rounder and who knew what they were doing. I couldn't really see how it applied to Alby, but there you go, you can't expect to understand everything life throws at you.

To say it was a happy crew would be the understatement of the century. It was amazingly happy even after we lost Danny on promotion, and he was replaced by Mike Fletcher. Mike was another stand up guy, as the Mafia would put it. We all knew him from our time in the Port. He loved rummage, he was enthusiastic, had a tremendous sense of humour, and he knew what he was doing. Although I'm not sure he really knew what he was taking on with us three. Although, as I say, we were a happy crew, we didn't start off too well. There was a dock strike going on when we started, so no new ships fresh from foreign shores, and we didn't have a seizure for 3 weeks. But once we started we couldn't stop. Our first success was on a little Danish ship called M/V Fueno. It was tied up somewhere in the middle of the river and we got on board before it could come alongside. We had a bit of a look round then my good luck kicked in and I decided to do the Chief Engineer. Unusually he had decided to put boards across the bottom of his wardrobe. Once the false floor was jemmied away there was his stash. But Bob went one better. In fact he went three or four better. He had decided he fancied the captain, purely professionally, not in the biblical sense you understand. And he convinced himself there was something dodgy about the magnificent table that he had in his day room. The table was double thickness, but Bob couldn't find a way into it. He managed to get a small mirror into one of the joints and felt that he could just see the corner of a cigarette packet, but he couldn't be sure. Eventually Bob told the captain that unless he showed him how to get into it he was going to have to damage the table to be sure there was nothing in it. Danny gulped and kept everything crossed at this point because he knew what Bob meant by "damage". The captain put his hands under the table and slid out a drawer that was thick enough to hold a packet of 20 cigarettes lying flat. And there was room for 50 packets. This was a truly magnificent concealment, which in later years would have been ideal for drugs. The captain had been present when the ship was being built, laid down is the nautical expression, and he had paid 300 Norwegian crowns or kroner which was worth about £300 at the time, to have the table made. Since then he had been going in and out of Par in Cornwall once a week. And on each trip he smuggled 1,000 cigarettes. He must have made his money back many times over. Nice work if you can get it.

We then went on a run that was to last the whole of the year, and we were by far the most successful crew in the Port. It wasn't just the quantity of seizures it was the variety and the fact that we made them from so many ships in situations where you wouldn't really expect them. I'll give you one example, and I've picked this one not just because it was my job, but because it also shows how I acquired the reputation as a lucky rummager. We were down at Tilbury Grain Terminal, and Danny and Bob were knocking off the captain of a massive grain carrier that was berthed on the outside berth. Alby and I were bored because it was taking a time. Presumably the captain wasn't responding to Danny's influencing skills. We'd done everything we wanted to do, and we obviously weren't going to get a beer, when we noticed a little coaster berthed on the inside berth. It looked like a Dutchman with about 6 crew members. So we decided to go and have a look. Small Dutchmen were always a good bet. And when I say this I don't mean people called Van Damme who are unfortunately short. When we arrived on board the ship was very very quiet, I went off to let the captain know we were on board and to find out where she was from. It turned out that she was from somewhere like Felixstowe and she had been on the UK coast for at least three months. But as the captain said:-

"If you want to waste your time please be my guest".

I went and had a word with Alby and he agreed it didn't look very promising, but he said he wanted to go and have a quick look at the forepeak. He had some mad scheme to search every forepeak until he found the massive seizure that they always looked like they should contain. Because of this I decided to go and have a look at the captain's cabin. There had been a strong aromatic smell of Drum tobacco which was a bit odd considering how long it had been on the coast. You would have thought that all their Dutch stores would have been used up long ago. Incredibly when I searched the cabin I found over 2,000 grams of Drum tobacco under the bottom drawer of his desk. It had almost certainly only just been put there; Dutchmen never used such simple concealments. It would have been buried somewhere deep, in the hold, the engine room, or maybe the forepeak and brought up when it was needed. We just happened to wander in at just the right moment. The point being that another crew at another time probably wouldn't have gone on board and certainly wouldn't have carried on when they'd found out how long she'd been on the coast.

Of course Bob and Alby saw it as more evidence of my lucky tag. Danny saw it differently, which is strange because it was him who first labelled me as lucky. He felt it was more about hard work, and the both of us, Alby and me, not wanting to sit on out backsides and do nothing. Danny wasn't a great one at giving direct compliments, but we decided that this was as close as were going to get, so we accepted it with gratitude.

**

It was 1970 and H M Customs and Excise was just waking up to the fact that drugs were being imported into this country. The first Act of Parliament prohibiting the importation of drugs had been put on the statute books in 1916, but it wasn't really seen as a problem until the late Sixties. Hence the "if you can remember the Sixties you weren't really there" adage. And what a lot of nonsense that is, I can remember it and I was certainly there. I can't remember much of what happened last week, but I can certainly remember the Sixties. By the end of the decade it was actually filtering through to HM Customs and Excise that most of these drugs would have to be imported.

On a Sunday morning in the middle of summer this manifested itself in a most peculiar way. Every Rummage Crew that was on duty that day was summoned to the Custom House for a hush hush meeting, no radios everything done by telephone. When we arrived we were told that a certain ship, the M/V Indian Success, had arrived in Tilbury that morning straight in from Bombay, and we had information that there were drugs on board. Not heroin or cannabis, nothing specific just drugs. So nothing too earth shattering in that message. However, and this is where it all became very strange, the information had come from a Polish informant. Now this was a bit odd because nobody knew where his information had come from or how he obtained his information, from what was almost certainly an Asian organisation. Then it became even odder. The Polish informant had offered himself as an *agent provocateur,* to go on board the Indian Success and try to buy the drugs. But, and this is where in hindsight it plumbs the depths of credibility, he would need money to make it appear that he was genuine dealer. And as he didn't have any money, would we all chip in? It was Sunday so there were no Banks open, no holes in the wall in those days. And guess what; yes that's right, he wanted us to give whatever we had on us that we could afford, so he could appear with a sum of money to enhance his credibility, and as I'm sitting here writing this I still can't believe it, the four of us gave a fiver each, which was a reasonable amount in 1970.

So off we went to Tilbury to stag the Indian Success. There were Customs everywhere but all out of sight from on board the ship. We observed the Pole go aboard. And we waited. And we waited. And we waited. Then surprise, surprise, a sack was thrown over the side of the ship on to the quayside. It was obviously not drugs. But we still waited; we were under strict instructions not to move until told. Two of our colleagues who had organised the operation were seen running up the gangway. And we waited. Then all hell was let loose and the radio ordered all Rummage Crews on board immediately. The Pole had gone missing. The sack only contained cigarettes. The drugs had gone missing. And most importantly as far as we were concerned the money, our money, was missing.

Eventually the Pole was discovered in a cabin, but without the money and with no drugs. His story was that he had had to give over the money as a sign of goodwill, as things were looking a bit threatening. The sack had been a trick to see if the ship was being watched. But there was no sign of any drugs. We then subjected that ship to a forty eight hour rummage, and by we, I mean all the crews involved, not just the Harpy Mobile. We did twenty four hours continuous rummage. No sign of the money, no sign of the drugs. It just shows how ignorant and naive we were, but it also shows our enthusiasm and yes dedication. I know what the answer would be if you asked a group of Officers to chip in nowadays. And I'm pretty sure it would end with, off.

However it wasn't an entirely wasted performance. It was on the Indian Success that I first encountered the delights of a "bone" curry. We were all eating lunch in the seaman's mess, tucking in with our normal gusto. When somebody asked the mess wallah what was in the curry. He didn't speak English so eventually a proper steward was called. Then we wished we hadn't asked. It turned out that there wasn't actually any meat. It was just a variety of bones that were boiled, mixed with various herbs, and produced as a curry. But nobody minded. After all, it was free.

**

But later on we did find some drugs. Bob had a very nice cannabis seizure in the linings of a porthole on board a South African ship in the West. We also found cannabis in the engine of the mechanical davit of a ship at Tilbury, but only after the dockers had complained that they couldn't make it work. And we did run into a Mr Louis Gnau who was a donkeyman on board a Ben Boat. Again it was one of those jobs that came out of our willingness to look, even when at first sight it seemed a waste of time.

A fresh Ben Line boat had arrived in South West India Dock. It was the Saturday of one of the Bank Holidays and we were looking for something to do. But not too much because we were off for the rest of the Bank Holiday, and we all had girlfriends, and better things to do with our time, so if possible we wanted a sharp away. When we arrived at the West we had our first disappointment. We could see she was light; that is she had already discharged her cargo; because she was so far out of the water. This meant she had come round the coast, probably from Hull and she would already have been rummaged, so all the easy stuff would be gone.

However we decided to go on board and do the engine room crew, on the basis that the engine room crew were the best bet if something had been hidden deep and had now been brought to the surface, just as it had happened with the captain of the Dutch ship at Tilbury Grain Terminal.

So we got into our overalls, Danny said he would organise some coffee, it was all very relaxed, we made our way down to the cabins occupied by the engine rooms crew, we were chatting about this and that, not particularly interested. Then Bob who was at the front opened the door into their alleyway, and it was as if we had thrown a grenade in, or disturbed a load cockroaches. There were Chinese running everywhere; in and out of cabins, up and down the alleyways, and most serious as far as we were concerned, in and out of the engine room. To which there were several entrances. As we went in after them we noticed one man run towards the engines then disappear altogether. As we were rushing down the gantries all three of us on different ones to try and head him off, we saw him running back up a fourth gantry, heading for the cabins. We promptly turned tail and rushed back up to the alleyway and of course by the time we got there, there was nobody to be seen and all the doors were shut.

Our somewhat relaxed manner had been completely turned on its head. We were rushing up and down the alleyway banging on and opening doors and checking who was in them. In the end we found a little wizened Chinese, they were all Chinese so no significance there, trying desperately to get of his overalls which were covered with asbestos dust. This was, we found out later, Mr Louis Gnau, and he had effectively just put an end to our weekend off. We searched his cabin without result. We searched all the other cabins and there were a few bits and pieces that weren't on the C142, hence all the running about, but nothing of significance. We then went into the engine room looking for somewhere that the asbestos dust might have come from. Sure enough the boilers were being stripped of their asbestos coating and near the engines on a platform were ten large sacks all full of asbestos. We had no choice, we put rags round our mouths, and we set too, emptying all ten sacks. You can imagine the state we were in there was asbestos everywhere. It was flying around in the air; it was in our ears, up our noses, and despite our improvised masks, in our mouths. Fortunately we didn't know about the danger of asbestosis in those days. We were picking it out and spitting it out for hours. I don't know how many pints we had to have to get rid of it.

Eventually Bob found a small package of what turned out to be Chinese Opium. It wasn't a commercial quantity but Danny suspected that as Louis didn't look like a user, it might be for someone over here or it might be a sample. Consequently as Mr Gnau had a book full of addresses in the London area, we spent the rest of the Bank Holiday weekend, charging him, taking him before a Magistrate, and searching lots and lots of Chinese restaurants.

So it wasn't all bad, we liked Chinese food, and we were on double time. I'm sure the ladies in our lives understood!

**

If we needed reminding that dugs were on the increase we had the evidence right under our noses. Our Investigation Branch had information that a lorry with two containers was bringing cannabis. They followed it from Dover and despite losing it a couple of times. Just how do you lose a massive articulated lorry? It was eventually apprehended and the containers were found to have about a ton of cannabis in them. The offenders were arrested and duly found guilty at the Old Bailey. The trailer which had also been seized was left on

Custom House Quay right next to the pontoon that led to the Harpy. After six months, surprise, surprise, nobody came to claim it, so it was decided to break it up.

One lunch time; probably a Friday as that tended to be paperwork day if we were off for the weekend; the three of us were on our way to a pub in Pudding Lane, when we noticed a couple of men with high powered drills about to start breaking up the trailer. Being curious, and obviously not very thirsty, we stood and watched. We were amazed at how easily the drill bit in to the frame and started churning out iron filings. We were even more amazed when the silver coloured filings turned a deep brown and because they were being subjected to a lot of heat, gave off the sickly sweet aroma of cannabis resin. The whole of the frame was full of resin. We tried to lay claim to the seizure as it would have been a feather in our caps, but we were told quite firmly by the Investigation boys to get lost. It wasn't that they wanted the glory they just wanted to be able to brush it under the carpet to hide their embarrassment at having missed it in the first place.

As a department we really were a bunch of amateurs in those days. But we were learning, fast.

**

Throughout all of this Bob, Alby, and I were inseparable, even though Bob was now living on Canvey Island with Martien his future wife. Our reputation for playing and working hard went before us, and was sometimes misunderstood. At one time there was a young lad called Ian Ord on one of the Harpy Station crews, and one day we were all getting changed at the same time. Bob being Bob was mucking about and camping it up in his underpants and putting on a bit of a show. Ian decided to join and started to respond to Bobs mock advances. Alby and I shook our heads knowing it would all end in tears.

Bob waited for his opportunity, then when the four of us were in the small room where we stowed our gear he started. The three of us were in our pants just about to go for a shower.

Bob   "Oh this is nice isn't it, all nice and close together"

Ian   "Oh yes this is very nice"

Wrong answer Ian.

Bob.   "I'll tell you what we'll do. We'll form a circle"

Ian, laughing.   "Yes we'll form a circle"

Wrong answer again Ian.

At which point Alby and I decided it was good to miss out on so we joined in.

Bob.   "First let's all hold hands"

Ian is still laughing, but now quite nervously.

Alby, Bob, and I hold hands. Alby and I each grab one of Ian's hands. Ian is very tentative, and he is now still laughing but very nervously.

Bob again.   "This is nice"

We all agree, Ian a bit half heartedly and with a sort of fixed grin on his face.

Alby locks the door and throws the key to Bob who puts it down his pants Bob now has the most enormous leering grin on his face..

Ian's laughter is now almost hysterical.

Ian.   "Come on lads let me out of here"

Bob.   "Don't you want to form a circle"

Ian. Now not only not laughing but looking extremely distraught. "No I don't ,I just want to get out of here"

Bob.   "You'll have to come and get the key" Pointing at his pants.

Ian.   "Come on lads a jokes a joke but I want to get out"

So bearing in mind he was new and obviously had pre-conceived misconceptions about the sexual orientation of men in uniform, and in particular we three, we had pity on him and let him go. And we could hear the roar of laughter from the rest of his crew when he reappeared. They had a pretty good idea what had been going on.

There was however a sequel to this story that showed how successful our wind up had been. Ian moved on to Luton Airport and one day he boarded the flight my future wife, Carol; who was a Dan Air Stewardess; was arriving on. She being the Number One was responsible for the paper work. He was being particularly officious and pedantic, so knowing the story, she decided to see if she could burst his bubble.

"Do you know Malcolm Nelson, Alby Kiy, and Bob Highstead?" She asked in all innocence.

"Huh" said Ian "You want to steer well clear of that bunch of queers"

"That's funny", Carol said. "I'm marrying one of them in two months time".

End of conversation.

Should Ian read this book he might be interested to know that all three of us have been married for thirty years and between us the number of children we managed to father almost runs into double figures

And Ian, just between you and me, when the three of us get together we still like to hold hands and form a circle.

**

On a similar theme; sexual orientation that is; Alby and I were doing a gangway watch on one of the big "A" boats in Victoria Dock on Sunday evening. The "A" boats came in from Buenos Aries, so they were at sea a long time; they had British crew, so they were a good bet. When they first arrived the best bet of all was the crew that were leaving as soon as she docked. So there was Alby and I checking everyone as they left the ship. It was all going very smoothly except that we weren't actually finding anything. Then along came two of the crew holding hands. Now remember this was 1970, we weren't as liberated as we are today. One was leaving and one was staying. They were distraught. They were both in tears. They were hanging on to each other as if their very lives were about to come to an end. And it went on and on. Alby and I kept an eye on them while we dealt with any other crew members who were leaving. At last it was time for the one that was leaving to tear himself away and make the long lonely walk down the gangway.

"Oh well", he said between sobs, "see you Wednesday".

His "friend" looked aghast when Alby and fell about in fits of laughter. We'd been sure this was goodbye forever and a day. But no just until Wednesday.

**

I think I should probably explain at this point that 1970 wasn't only a good year because of the work I was doing. It was also the year I met my wife to be, my lovely Carol. She was a Number One Air Stewardess with Dan Air. We met at the end of July, I had popped up to Luton for a party, and by the end of August we had decided to get married. And we did, we married the following January on the 23rd, at All Saints Church just north of Putney Bridge, in Fulham. She was and still is at heart a "Fulham Girl". People said it would never last, and we're still doing our best to prove them wrong .But not only did I get married on the 23rd it was a double celebration because I also became a dad to Mark Alan. Mark was Carol's son from a previous relationship, he was great, as bright as a button, amazing sense of humour for a five year old, and I was already turning him into a Spurs supporter. I loved him to bits.

Just as a matter of interest, All Saints Church is the one they used in the film The Omen. If only I'd known!

**

Sadly not every incident we were involved in had a happy ending. On the 23rd of October we rummaged a ship called the Pacific Glory. It was like a Christmas tree. There was contraband everywhere; on ledges, in cupboards in the mess, in the washing machine. We found thousands of cigarettes, nearly all "Lucky Strike". As most of the cigarettes were in places accessible to all members of the crew Mike managed to find twelve or thirteen owners, and by the time he had finished issuing the "pink raffle tickets" the ship was preparing to cast off.

I was due to see Carol, in Luton that evening, and by the time we got back to the Harpy I was running late. We had dropped Mike off at home on the way back from the Isle of Grain. Bob was off home to Canvey

Island. So rather than go through the process of booking all the cigarettes in, which would have taken another couple of hours, I decided to leave them in the boot of the Zephyr, which fortunately was enormous, and carry on straight up to see Carol. I decided it was safer to take the Zephyr to keep the cigarettes safe. Alby decided to come along for the ride, probably because Carol shared her flat with three other stewardesses, and there was always beer in the fridge.

Later that evening we were sitting around chatting and drinking, the television was on but nobody was particularly looking at it, when suddenly Mary, one of Carol's flatmates, said "Look at that ship on the TV". We all looked and sure enough it was the Pacific Glory. She had been involved in a collision just off of Ventnor on the Isle of Wight. She was ablaze, in danger of running aground, and thirteen members of the forty two man crew were dead. It was a very sobering moment. We had been laughing and joking with the crew only a few hours ago. Perhaps among the dead were the men we'd knocked off just before they left.

**

The year carried on at the same hectic pace, we were working long hours, Bob was getting ready to become a dad, and I was feverishly preparing for a wedding. Then there was an incident that could have had an impact on my whole future with Carol's family. It was the second week in December and we were rummaging a small German ship at Fulham Wharf, on the north bank of the Thames, just downstream of Wandsworth Bridge. As I have said previously Carol is a Fulham girl and most of her very large family still lived in Fulham at that time.

We were almost finished, Alby and I were doing the hold and we were about to go back up when I noticed a space in between the cargo that seemed to be full of packaging materials. Further looking revealed a large carton that later turned out to contain a thousand large cigars. Not a huge seizure but a commercial quantity nevertheless. Danny made a few enquiries but without success. We stagged the ship for a few hours in case the would be smuggler had other goods that he wanted to bring ashore, but again without success, so it went in as an unowned seizure.

End of story? Not quite.

About a week later I was at the Britannia Club, in Britannia Road, Fulham, just opposite Chelsea football ground. I was with my future in-laws, Madge and Arthur. They knew about the cigars but didn't think anything of it. I was standing around in the bar area having a drink chatting with some of the family. When one of Arthurs cousins, we'll call him Eddie, suddenly announced that there would be no cigars this Christmas as those b****** Customs had nicked the lot. Fortunately, on my advice, only the immediate family knew what I did, to the rest I was a Civil Servant. That normally was enough to shut people up because it sounded so boring, and it wasn't a lie, I really was a Civil Servant. I was looking directly at Arthur but he didn't even flinch. And although we were told in those days that we were never off duty, I decided that this was a time when I definitely was.

**

Life was a lot of fun but it did have its serious and even tragic moments. We were trying to get on board a ship in Rochester harbour one day, the three of us were sat at the back; I suppose I should say aft; of the Customs launch, as the crew tried to manoeuvre the launch into a position where we could get hold of the Jacobs ladder. We were just chatting about nothing in particular looking in the direction of the wheelhouse .Danny was standing outside of the wheelhouse and the skipper was having some trouble getting us alongside because it was quite choppy even inside the harbour. Danny looked back at us and shouted. "GET DOWN".

Fortunately there was a service element in the Waterguard and an order was an order, so we just threw our selves flat on the deck. When we got up the flag that we had been sitting around was floating in the harbour. We had swung under the bow of a light, that is unladen, barge. We were lucky. If Danny hadn't looked up at that precise moment we would have all been in the drink with the flag. And probably with severe headaches, if not something a lot more serious. Very sadly two weeks later the deckhand on that launch wasn't so lucky. He was taking the launch from one part of the harbour to another when he got into difficulties. The precise details aren't known because he was alone. But the launch was found drifting unmanned, and his body was found later. He had drowned.

This had been a dangerous incident for us, but it wasn't frightening because it happened so fast. What was frightening was running aground in thick fog on board a Spanish ship as she moved from the roads outside of Sheerness Harbour into the harbour. The fog was a pea souper, and we couldn't believe it when the Sheerness launch crew said they would take us out and put us on board the Spanish ship we were interested in. But they did. We climbed the Jacobs ladder and as she was stationary we started rummaging. We were all down below in the crew's quarters when we felt her start to move. Thinking the fog must have cleared we went topside to see how far out we were. All we could see was fog. I will never know what persuaded that skipper he could get into the dock with that visibility. Perhaps he was on a promise.

It was obviously a dangerous situation so the three of us, Danny had gone back with the launch, stayed on deck by the rail. We were watching what we thought was the horizon, when there was a dreadful crunching sound. The ship shuddered to a halt and amazingly lurched to one side. One moment we were looking out to sea, the next we were not only looking down at the sea, we were almost low enough to touch it. The ship hovered there for what seemed an age. The Spanish crew were in a panic, most of them were on their knees praying or crossing themselves and saying Hail Marys. Then just when it seemed impossible for the ship right itself, and that it must capsize, there was a loud groaning noise and the ship slowly swung back upright. The captain went hard astern and the ship freed itself fom the sandbank we had hit. Incredibly the captain carried on his way into Sheerness. He was definitely on a promise.

A similar fate to that which befell the launch hand also befell Ted Walters in the Royals. We were on board a City boat in the Royals one evening and Ted was also on board giving the crew issue of duty free cigarettes and spirits. These types of goods were placed under seal on arrival and could only be released under Waterguard supervision.

Ted was finished but we were rummaging until quite late otherwise we would have offered him a lift back to the office. We didn't know until the next day that he didn't make it back. He had tripped and lost his balance and fell into King George the Fifth Dock. His body was found a few days later. It was very sad. Ted was a smashing bloke, who had suffered terribly at the hands of the Japanese in the Second World War.

We never needed reminding that the docks and the river were dangerous places to work.

**

And so it went on. Mike took over from Danny and if anything things were even more hectic. Very often we would do a late shift down at the

Isle of Grain or Sheerness, or somewhere else on the North Kent coast, and because our route back to the Harpy took us past Mike's house. We would stop off and stay the night in his converted attic. Mike's wife Madelaine would feed us. We would hide our Brightstar torches so that Pete, Mike's son, couldn't find them. He had a fascination with torches and on one occasion managed to reduce the entire crew's torch capacity to a pile of spare parts.

We also managed to achieve what I believe to be a unique accolade. We were banned from a greasy spoon Transport Cafe. This particular cafe was owned by a lady who felt hers was an upper class cafe, if there is such a thing. And because it was upper class she refused to sell fried egg or bacon sandwiches. So to get round this, one of us would buy egg, double bacon, and four slices of bread and butter. Then we would then go and sit as far away from the counter as possible and make our own. We thought we were being pretty clever. Then one day, she must have been told what was going on, she suddenly appeared out of nowhere. She was extremely miffed; she told us we were compromising the high standards of her establishment. Then she threw us out and banned us.

The truckers thought it was hilarious. They didn't like us much anyway. Looking back it was pretty funny.

**

My last and enduring memory of the Harpy Mobile was having to pretend to be a courting couple with Bob. Now when you see this scene on the television or in the cinema, it's a man and a woman. The woman is normally attractive and there's sometimes a spark between them which this enforced activity brings to the surface. Well this was the Waterguard version. Bob and I were in a plain car, no Post Office van this time, outside of a pub in the vicinity of Victoria Dock. Mike and Alby were covering the second entrance in another car. We were waiting for something to be delivered from a ship in the docks. The pub was well known for selling dodgy gear. Be aware that the dock areas at night were not very safe so we were very much on full alert.

As we sat there we noticed a chap who had just gone in, come back out with a couple of others. They then had a very casual conversation and we could see the man who had just gone in nod very slightly in our direction and the other two taking their time looked down the street where we were parked. They didn't appear to be looking at us but we knew we'd been rumbled. We were watching them like hawks and as soon as they started to move in our direction, we grabbed each other in a lovers embrace. It was dark and the streets weren't well lit, so they probably couldn't see into the car that well, but it must have looked strange. Perhaps they couldn't see it was two men, or perhaps they could, seamen had a very liberated view about gays even in the early seventies. Anyway the good news was, that it worked. Although obviously there would be no dodgy dealings in the pub that night. What I never understood was why Bob felt the need to actually kiss me. He said it made it look more real, but as I've said before the jury's still out on that one.

In hindsight perhaps Ian Ord was right. Well about Bob anyway.

**

THE END OF AN ERA

End of an era might sound a bit melodramatic but that was how it felt. After the Mobile anything was likely to be a bit of an anti-climax, however life was still interesting and full of incident.

I was on a Harpy Rummage crew working for Alan Baker who was another smashing bloke to have as boss. The other permanent APO was Pete Clarke and this was his first rummage crew so I was very much the senior hand. I was newly married, and living in Woodford, Essex, I had become a dad, to Mark Alan, and I was studying for my promotion to Preventive Officer. So life had plenty of distractions.

It was imperative that I get my promotion first go because there was a huge re-organisation of Customs and Excise looming and the rank of Preventive Officer would disappear to be replaced by Executive Officer. Most importantly PO's would have certain Reserved Rights, and this would be last Promotion Board before the re-organisation. As it happened all three of us were successful. Alby became the last PO, because of his position on the APO list and I became the next to last, with Bob a few places ahead. So it was vitally important.

It wasn't for nothing that Carol wrote on my Definitions Book: "PO or PO", and on the other side of the page: "Study hard remember my housekeeping money", very single minded my Carol.

Although working with Alan was a lot more sedate than the Harpy Mobile had been, it was just right for me. Alan was a smashing boss and made sure that I kept up with my studies. He also made sure that I didn't switch off entirely, and this would have been easy to do with everything that was going on in my life at the time. During this short time there were still incidents that stand out as being worthy of a mention.

**

We were on a large British ship down at Tilbury. The Officers on board were British but the crew were mainly West African. I had decided to do the working alleyways which wasn't too strenuous and gave me the opportunity to pick up some easy jobs.

Along the top of the working alleyways were ledges that ran the whole length the centre of the ceiling. The ledges were actually trunking that enclosed all the wires and pipes that were needed to keep the ship running. This trunking was the perfect place for a quick stash. So what the sailors would do was keep their excess cigarettes, spirits, or whatever in their cabins, rather than stow it somewhere in the ship where it might get stolen by other members of the crew. Then if the ship wasn't rummaged they would take it ashore or sell it to the dockers.

However if the "blackgang" came on board they would quickly stow it close to their cabin, and the ledges were perfect for this because they were high and wide. The only way to check them out was to use your extendable mirror and your torch and painstakingly make your way along shinning the torch into the mirror. So this I duly set about doing. It was especially difficult because the alleyway was enormous and the ledge was high up and probably the widest I had come across. It was so wide that I had to check out both sides individually. So there I was making my way along waiting for the splash of colour that would have told me that I'd found cigarettes or spirits. Then I received the biggest shock of my working career. Suddenly I was staring at two big wide eyes that were staring straight back at me.

My first instinct was that it was an animal, but then I realised it was a man. I had found my first illegal immigrant. Now I couldn't get up there to tell him to get down. He didn't speak English, so all my shouting was doing no good. And, I found out later, he was stuck. Eventually someone answered my frantic whistles, a ships Officer appeared, and the illegal immigrant was freed from the top of the ledge. He was, we learnt later, deported on the same ship he came in on. This was my only human seizure in my career, although I did later manage to find a litter of cats in the Red Channel in Terminal Three.

The daft thing was that the rest of the crew, not the Officers, must have known about him, so if he'd just walked about in a pair of overalls, we would have just presumed he was a member of the crew.

**

The second incident was very scary and really quite dangerous. We were getting on board one of the larger City boats which had come round the coast from Hull, where it had discharged its cargo. So it was light and was right out of the water. It was one of the two biggest ships in the fleet, it was either the City of York or the City of Port Elizabeth. When we arrived it had only just come alongside and the gangway still wasn't down. But there was a Jacobs's ladder over the side. We needed to get on board straight away. Anything that had been hidden deep and brought up to dispose of in London would soon be returned to its deep concealment if we weren't quick.

The side of the ship was enormous as we looked up from the dockside, and it wasn't straight up. The side of the ship actually was convex, so as you climbed the ladder for the first half of the climb you were hanging backwards, and don't forget we all had heavy rummage cases hung round our necks. The trick was to always make sure you were hanging on with one hand, and once you had started, keep going at a steady speed even though you would get out of breath, and most important of all. Never, ever, look down.

Alan went up first, Guvvie always led the way. Then number three crew member went up, then number two, and then number one, in this instance me. So Alan was safely on board with number three man.

When number two, let's call him Pete, made the fatal error of stopping halfway. He was out of breath, which was fair enough, but then he compounded his error by looking down. And he froze.

So there he was half way up the side of one of the two largest City boats, hanging on a Jacobs's ladder with his rummage case hanging around his neck. There were all the dockers yelling and shouting, loving every minute of it. Alan was up above looking down and I was still on the dockside looking up. Pete was half way up looking scared.

The outcome, as I suspected it would be, was for Alan to instruct me to break another cardinal rule of climbing Jacobs Ladders, never more than one person on it at a time, and get on the ladder. Then climb up to Pete and dislodge one of his feet. You should never have two people on a rope ladder at the same time, not because the rope might break, but because if the top person falls he'll take the second person with him. Still up I went, cursing all the way, this really wasn't my idea of fun. But an order is an order and there really wasn't an alternative. Then having reached his feet I tried to move one of his feet whilst still holding on with my other hand, but his feet were planted firmly on the rung of the ladder.

Now this was getting serious. I was halfway up the side of one of the biggest ships that came into the Port of London. I had a heavy rummage case hanging around my neck. And I realised I was going to need both hands to give me a chance of moving one of Pete's feet. I was hoping that once I moved one it would break the spell and "unfreeze" him and he would make his way up as per normal. So in order to free up both hands I had to bring my hands round the back of the ladder and hang on with my arms while I used my hands to budge Pete's feet. I realised when I was doing this that when, or if, I did actually manage to move one of the feet it was likely to come away with a jerk. And when I say jerk, I'm not talking about the chap on the end of the foot. So at the back of my mind was the fact that when this foot suddenly released itself it was likely to fly back in my direction and kick me in the face. And all I was only hanging on to the ladder with was my arms, I didn't actually have hold of the ladder. The fact that I was still a non swimmer was irrelevant as we would be dropping onto solid concrete.

By now the seriousness of the situation had got through to everyone. The dockers were silent, the ship workers were silent, the sailors were silent, the only noise that could be heard was me telling Pete to move his f****** foot.

I think my influencing skills finally won the day. I had moved one of Pete's feet half way toward the edge of the rung. My plan was that once it was completely free I would hold on to it and shove it upwards onto the rung above. I imparted my plan to Pete, and I think at this point common sense finally got through and Pete realised that that would be extremely dangerous for both of us. He also realised that he was in a lot more danger if he let me carry on with my suggested plan of action than if he actually climbed the ladder. He would have probably lost his balance and might well have fallen on to me and taken us both down. So with me guiding his feet on to the rungs we slowly mounted the remainder of the ladder and finally slumped onto the deck of the City boat. I don't know why, but ever since then I've had a bit of a thing about climbing ladders, it was also shortly afterwards that I decided to learn to swim.

**

My final memory as an APO; and I've made it my last because I don't quite know where it fits in, or whose crew I was on at the time, probably Alan Baker's; was a quite extraordinary incident down at

Tilbury. We were on a Chinese ship, the Peoples Republic of China (PRC) that is. We were treading on eggshells because trade had only just started to flow and Diplomatic relations wouldn't be formalised for another couple of years in 1972. Mao was still alive and was very Anti-West, but he was coming round to the idea that he couldn't live in isolation forever. We didn't fancy the ship very much and decided not to do the cabins as this would probably seen as provocative. And the crew would be very unlikely to smuggle and risk the wrath of the Regime that would descend upon them if they were caught. I decided to go down into the holds even though they were being worked by the dockers at the time. This was a bit risky because cargo was being thrown around and pallets were being swung in and out. But it was a general goods cargo including a lot of electrical items, and there was a good chance that cargo would have been pilfered. The duty and tax on electrical goods was high in those days, as they were still seen as luxury goods. After a couple of hours the dockers decided it was "muggo" time. This is a tea break to you and me, but to the dockers it was "muggo". It was a nice day so they went topsides for it and sat in the sun talking about last night's football. I went up with them ostensibly to have a break myself but actually to see if anything was being removed and passed over to other dockside workers who would then take it off the ship. There I was enjoying the sun when the Commissar appeared. Now the Commissar was a political post that didn't exist on most ships. It was only seen on the ships from the Communist Block, remember this was at the height of the Cold War. Russia was still isolated, the Berlin Wall was still up, it wasn't that long after the Cuba crisis, and countries such as Albania still had no contact with the West at all.

Anyway back to the Commissar. His job on board was to make sure political correctness was maintained and in many ways he was more powerful than the captain. He was the eyes and ears of the Party. It was only on his authority that you kept your job as a member of the crew. So you can imagine, nobody on board was likely to upset the Commissar. So out onto the deck strides this fine gentleman, and the first thing he sees is all these dockers having their tea break. He can't believe his eyes. Nobody takes a break without his agreement. They don't have tea breaks in the PRC. They're lucky if they get a lunch break.

He tries to get them back down into the hold by telling them that isn't how things work in the PRC. He is the only person on board who speaks good English. The dockers respond with something that ends with off. The end of the incident you might think. The dockers weren't far away from going back anyway.

The Commissar disappears and returns a few moments later with his Little Red Book, Mao's bible. He then proceeds to march along the line of dockers reading at full volume the thoughts of Chairman Mao. It seemed to me that it was no coincidence that he was reading from the section that dealt with the idleness and laziness. Though I have to say I'm not too sure that he wasn't making some of it up. I have since read the Little Red Book and I couldn't find half of what he was quoting.

This was ruining the dockers muggo. The Commissar was almost goose stepping along the line and screeching at the top of his voice. Eventually one burly docker had had enough, he waited until the Commissar was within reach and he grabbed the Little Red Book and in the same movement threw it into the dock where it sank. Probably weighed down with all the knowledge it contained.

The Commissar was translucent with rage. He stood in front of the offending docker and gave him both barrels, half in English and half in Chinese. The docker looked him straight in the eye, even sitting down he was on a level with the Commissar, he stood up, and along with one of his mates, picked up the Commissar and threw him in the dock as well. As they were doing this he muttered something like, "Well if you want it that badly you better go and get it".

I thought this might be a good time to leave. Crew members were running around throwing lifebelts, although judging by the lack of urgency he wasn't the most popular member of the crew, and the dockers were making their way back down into the hold. This had all the makings of a political incident which I really didn't want to be part of.

I heard later that the Commissar was pulled out more dead than alive, but he survived intact. None of the dockers were reprimanded; wildcat strikes were very common around that time, so nobody wanted to upset them. And although it didn't develop into a political incident, the papers, especially the Daily Mirror, reported it extensively.

**

My time as an APO was fast drawing to a close. The interview/exam was looming on the horizon. Re-organisation was just around the corner. Times they were a changing, and sadly would never be quite the same again. In hindsight it was like Bilbo and Frodo leaving Middle Earth with Gandalf and the elves, in the Fellowship of the Ring. The interview day finally arrived. Off to Kings Beam House in New Fetter Lane, in London, with a couple of pints before I went in to relax me. Then like a lamb to the slaughter, to be grilled by a Collector, and two Assistant Collectors. This interview was about as far removed my first interview as it was possible to be. Nothing vague, nothing friendly, every question demanding a specific answer, nobody wanted to know which newspaper I read.

"No Mr Nelson what are the exact words you would put on the Duty Slip Receipt".

This from Ron Edmunds; who was later to be my Assistant Collector at Heathrow; when I tried to waffle my way through a question about the wording used on a Duty Slip Receipt when detaining firearms and ammunition.

"No what does it say in the Codes" The Codes being our books of instruction.

Waffle, waffle, from me.

"No what is the prescribed wording"

Amazingly I passed. The PO in Carol's message of encouragement translated into Preventive Officer. I was now entitled to wear a second stripe on my uniform, I would have my own seal, I would earn more money, I wouldn't wear overalls again, I wouldn't search ships.

My old working life was gone and I would be back on the merry go round. I would be saying goodbye to ships forever, and had I known that at the time, I would have been distraught. I loved ships, and being around them. It must be something to do with my surname. Heathrow was the only place I could be sure of getting a fixed place and by now Carol, Mark, and I had moved from Woodford to Fulham. There was another young Nelson on the way, so it made sense to find somewhere where I could settle. As I said previously it felt like Bilbo Baggins leaving Middle Earth.

**

4. Promotion and off to Heathrow.

PROMOTION/LUTON/LOMO

Promotion duly arrived on the 30th of June 1971. I knew it would eventually lead to a fixed post at Heathrow, we were now living just off of Wandsworth Bridge Road in Fulham, about 300 yards away from where I had found those cigars, so moving to Heathrow made sense. But before that move there was the usual mish mash of relief jobs.

So off to Luton for the summer, Alby and I shared a house for a while at Beechwood Green, but most of the time I travelled up and down from Fulham. I don't know why but somehow it didn't have the same attractions as on previous occasions, possibly something to do with being a married man, and an expectant dad.

Then at the end of the summer back to London and off to LOMO. The London Overseas Mail Office at West Ham, and what an eye opener this was. It was the first time that I had worked with people who weren't Waterguard. That, plus the experience of working alongside the Post Office workers, was a real education. The work was interesting, apart from the fact that there were no ships. But the management, and the restrictive practices of the postal workers turned it into a nightmare.

There were a whole bunch of us newly promoted PO's from London and Southend, and we had all come from an environment where we worked hard when there was something to do and we were allowed to relax when there wasn't.

The main problem was that the postal workers had been promised six hours overtime a day, eight hours on Saturday and eight hours on

Sunday during the pressure period just before Christmas. And when they were working we had to be there as well because the parcels were all coming in from abroad and had to be cleared by HM Customs. Now this wasn't a major problem except that because of a dock strike in the USA the amount of post was actually less than it was all the rest of the year. So the "Pressure" never actually materialised. But the post men and women had been promised their overtime so their Union insisted that they get it. This meant we had to be there as well.

It was especially hard for me because James Christopher Nelson had arrived on November the 28th and was having a great time keeping me and Carol awake at night. It was quite simple, after he'd had his six o'clock feed in the evening he just want to give full vent to his vocal chords until about one o'clock in the morning, and then he wanted another feed at five. I was then travelling an hour and a half each way, to LOMO and back, and doing a fourteen hour shift. The money was nice but a few more hours sleep would have been even nicer.

So there we were fourteen hour shifts with about enough work to keep us gainfully employed for four of those fourteen hours. And this was "Pressure". Every now and again the postman working with me would advise me to;

"Slow down a bit son"

It wasn't just that we only had enough work for four hours, we had to work at a pace that stretched it out over the whole fourteen. Utter madness.

The situation was exacerbated by a Surveyor who had no idea how to manage a group of PO's who didn't like having to hang around for ridiculously long hours with nothing to do. I should explain that a Surveyor was and is a rank one above a Chief Preventive Officer/Senior

Officer. We didn't have them at that time in London Port so this was new experience for me.

I'll just give you one example of how his intransigence compounded an already difficult situation. None of us were very good at getting in on the dot of eight o'clock. We weren't needed by the postmen until about nine, and we were more used to tides rather than clocks. But the Surveyor insisted. So after several warnings he decided that he would appear at ten past eight and draw a red line on the signing on sheet directly under the name of the last person to appear.

This cunning ploy would give him the names of all those who were more than ten minutes late. The next person in realised what the Surveyor had done and drew a red line under his own name and under the name above the line. This went on until the whole page was full of red lines. So the next day the Surveyor not only drew a red line he initialled it, pretty smart eh?

The next person in drew a couple of red lines above and below the red line that was already there, and, after a couple of practices, copied the Surveyors initial. By the end of the day the page was again covered with red lines, but this time it was also covered with forged versions of the Surveyors initials. Now this Surveyor was a pretty formidable opponent. So on the third day he drew a red line, initialled it, and used his own personal date stamp to authenticate the initial.

This could have been game set and match to the Surveyor, but unluckily for him the next PO to appear was Dave Lewis from Southend Airport. Dave was an easy going guy whose main claim to fame was that he could mimic the Four Seasons singing "Peanuts". And he did so whenever he entered the canteen or the bar, so during "Pressure" this was quite often. I went to see the musical "Jersey Boys" a few weeks ago and I was reminded of Dave and his rendition of Peanuts, it was much better than the chap on the stage. Anyway back to the plot. On this particular morning he had just had a nightmare of a journey coming up from Southend. So when he was faced with what seemed to be an insoluble problem he resorted to the only course of action available to him: violence.

He picked up the signing on sheet, tore it up in little pieces and threw it into the waste paper bin. And that was the end of that. No more red lines with or without initials and date stamps.

A good question would be.

"Why didn't he, the Surveyor, just stand by the signing on sheet, and note down all those who were late?"

Well firstly he wasn't happy with confrontation.

Secondly he wouldn't have been able to answer the "What's the point?" retort.

But thirdly and most sadly, he wouldn't have known what to do. He just hoped the red lines would make the problem go away.

I had just experienced my first brush with a beast that, sadly, was to become more and more common over the years. That is the incompetent and indecisive manager. Our merging into the general Civil Service was to make this manager more and more common.

**

It wasn't all a waste of time though. During my spell on "openers" I became aware of the various types of concealments I would find when I reached Heathrow. "Openers", was the section where parcels had been selected to be opened and inspected. During my brief time at LOMO I had various drugs seizures most of which were just seize and report. There being no point in charging the recipient as they would invariably claim that they had no knowledge of the contents of the parcel. I was relatively successful during my times on openers. It was all cannabis in those days very little cocaine or heroin. I did however have seizures inside homemade cakes; inside tins of fruit, although they were very amateurish compared with what I would see later in my career; in tubes of toothpaste; in talcum powder tins and in vanity bags, and on one occasion inside a doll. The only seizure I made that was followed up was a small amount of cannabis oil that I found in the cover of a photograph album. Strangely the destination was the Oxford Road in Reading, about a mile away from where I am sitting as I write.

The points of origin were also what I would come to recognise as high risk in the very near future; Kingston, Jamaica; Lagos, Nigeria; Karachi, Pakistan. Sometimes we were getting cannabis resin from Pakistan but we weren't seeing any heroin. When I left LOMO I didn't know it but it would be the last time I would work with Alby for over thirty years. By that time he would have a wife, Andy, and two children, Robert and Gillian. And I would have Carol, Mark, James my daughter Claire, and a granddaughter, Neoma.

**

Just to let the soft hearted reader know there was a happy ending to the lack of sleep situation. We were staying with my in-laws for Christmas, and Madge, realising we were both close to exhaustion, offered to have James in with her and Arthur on Christmas Eve night. Bliss. We woke up next morning at eight o'clock rushed into their room, to find all three of them asleep. Now whether or not James slept through, or he woke but wasn't heard; bearing in mind we had all been to the Britannia Club the evening before; we'll never know. But he never woke for another night feed from that day on.

It was the best Christmas present ever. Madge really was the best mother-in-law a man could wish for.

**

HEATHROW

It's January the Third 1972 and it's my first day at Heathrow. Little did I know that day that I wouldn't leave until September the 30th 2005, the day I retired. I would of course work in other places on a temporary basis, but I would stay fixed at Heathrow for 33 years and 9 months. Also little did I realise I was entering the most dynamic and exciting theatre of operations for someone who had joined HM Customs, Waterguard, "to catch smugglers". As I used to say to my trainees in future years; "If you find any of this work boring then take a long hard look at yourself and ask yourself if you're in the right job."

On top of the seizures there was the funny stories, the famous people, the international incidents, it was and is all there at Heathrow. When Samuel Johnson said;

"When a man is tired of London he is tired of life"

He was echoing my thoughts of Heathrow. If an Officer was tired of Heathrow then it is time to move on. Death, as suggested by Samuel Johnson, might be a bit extreme, but another job for sure.

**

I present myself to Frank Cox in the Admin Office in Terminal Two. Frank has a look about him that says. "I take no nonsense from anybody". And he didn't. But underneath that gruff exterior was, yes you've guessed it, a gruff interior. But he was a good hearted Geordie who would rather help you than hinder you and that's not something I could say about most Admin types.

Frank explained where my locker was, how the rosters worked, how many Sundays I did, and so on. This was all vital because there were no fixed posts. You did 3 months in a Terminal, then a month boarding aircraft on the Tarmac, that is dealing with health, stores, and crew. Then back to the same Terminal for 3 months, then another month on Boarding/Tarmac, then another 3 months back in the same Terminal, then a month on Boarding. After that you moved onto another Terminal. The net result being that you moved Terminals once a year.

I was also told that my Senior Officer was Dave Memery, although I didn't actually get to meet him for about 9 months. The first time I did meet him was when he was about to do my end of year Staff Report. He called me up, I was in Terminal Two at the time and he was in Terminal Three; SOs' didn't move round like the Officers; and arranged a date for us to meet. When we met we had a general chat about how I was settling in, and he asked me two questions about the Misuse of Drugs Act. I got one right and one wrong. This meant I received an average Staff Report. If I had got them both right, which I might have done had I been forewarned what the interview was about, I would have received a Good. And if I had got them both wrong I would have received a Poor.

None of this was Dave's fault; we were new to the staff reporting system in 1972. However had I realised what a disservice this was doing me I would have made sure I was working in Terminal Three a bit more often. You could do this because there were always people trying to swop out of Terminal Three. It was the Terminal where the vast majority of seizures were made and even at Heathrow there was a large contingent of POs' who weren't really interested.

I calculate that not getting a proper report in my first couple of years at the airport put my promotion back about fifteen years. I calculate this on the basis that some of my contemporaries were promoted around 1975 when HM Customs were looking for hundreds of SOs to go into VAT. When the list of promotees was posted that year there were so many names on it, it was subtitled "the pullover list". This was alluding to the fact that when uniform was in stock, lists were posted on the same notice board as the promotion list, and there were so many on it that one could easily have been mistaken for the other.

The first time the successful and unsuccessful candidates knew how they had done was when they either saw their name on a list, or didn't. No letters for the unsuccessful, your name simply didn't appear on the list. The successful candidates eventually received a letter confirming their elevation. So much for confidentiality, human rights, data protection etc. What would the political correctness lobby have made of that? Anyway I don't think I would have wanted to, or could have afforded to go into VAT. And that was the only career path for most of those on the "pullover list".

The work in the Central Area, that is the three terminals, and boarding, there being no Terminal Four or Five in those days, was as follows. Terminal One had very few seizures. Terminal Two had slightly more seizures than Terminal One and were of a better quality, by which I mean higher amounts of duty being evaded and some drugs. Then Terminal Three; lots and lots of good quality seizures of every type. By the time I was fully experienced working in Terminal Three it was like shooting fish in a barrel. Oh and Boarding or Tarmac as it later became known, where all we did was clear the crew and process the paper work on arriving aircraft; virtually no seizures at all, well not in those days, although this would change when the drugs scene developed. However there were plenty of refreshments, which was very nice.

It wasn't unusual to be offered a full glass of Chivas Regal, or a glass of Remy Martin on a BOAC or a glass of Moet on a BEA, both soon to join together as British Airways. On a Lufthansa it was beer, on a TAP it would be white port, on an Iberia it would be a "sol y sombre" or a Fundador. We all became connoisseurs of the international drinking. It was also steak on the South African, breakfast on the National, out of Miami, and curry on the Air India, so we never went hungry. Some of the waste on aircraft was incredible. On one occasion I was directed to an Air Canada that had gone technical and had had to return to Heathrow. The passengers had disembarked and the caterers were de-catering the aircraft. There were 450 gammon steaks with omelettes being thrown out.

During one of my first spells on Boarding on one shift I was teamed up with Jock Rainnie. Jock was an ex Black Watch, Regimental Sergeant Major. He had also been King Hussein of Jordan's 'personal bodyguard. So as you might guess he was a quite a tough nut, and he didn't suffer fools gladly. We boarded a BEA one evening and Jock was clearing the crew. Jock cleared everyone except the captain who had half a bottle of gin in excess.

Jock.   "That'll be ten shillings captain"

This was post Decimalisation but Jock was happier in old money.

Captain.   "Oh but surely Customs, its Christmas, isn't it"? It was early December.

Jock. "When you see me coming up those steps in a red cloak, and with a fluffy white beard, then it's Christmas, until then it's ten shillings".

I thought it was hilarious, so did the rest of the cockpit crew, but the captain struggled to see the funny side of it.

When I say Jock was a tough nut, it is probably the understatement of the century. He had a fall on his push bike one day on his way into work. He came in anyway. And he came in for the next three or four days. The pain was getting no better so eventually he went to the doctors. Diagnosis; Jock had been walking around with a broken ankle for four days.

When I eventually arrived in Terminal Three, Jock and I often worked together in the Red Channel. One day he was busy putting something away in his drawer under his till. His next passenger arrived put his case on the bench and started to open the case. The man was having a lot of trouble negotiating the lock with the key. I looked up and noticed that this particular passenger was a man of the cloth, resplendent in his dog collar and black cape. Jock hadn't noticed this. As the vicar continued to fiddle with his key, Jock muttered.

"You'd have no trouble finding the hole if it had a few hairs round it. Would ya?"

When there was no reply Jock looked up straight into the face of a very irate and very red member of the clergy. To his credit Jock also had the grace blush and make his apologies, this was accepted and the funny side appreciated by all three of us.

**

The life on Boarding was fun but it was hard on the liver and was very dodgy if you had a long drive home. Fortunately for me we were now living in Hounslow West and I could quite easily get in on Public Transport. This all changed when I moved out to Woodley, but there was a huge car share operation so I didn't actually drive that often. The drinking culture was ingrained in the Boarding Office. Officers not only accepted the free drinks on board the aircraft, a few of them would buy bottles if the bar was still open, or accept goodwill gestures if they were made. On one occasion I was boarding a BEA from Reykjavik with Ollie Campbell, a friend who I had worked with in LOMO. The flight was carrying the London Philharmonic Orchestra, it was all First Class, and it carried a Duty Paid bar. The Chief Steward, who neither of us knew from Adam, nodded at an unlocked bar box and said, "they're spare if you're interested". Inside the bar box were seven unopened bottles of spirits. Chivas Regal, Remy Martin, nothing but the best, and all duty paid. So technically we weren't breaking any Departmental rules if we accepted them. We tossed up for who would have the spare bottle and I won. This was actually irrelevant because of course we declined the offer!

Ollie was a classic case of how an environment like this can destroy a person, if they're not very careful. He was an excellent Officer when it came to finding drugs. But he just couldn't control his drinking. It destroyed his marriage and eventually he was dismissed from the Department for drink related misbehaviours. He died sometime later of a heart attack in a hotel in Bangkok; very sad. I had known him since he was a young man, he was good company, and had the ability to be an excellent Officer.

At the other end of the drinking spectrum there were Officers like Ken Edwards. Ken was a smashing bloke who was near retirement and had very little real interest in the job. One day I was in the Boarding office locker room getting changed when I suddenly heard someone say to Ken;

"Go on Ken have a drink you deserve it"

"Do you think I should, it's a bit early", said Ken. It was 06.45.

"Yes, go on"

There was then the unmistakable sound of something liquid being poured into a glass. This was followed by a long silence. Then Ken said.

"Well I really needed that, it's been a long night".

Then the other chap whose voice I couldn't quite place said;

"Well why don't you have another then. You've only had the one leg it'd be dangerous to hop around on one leg".

I should explain that in Customs jargon a leg was one drink.

"Do you think I should", said Ken.

"Yes, go on you've worked really hard this morning. You deserve it".

"I suppose I do really"

"Of course you do"

This was again followed by the sound of liquid going into a glass. There was another silence. And then the conversation started again. This time my curiosity got the better of me and I poked my head round the end of the row of lockers to see who Ken was talking to. Much to my amazement I found Ken was completely alone. Every time the second person spoke Ken lowered his voice and muttered into his glass. Ken was three sheets to the wind, and was justifying his continued drinking by having this phantom colleague persuade him just how much he deserved it. I left him to it. After all two's company and three's a crowd.

**

I spent a year or so getting my bearings and eventually my point on the roster took me to Terminal Three. I had arrived in the land of the "Seizure Kings". That small band of PO's who spent their whole working lives in the box i.e. an interview room. People such as Chris Isaacs, Jim Cairns, John Saunders, Dave Warren and Bob Snuggs. Bob would spend hours poring over the Exchange and Mart looking for guitars being sold too cheaply. Perhaps they had been bought abroad and the duty hadn't been paid. What Bob didn't know about guitars wasn't worth knowing. These people were my role models. Little did I realise that in a relatively short time I would be up there with them and by the time Seizure Rewards were abolished in 1979 I would have surpassed many of them.

It was to be fair, a little daunting at first. Although my name was known, mainly because I played football, I wasn't thought of in terms of seizures. I was new, I had come from London Port, and I wasn't a product of Heathrow. In short, in relation to seizures, which were the only measures that counted in Terminal Three, my pedigree was unknown and untried. That state of affairs didn't last long.

There were in Terminal Three another small group who were professional jockeys. That is, they were always available to act as a witness in a seizure. The reason for this being that the seizure reward was split five eights for the seizing officer and three eights for the witness. Hence the term jockey. Someone who rides on someone else's back.

This small band of jockeys would watch what was occurring in the Green and the Red Channels and miraculously just as the seizing officer reached the point where he would need assistance , they would be right there, willing and able to assist. They would have been watching the proceedings, they would have a good idea what goods were involved, and a ball park figure of what the reward was likely to be. Lots of officers worked in pairs, for example in later years I would normally team up with Brian Nunn a good friend of mine who lived not far away from me, more of Brian later. But for those who didn't have a partner the jockeys were always available.

Perhaps I should explain about seizure rewards. Rewards were an incentive that had been around from the fifteenth century. They were first introduced as an incentive to stop corruption within the Customs and Excise services, and because it was so dangerous. In 1792 when Rabbie Burns, poet and Excise man, was involved, with other Excise men and Dragoons, in the seizing of the brig "The Rosamond" there was reward of £120 split between the Excise men. This was a fortune in those days and the poets share would have represented about two thirds of his annual salary. By the time I arrived at Heathrow the maximum reward on revenue seizures was £40 split between the two officers. For drugs offences it was dependent on the weight involved but it was never more than £40. They were by then seen as an incentive for those who were prepared to work hard and take all the complaint files that they attracted, and they certainly did attract complaintst. After they were abolished in 1979; a process that was started under Jim Callaghan and completed by Maggie, so at least there was something Labour and the Tories agreed upon; the theory was that this would be addressed through Performance Related Pay. But being the Civil Service it never really worked and everyone received the same whether they bothered or not. It was a shame when they went because they were totally self financing. In at least three years I collected over £100,000 in fines restorations and received about £5,000 before tax in rewards. A rough calculation indicates that in fines alone I collected approximately five times as much as I received in salary during my entire career. Add to that money collected on goods properly declared, and smuggling that I prevented just by being there, I feel I was good value for money to the people who paid my wages. They were a fair if small reward for those prepared to put their heads above the parapet, and take the flack that went with them. I did actually top the £100,000 again later when I was in Terminal 4 but the vast majority of officers switched off, as indeed I did for a short while. As a lesson in how to totally de-motivate a workforce it was second to none. The counter argument of course was that we were only doing what we were paid for so why should we be paid extra. I'll leave you to decide where I stand in this debate.

Anyway I soon learnt who I could use as a jockey and who would help me with interviews, as these were a whole new ball game compared with dealing with seamen. I didn't exactly set the world alight in those early days in Terminal Three, but I was gradually finding out what was what and who was who. This whole process was helped when the powers that be decided to place everyone in fixed Terminals. Or "Terminalisation" as it was described. When I first heard this expression I thought I'd better check my life insurance, then it occurred to me that maybe I was about to appear in Fanny Cradock's ten favourite recipes. But no it meant we would remain in the same Terminal with the same Senior Officer for a whole year at a time. Note the CPO had now been replaced by Senior Officer or Higher Executive Officer (SO or HEO), the

Preventive Officer (PO) by Officer and the Assistant Preventive Office (APO) by Assistant Officer (AO).

One person I knew I could rely on in the box was my good friend Kenny Joy. Kenny was an Evertonian Scouser with a wicked sense of what was right and what was wrong, and this was to be tested to its limits before one particular seizure was complete. One Saturday I was in the Red Channel on an early shift when a gentleman who I later came to know as the Reverend R appeared before me. He had so much baggage that he couldn't get it on to a normal trolley so he had borrowed one of the porters Geest Trucks. I established that he had been to New York for a week and that he was normally resident in this country. He was a priest of a small army church in Wales and he had been away on "Church business", as he put it. He told me that he knew what his allowances were and all he had to declare was a parcel of books.

Now to say my suspicions were aroused is putting it mildly. The hairs on the back of my neck were standing up, and that was always a good sign. The reason for this reaction being that here was a passenger standing in front of me with at least ten pieces of baggage who had only been away for a week. Now why would anyone going abroad for a week need ten pieces of baggage. Exactly, they wouldn't, not even my Carol would need ten suitcases. For that reason I had to assume that there were items in the baggage that had been obtained while he was away. And it was very hard to think of anything that would be of so little value that it would be within the £28 "Other Goods Allowance".

When asked again if he had anything he'd bought or been given while he was away in excess of his allowances he again said he hadn't. Well to cut a long story short I searched the bags and found goods valued at several thousand pounds, and I found the receipts to confirm the value. Most of the goods were clothing and insignias associated with the

Church of which he was a priest. And as the Church wasn't a Registered Charity most of the goods attracted a combined rate of duty and VAT of over 30%. And as it transpired, he knew they did, although I wouldn't find this out until much later. This did put me in a quandary. After all this was a man of the cloth, even if it wasn't a denomination that I recognised. And as an ex Altar Server in the Church of England, I still retained the preconception that a man of the cloth would not lie, and would not try to break the law. How naive can you get?

I had a quick word with Kenny and we decided that at the very least we would take him into the box and see what he said under caution. This we did, but all we could get out of him was a denial that he had done anything wrong, and that he hadn't realised these goods were liable to duty, and therefore why did he need to declare them. He accepted that I had asked him if he had bought or been given anything else while he'd been away, apart from the books which he had declared. He accepted that they were worth several thousand pounds and that they far exceeded the £28 allowance. He actually admitted that in hindsight, when he said didn't have anything in excess of £28 that was incorrect. But it wasn't a lie. They weren't merchandise because they were for individual members of the congregation. He just hadn't realised there was any need to declare them. When faced with such a total lack of logic it is hard to make rational decisions. Kenny was convinced we should "knock him off".

Eventually I decided to leave the decision to the Senior Officer. Normally when you took the details to an SO to adjudicate you were convinced the passenger was guilty. On this occasion I was quite happy to live with his decision. You must remember he hadn't uttered those immortal words.

"I did it to avoid paying the duty", or "It's a fair cop guv".

So a fraudulent evasion offence was tricky. And he was in the Red Channel, therefore failure to declare in the proper manner i.e. in the Red Channel, was tricky. However the SO, Mike Rapley, decided that if we ignored his profession and looked at the facts as they stood, then it was safe to conclude that this was an attempt at fraudulent evasion. How right he was. Mike came in to adjudicate, and duly seized the undeclared goods and offered the Reverend R, the option of going before a Magistrate or paying a Compromise Penalty. The Reverend R opted to pay a fine.

That should have been an end to it. We would issue certain forms, the goods would be sent to the Queens Warehouse and the offender would pay the fine he had opted to pay. However the Reverend R needed many of the seized goods for a ceremony the next day. Now back in those days the offender had twenty eight days in which to appeal against the seizure, so the goods were kept until that time had elapsed. After that time the offender could buy the goods back from HM Customs.

After a degree of soul searching Ken and I moved heaven and earth to get Solicitors permission to release the goods prior to the twenty eight days elapsing. The main problem being to actually find a Solicitor, on a Saturday, when England are playing rugby at Twickenham. But eventually we found one who obviously didn't like rugby and he gave us permission to go ahead. We then hit another problem. The Reverend R didn't have any money. We needed cash. Cheques and credit cards weren't acceptable, and there was no such thing as a debit card back then. The Reverend telephoned one of his parishioners and arranged for her to come up from Wales with the money.

Great, problem solved. Not quite. When the parishioner arrived, the Reverend R had disappeared. Not being under arrest he had been allowed to leave the Customs area to go and have a meal, and he had done a runner. The parishioner was keen to pay the money, both the fine and the restoration, and take the goods, but we couldn't release them to her because she wasn't the legal owner. Although this had been a waste of time as far as the parishioner was concerned our conversation with her was very illuminating. We learnt that the Reverend R regularly dealt with postal importations of the very goods he had told me he didn't think he had to declare. He not only knew that duty was liable, he knew the exact rates, he had been given enough funds to cover the monies that were due, and on top of that he would have been aware that there was no duty or VAT to pay on the books he declared.

The declaration in the Red Channel had been an attempt at a bluff. He realised that pushing a Geest Truck through the Green Channel he would have stood out like a sore thumb and would undoubtedly have been stopped. So he thought that by declaring something on which there was nothing to pay he would just be ushered through as an honest but ill informed passenger. So when I started asking questions he was totally at a loss to know what to say. Hence his ridiculous lies. Amazingly about a month later I received a Red Complaint File. This was the highest level of complaint and this had come from the First Lord of the Treasury's office. Apparently the local MP had been present at the ceremony on the Sunday and when he asked why the uniforms weren't there the Reverend R told him that HM Customs had detained them for valuation. I was angry. Ken was apoplexic with rage at the injustice and hypocrisy, and he gave vent to his anger in his reply to the file. It was without doubt the best reply to a complaint that I ever saw. Normally one had to be very subdued and factual in how one replied. Ken put in everything every officer would have wanted to put in and then a bit more. He quoted from the translation of Daniel 5.25 in the Old Testament.

"Although I am not an especially religious person, I would like to state that if the Reverend R and I were hauled before the seat of judgement, I have no doubt who would be weighed in the balance and found wanting"

Opinions were just not allowed in complaint files, even if they were based on quotes from the Bible, but obviously someone up the line could see the injustice of us being complained against, and allowed Ken's response to stay with the file. We never heard another word about it.

**

I was now in the full swing of things Heathrow, our little family had moved from Fulham to Hounslow and then on the 17th of December 1973 we moved into our first house in Woodley, near Reading, Berkshire. Coincidentally we were only five miles away from where I had gone to boarding school twenty years before. What a day that was. Carol, Mark, James, Chelsea the budgie (the name wasn't my idea), and me in an Austin 1100. Eight days to Christmas; chaos.

**

TERMINAL THREE

I was now settled into life at Terminal Three, Heathrow. Terminals were fixed so there was no more moving about. It was 1975 and I was to stay in Terminal Three until 1986 when Terminal Four opened, although from 1982 onwards I would be mainly involved in the vocational training of new recruits and the developmental training of more experienced officers. Teams were fixed and I was on Mike Cox's team with a whole bunch of chaps who also lived in Woodley so I could car share. Mike was another great boss, I was pretty lucky throughout my career with the bosses I had. He was a master of the English language and had a vocabulary second to none. I was witnessing his offence action on one occasion and when I came to confirm his report I wrote.

"I was present when Mr Cox (Senior Officer) spoke to Mr Offender, and after referring to the Oxford Dictionary I can confirm his report"

Although he protested at this breach of discipline I know he was secretly delighted.

So there was Mike at the head, then there was Brian (Bite Your Legs) Williams, Russ Ayling, Joe Baird, yes the same Joe from the Waterguard Training Centre, John Aust, Peter Harland-Jones, Russ Ayling, Dick Powell, Mike Coulehan, and Jim Pressley. Poor Jim was later to be involved in one of my more embarrassing escapades involving a lot of bedroom furniture. Then later on Peter Norman, Anton Dworzak, Mike Ridley, Nat Lunny, and a new boy Brian Nunn. Brian was one of a new breed; he had come straight in as an Executive Officer, which was the same as Preventive Officer, from another Government Department. The OGD's or Plastics as they were known were part of the revolution that had begun in 1971 with the re-organisation of HM Customs and Excise, and the removal of the Waterguard. Brian Nunn and I, and our families, were to become great friends over the years, we lived about 200 yards from each other, we holidayed together, socialised together and our children remain friends to this day. Brian and I were to share many a seizure together and even though Brian left the department in 1980; mainly because he was obsessed with having a "company car"; and has the misfortune to be an Arsenal supporter, we are still close.

Change was rife during the Seventies not only did we have OGD's we suddenly had an influx of women Officers. Until then the only women had been Women Search Officers, but now we had become part of the general Civil Service the floodgates were open. The first to appear being Yvonne Chegwyn, Kathy Waldron, and Pat Trogg. On top of that our Asian contingent arrived. My good friend Paul Dhand arrived in 1973, along with Mr Sodhi, Mr Singh, Madan Jaggi and Mo Khan. In the last days of seizure rewards Paul would be the only officer in the country earning more than I was. Another close friend of mine, Chak Chakraverty, appeared a little bit later in 1974. You can just imagine the old timers shaking their heads.

"OGD's Plastics, Women, and Asians, what was the world coming to"?

I also came to know around this time a certain Mr Geoffrey Yerbury, Senior Officer, and later to become an OBE. Geoff was a remarkable man whose single mindedness in the pursuit of drug smugglers did more to drag HM Customs out of the dark ages, in respect of drugs, than any other single person. He was and is as far as I know a non drinker, he was obsessed with officers looking like and acting like members of HM Customs, and he was totally professional in everything he did.

"Do your jacket up, scruffy git"

He would mutter as he strode down the Green Channel on his way to target his next victim.

He studied the trends and actions of drug smugglers like nobody before him had, and he made a point of spreading his knowledge around. When high risk flights were going through he would be there.

"Go on, go on, stop her. Her, her with the green bag"

This would be Geoff. No subtle management influencing needed here, and none expected.

Geoff and I had an understanding, and I hope a sort of mutual respect. To the best of my knowledge I was the only officer to whom Geoff would actually point out potential revenue seizures. Normally he didn't think they were worth consideration and would only indicate where he thought we would find drugs.

**

It was a Saturday evening and I was off on the Sunday. For some strange reason, probably "sods law", bad things, by which I mean time consuming, always came along on the day before your rest day. For a lot of officers this was a good thing because it meant overtime, but for me it was bad because I actually appreciated time with my family.

I was stood at the mouth of the Green Channel watching the end of the West African flight from Lagos. There was only one passenger left and the rest of the team had disappeared to get on with whatever they were doing, probably not a lot. There was one passenger, who I later found out to be Catherine Madeke, and one enormous suitcase going round and round on the belt. I watched her for a while to see if she would claim the suitcase, and she was obviously watching me waiting for me to go. Eventually I cracked, I wanted her to pick it up to be sure she couldn't claim it wasn't her suitcase, but I couldn't hang around all night. I went over to her and asked to see her ticket. Attached to it was a baggage tag that matched the one on the suitcase, I also noticed that the ticket was cash paid. This wasn't looking good for Catherine, drug smugglers invariably used cash. She agreed it was her suitcase so we loaded it onto a trolley and wheeled it into the Green Channel. With a lot of effort I managed to get the suitcase onto the bench. A few questions established that Catherine was a Nigerian resident coming from Lagos to stay here for a few days. The purpose of her visit was unclear and she wasn't sure where she was going to stay. This was looking worse and worse for Catherine. So far she matched the perfect profile of a drug smuggler. I asked her the usual questions about the contents of the suitcase and she was vague, she was also unsure about whether or not she was carrying anything for anyone. I obviously wasn't going to get any more out of her so the suitcase was opened, only to reveal, that it was full of bananas! Nothing else, no clothes, no toiletries, no gifts, nothing but bananas. A bit perplexed, although not entirely surprised, having already seen cases full of dead monkeys and dead bats, nothing would surprise me too much, I said.

"Oh bananas"

Not very original but I really couldn't think of anything else to say, as all I could see was black slightly rotten bananas. However even that was wrong.

"No dey plantains" Catherine replied.

To the uninitiated we are talking about little curly bananas that can be eaten raw and big straight plantains that need to be cooked. These were the latter.

So a suitcase full of black rotten plantains. At this point Geoff Yerbury appeared over my shoulder.

"Get your knife into them" he said stating the bleeding obvious.

This I did, and amazingly instead of going through them like a knife through butter, the knife went about an eighth of an inch and stopped. Further inspection showed that each banana, sorry plantain, had been carefully sliced open down one seam. The flesh scooped out, filled with compressed herbal cannabis, then the seam sewn together, put into bunches with the stitching on the inside, and then allowed to rot. When all the cannabis was removed there was a total of forty two kilos of cannabis in the suitcase. This was then a record for a single suitcase, and I suspect it still is. You don't see many suitcases that can actually hold forty kilos of anything. It also made the BBC Television News as we were working to rule at the time and there was a lot of publicity about Customs Officers letting drugs flood into the country. Our Trade Union made sure the media were aware that this wasn't quite true, and the BBC duly reported it.

Anyway, back to Catherine. She had obviously been told that as long as she denied all knowledge of the contents of the bananas, sorry plantains, we couldn't put her in jail. What makes me think this, you ask? Well between 20.00 hours on the Saturday and 20.00 hours on the Sunday when we eventually charged her, her answer to almost every question was.

"You cannot lock me up"

Questions such as;

"Why didn't you pick up your suitcase when it was the only one left on carousel?"

"Why are you bringing a suitcase full of rotten plantains to the United Kingdom?"

"Who are they for?"

"Where are you going with them?"

"Why when asked about the contents of the suitcase, didn't you tell me it was full of plantains?"

"How did you get the money to pay for your ticket"? She was apparently unemployed.

Straight out every time.

"You cannot lock me up". "You cannot lock me up"

Even as I locked her up in the Police Cell after charging her, I could hear her, now shouting.

"You cannot lock me up"

When I returned on the Monday morning the Custody Sergeant, incandescent with rage by this time nodded at the cells and said;

"Listen".

Very faintly, I could just hear.

"You cannot lock me up"

"Either get her out of my cells pronto, or you'll be taking me before the magistrate for something a lot more serious than drug smuggling"

This from a very red faced Custody Sergeant. Apparently she hadn't stopped all night

The sad thing is that in the end Catherine was spot on. She appeared at Reading Crown Court, Artillery House, the foreman of the jury was a

Rastafarian gentleman, and she was found NOT GUILTY. Why our Prosecuting Council failed to dispute his inclusion on the jury I will never understand. She was travelling to the UK for no apparent reason with forty two kilos of cannabis concealed in rotten plantains. She couldn't or wouldn't tell us where she was going or who she was meeting. She didn't have a hotel booking, she had no money, and she had no credit cards, she was unemployed; not a crime but how did she afford the ticket. She couldn't explain why she didn't pick up her case when it was the only case there and it was very distinctive. Call me an old cynic but I suspect the jury might have got this one wrong.

I didn't look at Catherine as she left the dock but I suspect she was still mouthing in my direction.

"You cannot lock me up, you cannot lock me up"

We might not have been able to put her away but we did deport her, innocent or not.

**

On another occasion Geoff was responsible for ruining Sunday lunch for me and a friend of mine by the name of Bob Lugg. I had pulled a very wealthy looking chap coming off of the Miami. Miami because of its proximity to Colombia and the rest of the North of South America was high risk for cocaine and it was likely to be carried by absolutely anyone. During my search of his baggage I found a set of cocaine paraphernalia. A small set of scales, a mirror, a blade in a plastic frame, and amazingly the receipt showing the "head" shop where he had bought them. However there was no coke in his baggage and none on his person. Geoff authorised a full strip search.

At this point the passenger, who it transpired was the President of the Chase Manhattan Bank in this country, hadn't actually broken any laws. It is not an offence to possess the paraphernalia. However Geoff instructed us to get him in the box and see what he had to say under caution. It is amazing what some people say when told that they don't have to say anything. Plus there was always the possibility that he had something at home that was illegal, otherwise why bother with the paraphernalia.

This is where it went downhill for me and Bob. As soon as we were in the box and we had sat the passenger down he said he needed to use the toilet. We were just beginning to get swallowers so this wasn't a good sign. Although he did look a most unlikely looking swallower, we decided that we would have to go down the "swallower" process. We escorted him to the room housing the Portaloo. He sat on the toilet.

"Are you guys planning to stay here with me" He said

"We are"

"Well then I can't go with you here"

Back we go to the interview room.

Unfortunately the President had just spent seven days in Mexico City and all that chilli con carne was not to be denied. So off we go back to the Portaloo. As he sits and produces Bob and I look at each other. Through my mask I mutter.

"What a way to spend Sunday Lunch time" Sunday lunch time being my favourite drink of the week.

The plantains of Catherine Madeke. Showing how they appeared in the suitcase, how the stitching appeared and how the cannabis (Nelson H) could be seen inside.

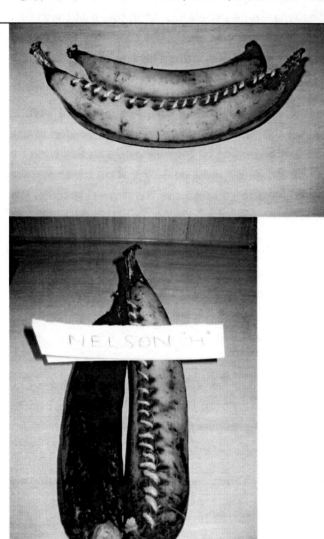

We then had to empty the plastic bag into a colander, beige plastic as I remember, they always seemed to be beige plastic, to this day I still can't have one in the house. Then we sprayed the faeces using a shower spray, down the toilet. There was nothing.

Geoff decided we would limit our action to seizing the paraphernalia. This was very magnanimous of him that the passenger hadn't actually broken any laws. But Geoff's attitude was.

"Go on appeal. I dare you."

Needless to say he didn't. And as Geoff said, "he was over his allowance anyway". I have to say that after that incident my Sunday lunchtime pint always tasted a little bit sweeter.

**

Life in T3 was dynamic. There was always something happening. Most of the old timers had opted for a quieter life in Terminal One or down on Boarding. Boarding was also where the really heavy drinkers ended up, there being a ready supply of free alcohol from the aircraft. That isn't to say that drinking didn't go on in the Terminals. Who can forget Yash's Bar; my friend and colleague, Yash Madan, had his own private bar in the locker room of Terminal Three. it was just that drinking was more of a recreation after the work had been done. The Investigation chaps had a particular affinity with Yash's and would be found in the locker room after the reason for their appearance was done and dusted. One of these Investigators, Peter Bennett, was shot dead by Lennie"Teddy Bear" Watkins in 1979 as he was trying to arrest him for being in possession of cannabis worth £2.5 million. I had only met Peter on a couple of occasions at Heathrow, but this was a reminder that we were involved in dangerous business where the stakes were incredibly high and people were prepared to kill to protect their investment and their liberty.

 Nights in particular, after the last flight had been put to bed and before the first one in the morning, gave ample opportunity for "Team Bonding". Curries were popular, and at one time on our team we had H M Sidhu an Assistant Officer who actually brought in the ingredients and cooked the food while we waited. Unfortunately Mr Sidhu found himself in trouble with the Department later in his career. He hired Wembley Arena for a particular singer to come over from India. He sold every seat in the house, but sadly hr forgot to hire the singer. There were a lot of angry people wanting their money back, and H M Customs were very unhappy that it was one of their staff bringing it into disrepute. There was a suggestion that there was never any intention to hire the singer, but there I go being all cynical again. Mr Sidhu's home was also registered as a temple which meant he didn't have to pay rates.

Some teams would have wine tasting events, some would have theme nights, maybe Caribbean, and some would just sit round and drink and eat. On occasion the bonding might have become a little boisterous I remember one time a certain team thought it would be a good idea to blow up pairs of surgical gloves and tie them to the air conditioning vents. It looked like there were lots of little men with white hands trying to escape from the air vents. The early teams didn't have to ask if they'd had a good night.

It was impossible to be bored. It was always exciting although not always for the right reason. For example the day the Ian Douglas-Hamilton decided to check if a detained firearm had been unloaded properly by pulling the trigger. I was in the General Office when he did it. There was a tremendous bang followed by.

Zing, zing, zing.

The bullet ricocheted around the office.

We all dived for cover. Nobody was hurt and the bullet was never found. What we said to Mr Douglas-Hamilton is unprintable.

There was a room lined with sandbags for the Air Marshalls to unload their weapons but Ian had decided not to use it. Nice one Ian. The situation with the Air Marshalls was always potentially explosive as we had men carrying guns through the Terminal and depositing them in a specially designed facility. The problem was we had no way of knowing who would be in there at any particular time. So we could have an El Al Air Marshall disarming at the same time as a Syrian Arab was arming himself. It's amazing that we never had the shoot out at the OK Corral.

Even if there were no jobs on the go or bullets flying around there were always interesting people going through.

The two most impressive people I ever met in T3 were Cassius Clay as he was then, and Ian Paisley. They both had a tremendous "presence" about them. It was as if they were above the things that trouble us mere mortals. I was clearing a member of the Ian Paisley entourage in the Red Channel, the airline had lost his baggage. Ian Paisley was standing a few feet away wearing a metallic green Macintosh apparently talking to another member of his group. I asked the chap standing in front of me if he had any cigarettes or spirits in the missing baggage. The man opened his mouth but no sound came out, then a voice boomed out from behind him. It was the Reverend Paisley

"He better not have. He better not have if he's travelling with me"

The man looked at me like a rabbit caught in a car's headlights. There was a nervous little tic in his right eye. I decided to have pity on him.

"I take it that's a no"

He nodded. I made a note on the C1488, the Mishandled baggage Form, if any excess cigarettes or spirits were found they were to be referred to me, and I would deal with it by post. He saw what I was writing and gave me a weak smile. When Ian Paisley moved away he explained that the Reverend didn't agree with smoking or drinking so even buying their allowances would be frowned upon. When the bag arrived there was only his Duty Free Allowance, nothing to get excited about.

The most polite and most gentlemanly VIP I met was Sir Laurence Olivier. A perfect gent even after I had snapped at him for approaching my bench without being called. He and his wife, Joan Bancroft, were so apologetic they made me feel about two feet tall.

The most obviously drunk was Sid James. He obviously didn't travel well. Or maybe he travelled too well. But he always had friendly word for the officers in the Green Channel. I think he felt he was amongst kindred spirits.

The most articulate; Clement Freud, I stopped him and asked where he normally lived. His reply;

"I like to think I don't live anywhere normally" With heavy emphasis on the, "normally".

The most artistic; Rolf Harris, he scribbled me a small cartoon, we didn't ask for signatures. Now he's a recognised artist it's probably worth something.

The tallest was Joel Garner the cricketer. Brian Williams had detained eighteen bottles of rum that Joel had brought in for the Bermudan High Commission. While he was packing them up I hid one under the bench. I did a quick count and said out loud.

"Seventeen bottles of Cockspurs, a nice present for someone at the High Commission"

Brian looked up. "No eighteen"

"No seventeen" I said.

He quickly counted them, and then before I could confess he bolted out of the Red Channel, rushed out into concourse, found Joel Garner, which wasn't difficult, explained that he had given him a receipt for eighteen bottles when there was only seventeen. Joel wasn't happy he was sure there were eighteen. And of course by the time he reached the Red Channel there was eighteen, I having retrieved the extra one from under the bench. Brian was very embarrassed, Joel was very confused, and I was extremely amused. I never did confess to Brian.

The sexiest person I ever met was Dolly Parton when she arrived in a shocking pink all in one jump suit. I was completely incoherent when questioning her in the Green. She must have thought I was speaking a foreign language.

The friendliest was Debbie Harry, more attractive in real life than on the screen, and very normal. Coming through the Green Channel on her own, no entourage she just seemed happy to chat and chat. I kidded myself that she quite fancied me. I just hope there wasn't an ulterior purpose.

The biggest liar; this is a footballer who I can't actually name for legal reasons, but lets call him John. John was a young lad at the time he had the misfortune to bump into me in the Red Channel in Terminal Three. He wandered into the Red because he was unsure of the allowances. I explained them to him, it was £28 other goods at the time, I explained what the £28 other goods allowance meant in great detail. He was coming back from New Zealand where he had been playing football for four months during the summer; this was when there was a proper break between the seasons ; and he was about to start pre season training with Norwich City who were in the old First Division. The reason I spent a lot of time explaining the £28 allowance was that John was wearing a fur coat which to my expert eye looked very new. It also looked very "fashionable"! Fur coats, especially wolf fur, were fashionable in the late seventies and early eighties. John listened to me then told me that he had nothing to declare. I asked him.

"So you haven't bought or been given anything in excess of £28 value"

"No nothing" LIE NUMBER ONE

"You haven't bought or been given anything such as watches, cameras, fur coats"?

"No" LIE NUMBER TWO

I then asked him point blank. "What about the coat you're wearing. Where did you obtain that?"

"Oh I bought that before I went to New Zealand" LIE NUMBER THREE.

"Can you tell me the name of the shop?"

"No I can't remember" LIE NUMBER FOUR.

I asked John to remove the coat. I examined it, and, brushing it with the palm of my hand, some hairs came away, a sure sign that it was very new. The pockets were pristine, there was no fluff. The cuffs and collar showed no sign of wear. The label was bright and also showed no sign of wear. It was brand new.

"Are you sure this coat is four months old?"

"Yes, I bought it before I went to New Zealand" LIE NUMBER FIVE

"This coat is new; I think you bought it in New Zealand"

"No it's four months old; I just haven't worn it much" LIE NUMBER SIX.

I searched his baggage and rubbed him down hoping to find the receipt, but no joy. The questioning was repeated and when we had reached something like lie number twenty seven I produced a document , a C104 and I explained to John that I wanted him to give me a written declaration regarding the coat, and that I intended to detain the coat pending proof of purchase in this country. He duly completed the form but just as he was on the point of signing; thereby making it a legal document that could be produced in a court of law; I explained that if he did sign it he was compounding any offence that he might already have committed. In layman's terms, so far I suspected him of attempted fraudulent evasion that is smuggling. Should he sign the C104 and it turned out to be false in any material fact, for example where he had bought the coat, then he would be guilty of knowingly and recklessly making a false declaration. He would be making things a lot worse.

"What happens if what I've told you so far isn't quite right"?

Eureka!

At this point these are just the words every Officer is waiting to hear. From then on it was plain sailing. Yes he had bought it in New Zealand. Yes it was a week old. Yes it was worth more than £28, actually approximately £1972 more. Yes, after I explained the £28 allowance he did realise it was liable to duty. Yes he supposed he had lied to avoid paying that duty. He only supposed that was why he had lied, just like most people in this situation he just couldn't quite bring himself to admit it was why he'd lied. Anyone who has had children will recognise this syndrome.

The last hurdle we had to get over was whether or not he should go before a Magistrate or pay a Compromise Penalty. He needed to speak to his manager. Let's call him Ken Brown. John spoke to Ken on the phone who then asked to speak to me. I explained the situation. Ken apologised to me. Ken spoke to John. A very chastened John paid a Compromise Penalty, and I suspect was put through some very vigorous pre season training on his return to Carrow Road.

Years later John was innocently caught up in a well publicised bribery scandal. I remember his brief describing him as being of unblemished character. Not quite unblemished I thought, perhaps John had forgotten a certain Malcolm Nelson, Officer of H M Customs and Excise, and a certain fur coat.

**

Bob had moved to Heathrow shortly after I did. He moved Martien and his ever growing family, now up to two, Monique and Jason, to Bracknell and tried to settle into airport life. This never quite happened. Aircraft just weren't for Bob and as he had no family ties west of London he had no reason to stay. Sadly for me in November 1975 Bob moved, now with another son Justine, to Great Yarmouth. Had I known what was going to happen I would have been even sadder.

It was the 22nd of November 1982 and Bob had just returned to Great Yarmouth from Dover where he had been working with the Investigation Division. Because he had returned unexpectedly he was the spare man. The Senior Officer or CPO, in charge was looking for someone to go on board a vessel berthed at Lowestoft to arrest the vessel on behalf of the Admiralty Marshall. Apparently the Master of the vessel, the Fishing Vessel GIRON, hadn't been paying his harbour dues. Two officers had already tried to serve the Warrant but had been unceremoniously thrown off of the ship. So of course there was Bob, six foot three, very experienced, not going to be thrown off or put off by anyone.

Bob boarded the GIRON and tried to serve the Warrant but before he could do so the master tried to put out to sea. Bob heard the engines turning over realised what the skipper was trying to do. Quick as he could he made his way down two decks towards the engine room. The alleyways were dark because the power was still only coming from the generator. As Bob went down a set of stairs he slipped. He caught his spine on the steps. He was badly hurt. His spine was irreparably damaged and he has lived with the pain ever since. That was Bob's last day as an active Customs Officer. He was unable to work and even after they had diagnosed the problem, although with no certainty, the doctors were unable to operate for fear of what other damage they might do. Eventually Bob was invalided out of H M Customs and Excise without any compensation from the Department. A nationwide appeal was conducted for Bob but only after I and a very good friend of Bobs' from his Heathrow days, Chris Hamblin, had threatened all sorts of things through the Customs and Excise journal "The Portcullis," and the national press. I remember a very strange conversation with Bobs' ex Surveyor during which every other line from him seemed to be.

"You can't do that"

"Just watch me" Was the reply.

Surprise, surprise, we then heard that a national collection was to be made on Bobs' behalf.

The GIRON with its Master disappeared for many years, apparently to the Gulf, when they did finally re-appear the Department took them to court, and sued for compensation on Bobs' behalf. But they, or rather Bob, lost. The defence was able to sew enough doubt and confusion as to who was responsible and how bad the injury really was, to get the verdict in their favour. Should any of those people who suggested, reported, or believed that Bob wasn't really that badly hurt, read this book, I would like to point out that Bob still has to use morphine, 27 years on. His and his family's lives are dictated to by the use of the drug. He hasn't worked, he rarely leaves the house, and his body clock is at variance with the rest of the world, in that our night is his day. If a special occasion, such as Christmas, is on the horizon, he has to manage the drug intake to be sure he able to operate on the same cycle as the rest of us.

Mr Justice whatever your name was, read this, remember Bob Highstead, and feel very ashamed.

**

Although it was mainly drugs and revenue goods there was also a great deal of variety in Terminal Three

Again it was a Saturday evening and I was off the next day. The MS777 was in the hall, this was the Egyptair from Cairo. Not high risk but still quite an interesting flight. I was in the Red Channel and as it was

Saturday evening, and as I was in the Red I was unlikely to get involved in anything too heavy. So during our break I had been to the bar with Brian Nunn and Mike Ridley. I was dealing with the queue, nothing too interesting was happening, and I was mentally winding down. Then an Egyptian lady came into the Red. Her name was Akila Nasser, funny how some names stick in the memory.

"Akila, which means intelligent" She told me.

How wrong can a name be?

I went through the normal questions. She was here to visit her daughter who lived here, she was staying a week, and she had some possessions of her daughters that she thought she should declare. Now because her daughter had changed residence to live here within the last six months, the duty liability depended very much on the type of goods, and how long they had been in her daughter's use and possession before she moved here. People coming to live here can't buy a lot of high value goods just before they move here and claim them as duty free under the Change of Residence Allowance.

So I needed her to show me the goods. She was carrying a sort of wicker basket as hand baggage and she placed this on the baggage bench, slightly to one side, whilst she opened her suitcase to show me the things she was bringing for her daughter. As I was leaning over to look in the suitcase, out of the corner of my eye I thought I saw the basket move. Remember I had been to the bar. I dismissed it and thought it must have been the light playing tricks. I carried on my inspection of the daughters possessions, and then I thought I saw it move again. I could have sworn I'd only had two pints, but I was seriously worried, was I seeing things, or worse still was my alcohol tolerance on the wane? The woman was nowhere near the basket, there was no breeze, I wasn't knocking it, this basket appeared to be moving entirely of its' own volition. As I was stood looking at it metaphorically rubbing my eyes and scratching my head, the cardigan that was draped over the basket appeared to rise up and then subside. My relief at realising that I wasn't seeing things, was quickly replaced with the awful thought that there was some living creature in the basket.

I looked at Mrs Nasser, no relation to the President, and she was looking extremely crestfallen. I pointed at the basket.

"Cats", she said as she removed he cardigan to reveal a mother cat and four tiny kittens.

She then admitted that she was bringing two of the kittens for her daughter and she hadn't wanted to leave the others behind in Cairo, so she brought the mother and the rest of the litter as well. She had carried them on the aircraft and had put the basket in the overhead locker. Apparently they had slept all the way from Cairo. She claimed not to know it was illegal to import cats into the United Kingdom. But her claimed lack of knowledge was irrelevant as it was an absolute offence to attempt to breach the quarantine regulations.

Her kind heart had cost her dear. She appeared before Uxbridge Magistrates Court on the Monday and was fined £50 for each cat. A total of £250, if she'd left the mother and the other two at home it would have only been £100. Sadly the cats paid an even higher price. The daughter couldn't afford to put her two kittens into quarantine for six months and the mother couldn't afford to have her three shipped back to Cairo so sadly the RSPCA had no choice but to put them down.

As I say. Akila means intelligent? This lady must have been the exception that proves the rule.

**

Revenue seizures were an endless source of amusing stories and the excuses people used for not declaring goods were both imaginative and ludicrous, as were the lines we used to persuade people to tell the truth and confess their sins.

I have been told.

"I thought it only applied to gifts" or on the other hand

"I didn't think it applied to gifts"

I have been told.

"I didn't think other goods meant cameras and things like that" or on the other hand.

"I thought other goods meant things like cameras not clothing"

I've been told.

"But officer I've worn it, surely that doesn't count"

Well actually it does especially as it's a £5,000 silver fox fur coat.

"I didn't think other goods meant things like clothing" Oh really, where exactly is the bit on the Customs Notice that says "other goods except clothing"?

Every excuse you can think of including.

"Mark Suter's (an Officer who was a very good friend of mine) my cousin, does that count"

Well no actually it doesn't, especially when I find out from Mark later, that he's a very remote cousin, who he doesn't particularly like anyway.

"But it's second hand officer" Well it might be but it's still a solitaire diamond ring worth over £5,000.

Perhaps the best excuse of all was a chap coming from Miami with a new set of Ping golf clubs.

"I just wasn't thinking officer, you won't believe me but"

"I probably won't but try me anyway"

"I called my wife yesterday, and as it was about two o'clock in the morning UK time I dialled the number of the phone we've got in our bedroom. And a man answered it. I just packed, jumped on the first flight out of Miami, and was desperate to get home"

"You're right I don't"

"Don't what?"

"Believe you"

He later paid a Compromise Penalty; he obviously didn't think the Magistrate would believe him either.

The difficult thing was to get people to admit that they had lied about the goods they were carrying. The favourite excuses were;

"I bought it in this country and took it abroad with me"

Or

"I it bought abroad ages ago but I've paid duty on it".

One day in the Red Channel I had the MP for Petersfield telling me that the camera he was carrying was his sons and he had borrowed it for the trip. He was sure his son had bought it in this country. Unfortunately for him during the ensuing conversation his wife let slip that their son was picking them up from the airport. My suggestion that I would go outside and check the MP's story with his son went down like a lead balloon. A very shamefaced MP admitted he had bought it in Singapore. Standards in the Palace of Westminster were obviously no better in those days.

They weren't always that easy. Passengers would lie and then refuse to admit the lie despite the most overwhelming evidence that what they were saying was untrue. We then had to persuade them that it was in their best interest to tell the truth, and to do this we would use a whole range of arguments.

I remember being involved with another one of the Woodley commuters, Mike Coulehan, with two men of the cloth from Northern Ireland. The fathers were bringing back two sets of brand new golf clubs. We knew they were brand new, we knew they were bought in the USA. The trouble was we couldn't persuade the fathers that we knew. They thought we were making an assumption. Eventually the conversation with the more senior of the two went like this.

"Father I know you're lying"

He nods but says nothing.

"What is more I know, that you know, that I know you're lying"

Father says.

"To be sure moy son, but it's loike a roundabout, once you get on how'd ya get off again"

"You tell the truth, and that's the end of the ride."

"I guess this is the end of the ride"

And tell the truth they did, they just needed persuading that we really knew the clubs were new, we weren't just guessing. They had been asked to buy the clubs for some parishioners and they thought they would save them some money. They do say that confession is good for the soul. But it isn't always too good for the Bank Balance.

Mike was a smashing bloke, even though he was a Yorkshireman, later in his career he was treated disgustingly by the Department. He and another Officer, Brian Seymour, were accused of fiddling their expenses. They were both on the Cutters, Brian was Captain and Mike was Chief Engineer. They were accused of travelling by train from somewhere like Aberdeen but claiming the air fare. It was true; they had booked flights and then changed to the train at the last moment. But what the investigators, Dave Down and Pete Wiles from London Port, hadn't realised, was that far from fiddling money out of the Department, they had actually done themselves out of money. The train fare was more expensive than the air fare. By the time Messers Down and Wiles had realised it they wouldn't back down, so Mike and Brian were guilty of providing a false travel claim. Brian was demoted from Officer to Assistant Officer, and Mike lost several increments. I knew Dave Down really well from my West India Dock days and his behaviour bewildered me, he was a really top guy. However nothing surprised me with Pete Wiles, I had also known him in London Port. Ironically Dave Down once threatened to fill him in when he accused me of reneging during a game of Chase the Lady. This was just about the worst insult you could throw at a member of the Waterguard, Chaser being almost a religion.

Sadly Brian couldn't handle the demotion and he resigned and started his own building firm. When we were still in London, Alby, Bob, and I, took Brian out for his stag do. By the end of the evening he was begging us to let him go as he had to get up in the morning for his wedding. Eventually he escaped out of the toilet window in the pub we were in, and I can still see him now in the distance, running down Borough High Street towards the Elephant and Castle, as if his life depended on it.

Anyway back to the plot. The bluffs used by officers to persuade potential offenders that they knew something that in reality they only suspected were many and varied. I'm sure it's where the expression "bull***t baffles brains", comes from.

Anything that had a serial number on was easy. For one thing the number would almost certainly indicate the year of manufacture. So if a person was claiming to have bought the camera, radio, golf clubs, or whatever, at a certain time in a certain place, we could probably tell if the date was correct. And we could use that number to put pressure on the person about where they had bought it. The conversation would o something like this.

"You see this number here"

"Yes"

"That tells me when it was made and it tells me where in the World it was distributed to"

"Really"

"Yes really. And I can see from this number that it wasn't distributed to the UK "

At this point you don't want to be too specific because you might give the whole game away. So I'm only saying it wasn't distributed to the UK. If I say it was sent to the Far East but he bought it in the USA he might realise that the number isn't the font of knowledge that I'm pretending it is.

"Oh"

"So if you insist that you bought in the UK before you left. Then we have a problem don't we"

"Yes"

"Or rather you have a problem because I am going to ask you to put what you have told me into writing, and then I am going to detain the camera until you can produce proof of purchase in this country".

"What if I can't find the receipt?"

"Then we will call the shop"

"Yes but I'm not sure what shop"

"Well we will have to contact the manufacturer. The serial number is unique, so they will be able to tell me exactly where it was distributed to and when"

You are very unlikely to do any of these things; it is all a bluff to get the potential offender to admit the truth. Nine times out of ten it worked. If there wasn't a number as with golf clubs and fur coats, then you would use the model or the style and try and impress on the passenger your knowledge of what models were available in different parts of the world. Ping was the only exception and they did have serial numbers. Again you would try not to be too specific, a line such as;

"I'm not very happy about these clubs Mr Offender. You say they were bought in the UK but to the best of my knowledge this particular model is only available in the States".

If it was fur coat or expensive clothing then you would use style rather than model. Or with a fur coat you might ask where it is stored during the summer. Most top quality fur coats will be refrigerated in the summer. Fur also continues shedding hairs while it is new and a gentle rub will actually dislodge a few. Another clue might be the pockets as they will show no signs of wear and tear on a new coat.

Jewellery was easy because of the hallmarks. Jewellery bought legitimately from a retailer in this country will have a hallmark. It did however become much trickier when we recruited our first Asian officers. We suddenly found out that all this jewellery being worn by Asian women was 22 or 24 carat gold. It was such a bright yellow colour we had always assumed it was rubbish so we had ignored it. This presented us with problems because a lot of it could be allowed in as part of the Change of Residence Allowance on marriage, and of course it had no hallmark. As a consequence whenever we stopped an Asian lady with a full set of jewellery we were invariably told it had been imported previously and passed free. The difficult thing then was, in the absence of any serial numbers or hallmarks, to persuade them that you knew it was new.

Some officers resorted to shouting and bullying, although to the best of my knowledge this was very rarely successful. I remember going in the box with an Officer by the name of Barry Terry. Barry felt if you shouted loud enough you would get a cough, later in my career I would have the same problem with my Russian trainees. At one point he was bright red, wild eyed, and the veins on forehead were standing out. I stopped the interview, got him outside, and told him to calm down. I went back into the box and said without realising how effective it would be.

"Look when he comes back in just answer his questions as truthfully as you can or he's going to get really angry." Unwittingly I was going down the good cop bad cop routine.

It was a man and wife, which was unusual, they just looked at each other, they must have been thinking.

"You mean he wasn't angry before!"

When Barry came back they gave a full admission. They obviously didn't want to see him get really angry.

That wasn't really my style. So I had a little fairy story that served me well. I used to convince the passenger that jewellers use a particular paste when fashioning jewellery and that when they had finished they would polish the jewellery to remove the paste. Now although to the naked eye it would appear that all the paste had been removed some would remain for up to six months, by which time it would evaporate. By applying certain chemicals our forensic scientists could ascertain whether there was any jewellers paste present. If there was then the jewellery wasn't as old as the passengers were telling me. This served me very well over the years and was much more effective and civilised than banging the table. On one occasion it almost worked too well. I was working with a colleague and friend, Inder Alagh. I must have been convincing because as we were getting ready for the Senior Officer to come in he said.

"That's amazing I never knew that about the jewellers paste". The client just looked at me. He knew he'd been tricked, but it was too late. He'd coughed by then.

I've talked about all the different excuses I've heard all the silly answers but only one person ever left me completely lost for words. Catherine Madeke came pretty close with her suitcase full of bananas which were really plantains. But one young lady who we will call Miss Option for reasons that will become apparent succeeded in silencing me completely.

It was an average job, just a small amount of undeclared jewellery and some clothing. Miss Option was an ex air stewardess so it wasn't difficult to prove that she knew what she was doing and she duly admitted to trying to avoid paying duty.

I told her that I was going to report the matter to a SO and he would come and listen to the facts. What happens then she asked. I tried to explain to her that she would be offered certain alternatives. That is she would be offered the option of going before a Magistrate or paying a Compromise Penalty. We were not supposed to go into too much detail otherwise we could be seen as pre-empting the SO's decision. But in cut and dried situations like this, rather than put the offender in fear of their life and liberty, we would explain the option. The trouble was that every time I started to tell her the alternatives as soon as I said she would be offered the option of going before a Magistrate, she said

"Yes I'll do that"

"What do you mean you'll do that you don't know what the alternative is"

"No it's alright I'll go before a Magistrate"

"But you can pay a Compromise Penalty as an alternative"

"Yes I know. I was in a bit of trouble at Gatwick coming back on a night flight. I was offered that chance to pay a penalty then. But I'm not doing it again"

"What do you mean?"

I was totally confused. Then in words of one syllable she explained to me what exactly the penalty she had paid was. Needless to say it didn't involve any money, or any official records. Some frustrated Officer had taken advantage of the situation and had taken a penalty that had satisfied them both. Although obviously he more than her as she wasn't interested in doing it again. Or perhaps it was just me she didn't fancy. I discontinued the conversation, mainly because I couldn't think of what I could possibly say. I left that to the SO who was a certain Mike Cox, who as I've explained previously had a wonderful way with words.

**

Brian Nunn and I worked very effectively as a team for a number of years. We were both driven by the same desire not to muck about. Some Officers liked to take their time about things and stretch things out as much as they could, ostensibly to make sure they didn't make mistakes, but in reality to see if they could make any overtime out of it. Brian and I were more interested in getting home to our young families.

One day Brian and I were involved in a jewellery job off of a Sandfly, a Sandfly being a UK resident currently working in the Middle East or the Gulf of Arabia. Just as we thought we were bringing it to a close we rubbed him down and in his pocket we found about twenty grams of cannabis. Not a commercial amount but enough to make sure we didn't get away when we were supposed to. This was before the Compromise Penalty on small amounts for personal use was introduced, so it meant we had to go through the full procedure. Arrest, Charge, up before a

Magistrate, Witness Statements the lot. The only reason I mention this rather small and insignificant seizure is that it was responsible for me being more embarrassed than at any other time in my entire career.

We had done it all, interviewed him, bagged up the exhibits, locked up the drugs, etc. All that was left was to take him to the Northside Police station and charge him with the offence. This we did. It was all going like clockwork when we reached the point where he had to have his mugshot taken. The offenders name was Norman Shannon. I was looking for the letters to put in front of him to identify the mugshot. I was totally unaware that the room had filled up with burly policemen. Brian asked if I was nearly ready.

"I'm just looking for another Nnnnnn." I said.

Both Brian and I had young children who we were in the process of teaching to read. So I didn't just say N. I pronounced as would have done to one of our tin lids. Brian knew what I meant. But the six boys in blue who were watching me just shook their heads. I had just confirmed all their suspicions about HM Customs. Result; one very red faced Malcolm Nelson and the more I tried to explain it the redder I went.

**

Drug offences tended not to be so amusing. For one thing the crime was much more serious and the penalties consequently much more severe. However there were some light-hearted moments. I was carrying out an interview on a Mr Nosiru who had come from Lagos with half a kilo of heroin inside the tube of a television set. My witness was Zara Khan a lovely lady who was new to Customs at the time.

The interview was following the usual pattern.

He was bringing the TV for the friend of a friend in Nigeria, but he wasn't sure of his name or where he lived.

He was on holiday but he didn't have a hotel booked and he couldn't explain how he was going to manage as he had almost no money on him.

No he knew nothing about the contents of the TV.

He had only taken possession of the TV at Lagos airport. And so it went on. I came to one piece of potential evidence, a photograph that was in the top pocket of his jacket.

"Who is this in this photograph?"

I inform the tape recorder that I am showing Mr Nosiru a photograph of a man.

"What dis photograph?"

"Yes. There is only one photograph"

"What de picture here"

I explain to the tape that there is only one picture.

"Yes. Who is it in the picture?"

"Who is dis in de picture?"

Nosiru is apparently deep in thought.

"Yes who is dis; I mean this, in the picture"

"Dis picture here"

Nosiru is still apparently deep in thought.

"Mr Nosiru. The man in the picture who is he"

"Ah de man in de picture"

This said in such a way that you would think there is a whole lot of women with one man in the picture. I explain to the tape that the picture shows one man all on his own. We go round in circles for another two or three minutes then I'm told.

"Dis man here, he my brudder"

"This man in the picture is your brother"

"What dis picture here"

"There is only one picture"

"Yes dis my brudder"

"So the man in the picture, he is your brother. What is his name?"

"What de name of de man in de picture"

"Yes the man you say is your brother what is his name."

"He my most favourite brudder"

"What is his name?"

"What de man in picture, his name"

"Yes the name of the man who you say is your most favourite brother?"

The reason for all this fencing is that Nosiru hasn't got a clue who the man in the picture is. He has been given a picture of the man who will meet him but that's all. After another five minutes Nosiru changes tack. He suddenly starts wailing and banging his head on the wall. Now you must remember this is being recorded and it is not going to sound very good.

"Mr Nosiru, stop banging your head on the wall"

Then to the tape.

"Mr Nosiru is banging his head on the wall."

Nosiru carries on wailing and then starts banging his head on the wall again.

"Mr Nosiru stop banging your head on the wall"

Then to the tape.

"Mr Nosiru is still banging his head on the wall"

Then Nosiru does it a third time. At this point I say.

"Mr Nosiru stop banging your head against the wall"

Then I muttered under my breath, or so I thought.

"You're damaging the wall".

Unfortunately it wasn't as quiet as I thought it was and my comment was very audible. The defence made quite a lot of my sotto voce remark when we reached Isleworth Crown Court. It was suggested that I didn't take the situation seriously enough; that I was racist; that I was an unfeeling so and so with Nazi style tendencies etc etc. However the jury and the judge seemed to see the funny side of it. Nosiru got seven years and I was commended by the judge for the patience I had displayed during the interview.

**

Getting away from seizures and smugglers for a bit I spent some time acting as a Senior Officer. This was my first taste of management and it was something I grew to like. My first spell in Terminal Three put me in charge of my good friend Paul Dhand, as well as Tony Griffiths, Ken Faulkner, Des Latimer, and Yash Madan, all of whom were also all friends of mine. It was a quite unremarkable couple of months except for an incident that was all about decision making in an area where I had little or no experience.

It was as a Saturday morning in the middle of August and I was the Duty Senior Officer. There was no Surveyor on duty in those days so I was the Senior Customs official on duty. Someone, I don't remember who, rushed into my office and said. "There's a bomb in the Green Channel x-ray machine". This was just what I wanted to hear.

In those days we were talking IRA not Al Qaeda, and I had actually witnessed the bomb exploding in the Terminal One car park, so you can imagine my delight. It was a Saturday, Terminal Three had about eighteen thousand passengers passing through; at that time Heathrow was the busiest International Airport in the world, and Terminal Three on it's own was the second; and we had a bomb in the Green Channel.

I quickly ascertained that a British Airports Authority (BAA) Security Guard had seen a suspicious looking attaché case on its' own in the Terminal Three car park. So what does he do? Does he leave it there where all it can do is blow up a few cars, and contact his control centre? No of course not. What he does is, he picks it up and brings it into

Terminal Three where if it is a bomb, it's got eighteen thousand people to maim and kill. Then he walks into the Green Channel and puts it into our x-ray machine. Whereupon he confirms that it is a bomb. We of course have no idea what the x-ray image of a bomb looks like, but BAA Security are trained for situations such as this.

I then instruct my officers to seal off the Red and Green Channels and evacuate both Channels and the offices immediately adjoining the channels. I inform the BAA Duty Manager who tells me that I can't do it. He's got Jumbo jets arriving every three minutes and the Immigration Lounge is already full. Eventually he sees sense and starts to divert passengers to Terminal Two while we wait for the Bomb Squad to arrive from up town.

An hour and a half later the Bomb Squad finally make their way through the chaos that has taken over the airport outside of the Terminal. They kit themselves in their bomb proof gear and make their way tentatively into the Green Channel. They are prepared to destroy the x-ray machine in a controlled explosion if necessary. Over the radio they confirm that the x-ray picture indicates an explosive device. They then decide to move the case from the x-ray machine and put it on a bench. One of the squad returns to the back office where we're waiting. He tells us that although it looks like a bomb they can see no signs of wiring to indicate that it is booby trapped. Because of this they are going to open the case and that is why he has left his mate alone. If it does explode they only want one of them to go up with it.

It was so tense; the amount of explosive indicated by the x-ray will be enough to demolish the Red and Green Channel and the room above. We're about 60 yards away with several walls in between, no CCTV in those days. The only link we have is the radio between the two members of the bomb squad, and we're getting a ball by ball commentary.

"He's undoing one lock."

"He's undoing the second lock"

You could hear a pin drop.

"He's listening for any noise of a device that he might have triggered"

"He's lifting the lid to half way"

"He's listening again"

"He's lifting the lid all the way"

"He's laughing his bloody head off"

"WHAT"

"He's found two bottles of aftershave and an electric alarm clock"

You could feel the relief, the laughter was slightly hysterical, and the BAA Duty Manager was beside himself with a mixture of relief, annoyance, and a fair bit of," I told you so". He never thought I should have closed the Terminal.

I was assured by the bomb squad that I had acted correctly. The Security Guards assessment had been correct, in as much as the image shown from the x-ray matched their Training Manuals version of a homemade bomb. Two sticks of whatever explosive, that is the bottles of aftershave, a detonator combined with a timing mechanism that is the alarm clock. However this support didn't stop the BAA Duty Manager filing a complaint against me because of my decision to shut the Red and Green. In his complaint he managed to completely ignore the fact that one of his Guards had brought the case into the Terminal in the first place.

I'm pleased to say my bosses treated the complaint with the contempt it deserved, and my decisions to firstly shut the channels and secondly not to re-open them when under pressure from BAA had been vindicated.

**

Before I leave Terminal Three I must talk about the incredible characters who worked there. It is the people that make anywhere memorable. Some I have already mentioned; Geoff Yerbury responsible almost single handedly for dragging us into the world of the drug smuggler and Yash Madan with his famous bar in the locker room.

Then there was Pete Alexander, I was witnessing a fur coat job of his when the offender gave a particularly stupid answer. Pete put his pen down looked her straight in the eye and asked.

"This mental institution (she had given her address as a well known institution for the mentally challenged). Do you work there or are you an inmate?" I was also with him the day he was trying to repair a priceless antique; that he'd seized and dropped; with a tube of super glue. The antique was on its way to the British Museum.

Neil Benson. A plain speaking Yorkshireman who not only called a spade a spade he was on occasion downright rude, and rather prone to making racist comments. He was an average Customs Officer but a magnificent violinist.

Pete Rogers was a guy in a million. It was actually when he was in Terminal One when he played the best practical joke on a Senior Officer that it was my privilege to witness. Pete had a potential offender in the box and the man was suffering with a complaint that caused him to bleed profusely from the mouth. Pete left the box and told John Liggett the SO that he had a problem. John followed Pete into the box. As soon as they entered the room Pete yelled.

"And if you don't answer my bloody questions I'll hit you again"

The man looked up with blood streaming from his mouth. John went white. Pete burst out laughing and John realised he'd been had.

There was Ian Douglas-Hamilton the Officer who preferred pulling the trigger to the more conventional ways of unloading a firearm

Mike Ridley was on our team, he was completely off the wall. When asking a Jamaican man;

"What's this?"

As he pointed at a parcel of herbal cannabis, the man replied;

"Dat's cat food"

"Well you must have a f******* happy pussy", was Mike's reply.

Mike Roffe the only Partick Thistle supporter I've ever met. Mike had a passion for English mustard and French Brandy. He and I demolished a quart bottle of Cordon Bleu brandy between us one afternoon. We were so drunk we managed to convince ourselves that we were both sober. The power of alcohol is amazing.

There was Martin Quek. "Rittle slant eyed git", as he was affectionately known. One Sunday morning I was the duty senior Officer, not a Senior Officer, but the senior Officer on duty. I was on 7/3 shift. At 07.15 my telephone rang. It was "rittle slant eyed git", ringing to say he wouldn't be in that morning.

"But it's double time", I said

Martin explained. He was in a card game somewhere in Greek Street, Soho, and he was winning so much the other players would be extremely unhappy if he tried to leave. Martin was also the person who translated for me when inadvertently I knocked a Chinese student's camera on the floor.

"Why you flow camela on froor?" demanded the student.

Martin lent across and translated. He was also the only person to take money off of me playing table tennis.

Tony Corless; Tony was a Scouser who had unique way of dealing with bills. Once a month he put them all in a hat and drew out as many as he could afford that month. He explained this to an irate garage mechanic who he owed some money to. When the man became abusive Tony warned him that next month his bill wouldn't even go in the hat.

George Atkinson was the captain of our football team. He was like a lump of granite. He was responsible for the only serious injury I ever suffered, and we were on the same side.

Then there was Brian "bite your legs" Williams, he who I had so embarrassed with Joel Garner. Brian was famous or infamous for having been put before a court martial when he was on active service in Cyprus during the EOKA uprising. Brian had been leading a platoon that was ambushed and had issued the order. "No prisoners". He was cleared at the court martial, mainly it is rumoured because of a threatened mutiny. Brian's logic being that as the terrorists took no prisoners why should we.

There was Pete Whyman who sadly suffered a stroke and was never quite the same again. One day I was at the front of the Green watching a lady in a splendid fur coat which I couldn't recognise. When she finally collected her baggage much to my chagrin she headed for the Red. I waited a while and then went into the Red purely to find out what sort of fur the coat was made of. There was the lady being dealt with by Pete. I strolled over and picked up the receipt. It showed one "Nutria" fur coat.

"Nutria, I've not heard of that. What animal is that?"

The lady replied in a very upper class accent that she had no idea.

Pete, who was facing away from the lady suddenly said.

"Nutria, that's a water rat"

The lady's face froze, and there was a deathly hush. Getting no response Pete who was still facing away from us looking at his till tried again.

"Yes, nutria's a water rat"

The expression on the lady's face now has a fixed look of horror on it. Still getting no response Pete swings round on his stool and tries again.

"Yes. They're bleedin great water rats. That's what they are."

The lady's voice was pure ice as she replied in her fine, clipped Rodean accent.

"Thank you, thank you very much Officer. You've made my day"

"That's alright, no problem" said Pete totally unaware of the trauma he had just caused.

Anton Dworzak was renowned for the way in which he knocked a door off of its hinges when chasing a drug smuggler who was making a break for it. The offender swung the door back behind him and Anton caught it right on the edge with his forehead. He hit it with such force that he was knocked out and the door was unhinged. The offender was charged with an offence against Section 16 of the Customs and Excise Management Act. Assaulting an Officer.

Anton's best friend Peter Norman also managed to get his blood all over the floor on another occasion. Peter was Duty senior Officer. That is to say he was the most senior of the Officers on duty, not that he was a Senior Officer. He was the Officer who sorted out meal breaks and thing like that. Anyway that's twice I've tried to explain that now, so I expect that's as clear as mud. Peter was in the DSO's office when the noise of breaking glass could be heard coming from the Red Channel. This was purgatory for someone who liked a little drink now and then. So Peter rushed out into the Red and promptly slipped on a lake of white Wray and Nephew over proof rum. He managed to cut open the top of his head and get blood everywhere. What had happened was that an Officer by the name of Mr Bamrah was dealing with a lady from Kingston, Jamaica, who had declared a lot of white rum. When she was told how much it was going to cost she had protested very volubly. Working next to Mr Bamrah in the same till was Mr Doolub. Hearing his friend being berated by this large Jamaican lady, Mr Doolub turned round and drawing himself up to his full five foot two inches, imposed his authority on the lady passenger.

"If it is the law, then it is the law" By this he meant if that's what you've got to pay then that's what you've got to pay".

The large Jamaican lady was not impressed. She took one look at this little pipsqueak in a uniform and picked up a bottle and smashed it on the floor. Nobody did anything so she picked up another bottle and smashed it on the floor. Still nobody did anything. Bamrah and Dooloub just stood and looked. She picked up all the loose bottles and smashed them all. She was just beginning to open one of the cases of rum when Peter appeared and did his dying swan impression into the lake of Wray and Nephew. By this time those of us working in the rest of the Red Channel had also arrived so the situation was brought under control. There was some discussion as to whether or not the lady should be charged with obstruction but it was decided not to. It was thought that there was more chance Bamrah and Doolub's inactivity would bring the department into disrepute. She was however charged the duty on all the bottles of spirits including those she had destroyed.

On the subject of breaking bottles there was Ken Farrimond who hearing an argument going on behind him in the Green Channel, turned round just in time to catch a bottle of gin that a passenger had just hurled onto the hard ceramic tiled floor. Even though it was glass the bottle bounced and Ken pulled of a catch that a test cricketer would have been proud of.

Then there was my good friend Paul Dhand who had an agreement with his SO, Geoff Yerbury, he was allowed to leave the Terminal every day he was on an early shift to take his children to school, as long as he got a job every day. This he did, with no trouble at all.

Last and not least there was Jock Rainnie and Geoff Yerbury, both previously mentioned.

**

During my time in T3 my home life had progressed much like other peoples. There were highs like when my little princess Claire Annalise was born on the 3rd of July 1975. I can't put into words the pure joy I felt when I first held her in my hands. And there were lows such as when Carol and lost a child before we had Claire. I don't think I realised at the time just what a blow the miscarriage was. We had the two boys and we soon had Claire so there wasn't time to dwell on something that in hindsight was a terrible incident in our young lives. During this period we also acquired our first family dog, a collie cross by the name of Nookie. Named after the bear. She was followed by Nellie; one of Nookie's pups from the three litters she had, Mollie; a Springer Spaniel; and Daisy, who at the time of writing this is still with us.

Then in August 1980 we threw a huge surprise family party for Madge and Arthurs 40thanniversary. It was tremendous occasion, everybody was there, it was held at our house and we had tents in the garden so everyone could sleep over. Madge and Arthur were overwhelmed; they loved every minute of it. To this day whenever I hear "Dancing Queen" I can see Madge jigging away with a glass of gin and tonic in her hand.

Three weeks later, on August the 29th Madge was tragically killed in a car crash on the A303 near Wincanton. Arthur was driving with Carol's uncle John in the passenger seat, Madge and Dolly, Johns wife, were in the back. They were on their way to Cornwall and they were being followed by Carol's sister Rosalyn and her husband Ray and their two children Paul and Emma. It was raining and one of Arthur's tyres blew out. The car careered across the central reservation and into the path of

the oncoming traffic. Madge was killed more or less instantly. Dolly
spent months in intensive care. The two men walked away with a few
scratches and bruises.

It was the breakup of the family as we knew it. Arthur never got over it,
he always blamed himself. He had no reason to, nobody could have
done more to keep that car going straight. Carol was devastated, not
only had she lost her mum. She had lost her soul mate. Again, in
hindsight, it was the beginning of the breakup of the family. As I have
said Arthur never recovered, Dolly was never the same again, and after
she died John moved out to Australia to be near his eldest son Brian. As
for my Carol, I know she will miss her mum until the day she dies.

**

TRAINING AS TRAINER.

It was 1982 and I was looking for a new challenge. I'd been in Terminal
Three since we had fixed stations, it was still the best Terminal to work
in but it had become a bit too easy. Apart from the work in the Red and
Green, I had been the Accounts Officer for a while, the Mishandled
baggage Officer, which meant I was working with the airlines to clear
baggage that had become separated from their owners, for a while. It
actually gave me an insight into policy making and was really my first
experience of being able to influence changes rather than just suffering
them. Whilst I had this role British Airways (BA) decided that they
wanted to centralise all the mishandled baggage that hadn't been
cleared within three days. By centralise they meant bring it into one
warehouse. Whereas the practice at the time was to hold it within the
Terminal or return it to the home base for the airline involved e.g. Iberia
bags would go back to Madrid. As BA acted as agent for most of the
airlines in Terminal Three this really meant a lot of bags. The sticking

point was that BA wanted to place the Baggage Warehouse off airport and we wanted to keep it airside so it was under our control. This was my recommendation as the Mishandled Baggage Officer for Terminal Three. At the outset the negotiations were led by old boss from West India Dock, Vic Roberts, he was Assistant Collector now but he moved on before we reached decision stage. The negotiations were concluded by my adversary at my PO Interview, Assistant Collector, Ron Edmonds. It was a fascinating study in two completely different negotiation styles. Vic Roberts all full of bonhomie and giving the impression that no particular point was a showstopper, then there was Ron Edmonds, sharp, business like, never giving an inch. Between the two of them we got exactly what I recommended, and we still have the Baggage Warehouse airside and under our control.

The other notable incident during my tenure as Mishandled Baggage Officer was Operation Snowball. This was an operation involving our Investigation Branch and resulted in three members of the BA Terminal Three Mishandled Baggage Team being arrested, charged, and convicted for smuggling cocaine. Fortunately for me it had involved suitcases that never actually reached the Reclaim Area and were taken off airport through one of the many gates. We called these "rip off" bags, because they were literally ripped off of the baggage carts as they made their way across the Tarmac. However I learnt later that I had been under investigation because I was seen spending so much time in the area where the three men worked.

**

One incident in particular exemplified my need to move on. I was moved to Terminal One for a short while because of staff shortages in that Terminal. I wasn't happy. Jobs were hard to come by and they were normally of poor quality. On top of that car sharing wasn't possible because I was away from my team. I was getting in late almost as an act of defiance. Then one day as I was walking from the car park to the Terminal I bumped into John Mason, one of the Terminal One Senior Officers. I was twenty minutes late. He pointedly looked at his watch and asked in his broad Yorkshire accent;

"Do you normally get in at this time?"

"No, I'm not normally this early", I replied.

As soon as I said it I knew it wasn't a smart thing to say. But the sad thing is, John never said a word. He didn't even report me to Ken Williams my own SO. But I knew it was wrong, and it was a sure sign that I was too comfortable and over confident in the job I was doing.

**

So looking around for a new challenge I decided to apply to become a trainer and I went on an Occasional Speakers course, at which I have to say I wasn't an unqualified success. In fact the feedback suggested that if I was to get involved in training I shouldn't give up the day job. Nevertheless I persevered and eventually I was called up to be Practical Trainer. This meant at the end of the Preventive theory course I would take three trainees under my wing and lead them through their first practical experiences in being a Customs Officer.

My first three trainees were Steve McLaughlin, John Button, and Roy Coombes, and we had a ball. Now I don't know if I was a natural, as suggested by Jack Luddy the Senior Officer at the Training and Development Unit (T&DU), or just plain lucky. But everything I did seemed to work. For instance the most nerve racking moment for the trainees was the moment they had to stop their first passenger and actually talk to them. So there we were doing the walk round, I was showing them the Terminals and explaining which flights went where, when we ended up at Terminal Three. It was about 30 minutes from the end of the shift and I told them to watch the officers and see how they stopped and questioned the passengers. Then, entirely unrehearsed, I stopped a passenger and led him over to Steve, then I did the same with the other two. Although the questioning was rubbish, it served its purpose and the ice was broken, the fear of the passenger was gone. Three or four days later we bumped into one of the other groups and they still hadn't stopped any passengers, and stopping their first one was all they could talk about. My three were already talking about incidents and detentions of excess goods, no seizures at that point, but they were to come. I didn't need to ask who the happier trainees were and who were getting the most out of their practical training. I felt smug about it, and I still do because the trainer with the other group was the lead trainer from the Theory Course.

That first lot of training went really well, lots of seizures, we actually thought we had a drug seizure at one time and then fortunately further tests on the substance showed it not to be cannabis. I say fortunately because somehow or other we lost the potential offender. We were operating altogether in the Red Channel when a little Asian gentleman came in and made a declaration of some souvenirs he had bought in India. Among them was an ash tray: it was solid and the middle of it appeared to be made out of a compressed herbal substance. So Steve and I went to test the substance leaving John and Roy with another Officer in the Red with the passenger. We tested the substance for cannabis and it reacted with a strange sort of wishy washy orangey pink colour. Not the pure pink colour of cannabis but positive enough to be worth looking into. I went back to the Red Channel to tell John and Roy to bring our Asian gentleman into an Interview Room whilst Steve and I carried out another field test.

Imagine my horror when I got back into the Red to find our Asian gentleman had gone. Apparently John and Roy were being kept occupied by the Officer I'd left them with, and the passenger had just picked up his bags and left. We rushed outside but there was no sign of him.

My feelings as we returned to the Customs Area had done a complete about turn. From hoping that further tests would prove positive for cannabis I was now desperately hoping they wouldn't. And luckily for me the tests proved negative; but what a good teaching point. We had all assumed that someone was keeping an eye on the passenger when in fact nobody was. Steve went on to be a really top drugs seizing officer and to the best of my knowledge he never lost an offender. It was obviously the training.

We had a "wash-up" every day, in the bar of course, this was when we went through what had happened during the day and we listened to Roy's stories. Roy had been a musician and an actor in a previous life and he regaled us with stories of the time he was the Sergeant Major in the Hoover advert on TV. And when he was the man in the swimming pool, under water, reading his Daily Telegraph. But funniest of all, were the stories of when he was the third Triffid from the left in the final scene of the "Day of the Triffids". Whenever I see there's a re-run of the Triffids I just have to watch the final scene where the Triffids are doused with sea water and they wither and die. I watch Roy, third from the left, staggering towards the camera, and I remember us all crying with laughter as he described it.

We had a wonderful period of training. If nothing else it brought home to me just how much there was for them to learn. John had a passenger in the Red with a camera he said he had bought in this country. John searched his baggage and found a receipt showing that he had bought it from "47thSt Photo", a camera shop in New York. I sent Steve in with John to act as the witness. This was the first time they had flown solo, in all the previous jobs I had either carried out the interview or I'd acted as witness. I was pacing up and down the corridor like an expectant father. John kept popping in and out. "Shall I ask him this, shall I ask him that, can he have a cigarette, etc". John finally came out admitting defeat. The passenger wouldn't own up to anything. He didn't know he had to declare cameras, he didn't know they were liable to duty, he didn't know his allowances, he didn't know what day it was, he didn't know where he was. In fact he was having trouble remembering his own bloody name.

"Have you asked him why he lied about where he had bought the camera"? I asked John.

"Er no, I haven't"

"Might be a good idea "I suggested.

Two minutes later I was informed that the client had "coughed"

The other thing that happened on that course that convinced me I was lucky, and that convinced Jack I was a natural, was when the course re-assembled for the wash-up. We were all together in plenary session looking back at the practical training, when suddenly Jack turned to me and asked me to give the group feedback on how my three had performed. I was completely unprepared for this. Apparently at this point I was supposed to give a breakdown of what we had achieved and any particular teaching points that had arisen. So not quite knowing what to say I turned to my three and asked them to tell the rest of the group what they thought they had achieved. This they did at some length which gave me time to get my wits together, and as it turned out all I had to do was re-enforce one or two of the points they raised. Jack told me later it was the most successful wash-up he'd taken part in and it was the first one where the trainees did more talking than the trainers. He decided it was the way forward for all future wash-ups. This might all seem a bit obvious now, but remember this was back in the days when trainers talked and trainees listened.

From there I went on to theory training; first with Matt Bermingham and Mike Thompson; training Assistant Officers, it was like working with Bilbo and Frodo Baggins, they were a brilliant partnership. Then with Mike Carr as lead trainer, and Joe Baird, training on Officer Preventive courses. Then came the time when Joe and I decided we'd had enough of doing it how other people said it should be done, so we went to Jack to ask for a course where we were the leaders. We had a lot of ideas about how to do things and they didn't really fit with Mikes' style of chalk and talk, or with his habit of discharging firearms during the "Arms and Ammunition" session.

This did put Jack in a quandary because Mike was "Mr Training" and was prepared to run course after course, whereas Joe and I always wanted to keep in touch with the real world, so he didn't want to upset him. So he bided his time and waited for the opportunity when there were two courses to be run, one at Heathrow and one at Gatwick. Then he asked Mike to do the one at Gatwick and us to do the other. This appeared to satisfy Mike, but as it turned out it obviously didn't. When Joe and I arrived on the Monday of the three week course we found that Mike, bless him, had removed every bit of training material that he could find. It wasn't a nice thing to do. There wasn't a manual to be found. No module, no exercises, no teaching points, no programme, no guidance, nothing. The cupboard was quite literally bare. Now we'll never know if Mike did it out of spite, but it was unusual when training at Gatwick to take everything with you, as they had their own material. But it didn't really matter as Joe and I had been to the T&DU the week previously and we'd copied everything we needed. We must have had a sixth sense, maybe Mike seemed to be taking it too well, or maybe we were just acting like Customs Officers, and trusting nobody.

It was just after this first course that I witnessed one of the funniest incidents I ever had the pleasure of seeing in a training room. I was actually on a course designed to show me a variety of training techniques. On day three all of us trainees had to give a short presentation using demonstration as technique. It was all going quite smoothly, the trainer, Muriel, was videoing us all so we could see how we came across on the screen, everyone was doing rather well. Then it all went pear shaped. One of our colleagues, Colin Russell; who was a Merchandise in Baggage trainer; had decided to demonstrate how to build a brick wall. He announced what he was going to do. Muriel started filming. We all settled down to be entertained. Colin disappeared and returned with a wheelbarrow full of bricks, and with a bag of sand and cement on top. He laid out a large sheet of plastic and proceeded to lay the bricks out as if he was building a brick wall. It was all going rather well. Then Joe asked him what you had to do when the wall came to an end. He must have been the only one listening and he had realised that if you overlapped bricks then when you reached the end of the second tier the bricks wouldn't match.

"You just chop one in half" he said

"Is it that easy" asked Joe.

"Yes, just give the brick a couple of sharp whacks with the trowel"

"Will that really break a brick?"

Colin said he would show us, which was a good idea as this was supposed to be training by demonstration not question and answer.

He took a brick in one hand and his trowel in the other. He gave the brick a couple of sharp whacks. Nothing. He hit the brick harder. Nothing. In the end he put the brick on the floor and was holding the trowel with both hands above his head and hitting it with every ounce of strength he possessed. Bits were flying everywhere; Muriel was defending her video camera like Wonder Woman deflecting bullets. Joe, Chak, and I were in fits of laughter. Tears were literally running down our cheeks. When eventually Muriel called a halt to the mayhem there were bits of brick all over training room, all over us, and all over Muriel and her camera. But the brick remained stubbornly in one piece, albeit considerably smaller. We insisted in viewing the video and I still have this image of Colin, teeth gritted, with his hands above his head hammering the brick with all his might. There were all these little bits of brick flying towards the camera and every now and then Muriel's hand would zoom into view as she tried to protect the lens. There were some very relevant teaching points to take from this session but we were all having too much of a laugh to appreciate what they were. I'm not sure if I ever thanked Colin, but if I didn't, and perchance he reads this book. Thanks a bundle. To quote the advertisement on the TV: a barrow load of bricks - £5.95; Muriel's video cameras - £250; the unbreakable brick – priceless.

**

Joe and I were doing more and more training, we really had the bug, it was so satisfying seeing new entrants coming in absolutely clueless and watching them pick up the baton and run with it. There was of course also a downside, some people were never going to make it as a Customs Officer but in those days there was no machinery within the training programme to weed those people out. It was something that when I reached the heady heights of Assistant Collector I was able to do something about, but that wouldn't be for another twenty years, so in the meantime we had to soldier on.

The Preventive Courses lasted three weeks and were very intense for both us and the trainees. Joe and I had our own methodology, some of it deliberate, and some of it by accident. For example one day we decided that this particular group needed more practice at dealing with Red Channel declarations. So while Joe was going through the theory I quickly put together a variety of declarations that they would have to assess. I came up with about a dozen of these exercises which we put out to the group after Joe had finished his theory. The first two or three were fine and everybody settled down to work them out. Then as they moved down the list they started to ask questions to fill in gaps in the information that I had inadvertently omitted. Perhaps I had forgotten to put how many people were making the declaration, or where they were coming from, or how long they had been away. Joe with a massive grin on his face told them how pleased he was that they had spotted the deliberate omissions, but I don't think they were fooled. But what we found out later was that this was the best way we could possibly have approached this particular topic. It got them thinking, asking questions, working on the hoof. From then on it really was deliberate. It certainly made it a lot easier for us, if we did forget something nobody knew if it was deliberate or not.

But that was how it went, without realising it we were adopting the methodology of self learning, and not spoon feeding the trainees. In one area, the questioning of passengers in the Green Channel we re-wrote the Codes to a certain extent. The section of the Codes that covered passengers and their Baggage,CC1.4 ,laid out the prescribed questions for officers to ask in the Green Channel. Trainees were told to memorise them. Joe and I turned it on its' head and told the trainees to forget about prescribed questions and think about what they needed to know to assess that passenger. They had a passenger with a trolley and a suitcase. What did they need to know about that passenger to be able to decide whether or not to turn them out, that is search their suitcase, and in the event that they had more than their allowances, to be able to knock them off successfully. This is now the accepted practice. Previously trainees would learn the questions parrot fashion and half the time would be concentrating so hard on remembering the questions they paid almost no attention to the answers. I recall Jack asking me why we had done it. It was a big step to ignore the Codes, and Jack needed to know we had good reasons for what we were doing.

"Because it works" I said.

That was enough for Jack. He was a smashing Senior Officer and for a long time he acted as the Surveyor at the T&DU. He was one of the main reasons I enjoyed my early training so much.

He was also the reason that I moved into Developmental Training.

"How do you fancy moving on and doing some Induction training", he asked one Monday morning when Joe and I weren't quite awake. Up until then we'd only carried out vocational training.

"Yes I'm up for that. Er, what is it exactly?"

In those days Induction training was about taking those people who had mastered the job they were doing and getting them to look more deeply at their role within the Department, looking at the values and the behaviours that were expected of them. You can imagine with a lot Customs types all they wanted to do was catch smugglers, so this was bit of a poisoned chalice. Still I was at that stage in training where I was up for anything. So off I went to Harrogate for an Induction Workshop. What an eye opener this was for me. It was the first time I had really mixed with Customs and Excise people apart from those of us in uniform, and I spent most of the week wondering if I really was hearing what I was hearing.

In a nut shell the workshop was all about seeing if we had the inter-personal skills to be able to assess whether or not people in the groups could handle the sort of issues and confrontation that sometimes surface in these types of forum. And if we could make that assessment, to see if we could manage to control the discussion without it getting out of hand. So the idea in the Workshop was for the trainers to manufacture situations where they knew confrontational statements would be raised, then to see how we dealt with it.

Now bearing in mind we had people from all parts of HM Customs and Excise it wasn't too difficult for the trainers to generate some confrontation because there never was much love lost between the various sections within the Department. Customs didn't particularly like VAT, they were indifferent about Excise, and they sort of tolerated the rest. Nobody liked Customs because they thought we were elitist, in particular they didn't like Heathrow Customs because they thought we were elitist and insular. And they were right, we were. We produced ninety percent of the departments smuggling results so we thought we were entitled to think we were a bit above the rest. Especially VAT. There was also a fair bit of jealousy because we were on shift pay and overtime and most of the department wasn't. Especially VAT, who thought they should be.

So it didn't take me long to realise I was in a minority of one, and consequently I had to tread very carefully. I was also one of only two people in the group who had no experience of Induction training, the other being a chap from Dudley VAT, Joel Farnworth. Joel went on to be a magnificent developmental trainer and later on he produced a management training programme titled Developing Professional Managers (DPM) which was the best training I was ever involved in.

There was a session on "Conflicts within the Department" which I knew was going to be tricky. Not surprisingly the discussion moved round to the inequality of pay. Suddenly a Senior Officer from VAT, Hugh Ryan, who later went on to be head of the Overseas Training Branch, told the group that not only did he resent the higher rewards the Uniformed (Customs) Branch received. He resented the fact that they didn't earn them, or deserve them. I was a bit surprised at this direct challenge.

"What in particular are you thinking about Hugh when you say we don't deserve them", I asked

"Spanish practices ". He snapped back.

By Spanish Practices he meant that we were paid for night shifts, but if there were no flights at airports, or in the case of ports no fresh arrivals, we would get our head down. Now I'm not defending this, but unless we had outstanding paper work to do, if there were no smugglers to catch, it was human nature that we would relax, and in some instances this relaxation would include a short spell of unconsciousness. The other side of the coin was that we were liable to have to extend our shifts if we were in an offence situation when the shift ended. Yes we received overtime, but that didn't make up for not being present at a birthday party or missing the one swimming lesson when your son or daughter achieved his or her bronze medal; so swings and roundabouts. Later on we did receive flexibility payments to compensate for extended shifts but not then.

As I was working out the best way to respond without rising to the bait, a Scouser by the name of Vinnie McCarthy said through clenched teeth. I found out later he was ex Waterguard.

"What about POETS day then?" There was a heavy silence. I didn't have a clue what he was talking about.

"What about POETS day then" This time directly at Hugh Ryan.

I didn't realise until later that he was telling Hugh that he was a hypocrite. Vinnie was getting irate, but as he was now in VAT he was in a position to goad all the other members of the group who came from VAT. Still no response from Hugh, then a lot of VAT types all speaking at once.

It turned out that the common practice in VAT in the early years was for the Senior Officers to arrange all their visits from Monday to Thursday, do their paper work Friday morning, and on Friday afternoon, P**** Off Early Tomorrow's Saturday. See we all had our skeletons in the cupboard and it really is dangerous to throw stones if you live in a glasshouse. I found out later that Hugh Ryan, who was a typical bully, had an irrational dislike of anything to with those of us who wore the uniform. I think he must have been frightened by a sailor when he was a little boy.

The session was very tense, towards the end of it, I was asked by one of the trainers how I'd managed to be so restrained.

"Quite frankly I didn't have a clue what anyone was talking about" I said.

There was a lot of very relieved laughter and the bubble had burst, and I learnt an awful lot about the value of not jumping in when provoked, and the value of laughter in stressful situations. Vinnie was a very interesting bloke, I learnt later that he was actually moving house that day but he had decided his wife would cope better without him so he came to the Workshop instead.

Joe, who was on a different workshop, and I obviously did something right, because Jack soon received the thumbs up to use us on our own Induction programme, and this was something that had never been attempted previously at Heathrow .

**

Training could be very stressful for both the Trainers and the Trainees so Joe and I always tried to keep things as light as possible. Our first training room had a massive double roller blackboard, and on the first morning Joe's favourite way of testing the groups sense of humour was, before the group came in, to write on the side of the blackboard that couldn't be seen.

HELP I'M A PRISONER IN A BLACKBOARD FACTORY.

He would then find a pretext to turn the board over whilst appearing not to actually look at the board himself. We always thought that the groups that found this funny would be alright and those that didn't were going to be difficult.

On one occasion the group were such hard work for the first week that on the Friday I brought the family dog, a black Collie cross called Nookie, into the classroom. She was very well behaved so I sat her on a chair facing the class, I then wrote on the blackboard.

I'VE GIVEN UP WITH YOU LOT SO I'M GOING TO SEE IF MY DOG CAN DO ANY BETTER.

I then hid behind the fire escape and watched the group's reaction as they trickled into the training room. There was a lot of whispering, lots of strange looks at Nookie. Nobody knew what to do.

Nookie just sat there looking at them.

The group went quiet and it really looked like they were waiting for the lesson to start. Then the game was up. One of the brighter members of the group realised that Nookie kept giving nervous looks in my direction. He noticed the fire door was slightly ajar. Then he stood up and said in a loud theatrical voice.

"Well I think it's a good idea the Trainers were no bloody good anyway"

The group thought this was hilarious. I stepped out from behind the door and there was uproar. It had taken a week and needed the help of a very intelligent dog called Nookie, but at last the ice was broken.

It was about this time that Prashun (Chak) Chakraverty and I became good friends. We had worked together in Terminal Three and he had done some Preventive Training with Mike Carr. He worked with Joe and I on a Preventive Course and then he and I led one between us while Joe was working down in Gatwick. I remember we picked the course up very late and we were rushing like mad to get ready for it. Anyone who knows Chak will admire his many fine qualities but will know his ability to rush is not one of them. However he knew his stuff, he was very successful at finding drugs and had some remarkable jobs under his belt. He was also extremely articulate and spoke the Queens English impeccably. I was in court one day with a group of trainees and Chak was in the witness box. The defending counsel was doing his level best to accuse Chak of planting evidence. Chak turned to the judge and said in his finest Oxford accent.

"Your Honour that is a complete farrago of twisted facts".

The court went completely silent. Nobody had a clue what he was talking about, but it shut the defending counsel's mouth and earned Chak a commendation from the Judge. He was however, and I hadn't realised this until then, a bit of a worrier. During our prep days he was constantly worrying about the limited amount we could hope to get across because of the lack of preparation time we'd been given. Eventually I wrote across the White Board on which we planned the course, in large bold capital letters.

OBJECTIVE: AT THE END OF THIS COURSE THEY WILL ALL KNOW A F****** SIGHT MORE THAN THEY KNOW NOW.

This wasn't exactly trainer speak but it had the desired effect. Chak calmed down, stopped worrying, and we had remarkably successful course. We did however get a lot of funny looks from everyone who came into the trainer's room.

**

The Induction Training really took off especially with the Assistant Officers. They took to it like ducks to water. It was also where we saw the greatest success. Most of the AOs were young and therefore more receptive to the ideas that were being put forward. I remember a Surveyor, Harold Mitchell, calling Jack and complaining that Joe and I were being too effective.

"Why what's the problem?" asked Jack.

"Every time one of my AOs goes on an Induction course they won't stop talking to me when they come back"

One of the favourite sessions was "How to manage up". Most AOs didn't realise it was possible to manage their Manager. But once they did they couldn't wait to put it into practice. Hence Harold Mitchells discomfort.

Harold was a good bloke who confessed to me one day that he was prone to wandering around the Custom House with a "Post It" in his hand. He did this on the basis that if you were carrying a "Post It" then everyone thought you were busy doing something and left you alone. Good psychology Harold.

AO Induction also gave us what I always saw as one of our most satisfying successes. A young girl by the name of Charlotte Lockwood, now Fielder, came on an Induction course. Charlotte was born with an upper limb deficiency and seemed to assume that this would always restrict the areas in which she could work satisfactorily. I'm not sure what was said or how the message was put across but Charlotte left the course convinced that she could actually do whatever it was she wanted to do. Soon after that she applied to move to the Preventive Service within the Terminals. In fact she applied to become a Customs Officer. Her application was successful and Joe and I had the pleasure of carrying out her Preventive training as an AO. Later on she was my AO on a team in Terminal Four and she became the only person I ever assessed as Box One on her staff report. That wasn't just the only Box One I gave while I was in Terminal Four, but throughout my whole career. I was always hard to please. That year she had a phenomenal record she had several commercial drugs seizures, which was incredible for an AO because their Green Channel opportunities were quite limited. She wrote the Cash and Lock-Up, and the Outward Baggage, Seat Instructions, we were in a new Terminal and they had to be written from scratch. And I used her to mentor new EO's when they carried out their first interviews, she was the only AO ever used in this role. She carried this role out both bravely and without prejudice which was not easy bearing in mind that the people she was mentoring were all of a higher rank than she was. I remember on one occasion I asked her to go in with a new Officer, let's call him Prem. They'd only been gone about ten minutes when Charlotte appeared in front of my desk. I was acting up as Senior Officer at the time.

"What's up?" I asked.

"I think Prem should either go back for re-training or he should just leave" Charlotte said.

"What's he done then" I asked.

"Well he's asking leading questions and when he doesn't get the answer he wants he's making them up"

"Making them up....., like what?"

"Have you ever had a client quote a Section of the Management Act?"

The Customs and Excise Management Act 1979 being the piece of legislation that framed the offence of fraudulent evasion, and non-declaration of unaccustomed goods. Now these were pretty serious allegations. Charlotte had made up an excuse to leave the Box so Prem was unaware what was happening. I told Charlotte to go back into the Box and said she should suggest to Prem that it might be a good time to show me his notebook. This she did and a few moments later Prem, whose Preventive training Joe and I had only recently delivered, appeared before me with his notebook. Sure enough there it was.

Question. "Why didn't you declare the excess goods?"

Answer. "I did it to evade the revenue contrary to section 170 of the Customs and Excise Management Act 1979".

"Prem, this is amazing I know some Officers who wouldn't be able to quote the Act like that. You didn't put these words into his mouth did you?" I asked him.

"Oh no" He replied.

I then instructed Charlotte to re-interview the passenger. The passenger duly coughed and paid a Compromise Penalty before going on his way. Prem insisted that he hadn't asked leading questions and the passenger had quoted the Customs and Excise Management Act. I recommended to Prem's Senior Officer that Prem should be closely monitored and should only be allowed in Interview situations as the witness. As I said previously in those days we had no system for removing unsatisfactory trainees. Prem later became famous in T4 when his coffee mug was lent to a swallower to allow him to wash his private parts. I don't know if anyone let Prem know it had happened but we all kept our mugs in our lockers after that.

Charlotte was a remarkable Assistant Officer, she was then promoted to Officer and had to undergo the Mike Carr experience when she was trained. This experienced involved having firearms discharged during the Arms and Ammunition session for no apparent reason other than to scare the living daylights out of the trainees. Just to repeat myself Mikes methods were about as far removed from mine and Joe's as it was possible to be. Charlotte is now a Senior Officer and continues to justify that very rare Box One.

** **

Training wasn't all hard work. Sometimes it was hilarious. One day I was training on an Advanced Preventive Course. This course was for experienced Officers who needed to improve. Part of the course involved interviewing a suspect (a role player) whilst being televised. The rest of the group watched on TV and later gave the interviewer feedback. It was nerve racking for the interviewer and had to be managed very carefully by the trainers. But these were experienced Officers and had to be able to deal with stress. There I was half watching the interview, and half looking out of the window, when I suddenly saw two Immigration detainees, who were housed in the block next to our Training Centre, scale the fence and the barbed wire and make a run for it. I couldn't believe my eyes. These blokes were gymnasts; the wire was at least sixteen feet high. I grabbed the telephone and raised the alarm. The interview was suspended and there we were all running around like headless chickens trying to find two men who both looked like "Gary", the illegal immigrant of "Only Fools and Horses" fame. One was caught wandering up the A4 thumbing a lift. Unfortunately the car he tried to get a lift in was one of our unmarked cars. All he could say was, "London". The two Officers nodded and drove him straight back into the Immigration Detention Centre at Harmondsworth. But despite the best efforts of at least twenty members of Her Majesty's Immigration Service and twelve Customs Officers, all running around shouting "Gary" at the top of our voices, and looking very much like Mack Sennett and the Keystone Cops, the second "Gary" was never seen again.

**

To conclude my foray into training for the time being; although I did return later to deliver the DPM training I mentioned previously; a short story to demonstrate how trainers need eyes in every part of their anatomy.

I was showing a group of trainees the drugs case. This was case showing small samples of the most popular types of prohibited drugs. There was heroin, opium, cocaine, cannabis resin, oil, and herb. There was LSD, Speed, and all sorts of synthetic drugs, about thirty different samples. The idea was that the samples were passed around amongst the trainees; they got to look at them and get an idea of what they were looking for. Of course as this process was taking place they were firing questions at me;

"How much is this worth?"

"Where does this come from?"

"Does it always look like this?"

As I turned from answering one particular question I just caught sight of a trainee, Derek Bowen, putting the cocaine sample up to his nose, obviously about to have a good sniff at it. As I shouted, "Nooooo", two of the other trainees, Garth Powell and Martin Yates leapt upon him and caught him just in time.

Jack said I was a natural. I thought I was lucky. I certainly was that day. I remain eternally grateful to Garth and Martin, just think of all the forms I would have had to fill out if I'd lost a sample, let alone lost a trainee.

**

Just one last memory before I leave my training career for the time being. My long suffering Senior Officer, Ken Williams, allowed me to do as much training as I wanted to do, on the understanding that whenever I was working in the Terminal with the team I made a Seizure. This normally meant Sundays as training only went ahead on a Monday to Friday basis. On one occasion I'd been letting things slip. Ken left a very succinct note in my pigeon hole.

"You owe me three" it said.

No explanation. None was needed. Not even a signature, just his date stamp. Remarkably I made three Seizures that day. Not very good ones, two revenue and a personal use cannabis job. But nevertheless they were seizures and they fulfilled my side of the bargain. The next week when I turned up on the Sunday there was another note from Ken.

"Nelson, you're taking the p***".

No explanation. None was needed.

**

TERMINAL FOUR

In 1986 Terminal Four opened and I was looking for a new challenge. I moved over to Terminal Four with the rest of the team I was on at the time; Joe, Pete Norman, Anton Dworzak, Bob Lugg, Brian Williams, and Charlotte who was one of our AOs. Our new Senior Officer was Jim Mitson. Jim's biggest claim to fame was that at one time when he was acting up as a Surveyor he was the highest paid Customs official at Heathrow. He was also another great boss, and although we did have our differences, there was a lot of mutual respect between us.

So there we were in a brand new Terminal, only three airlines, British Airways, KLM, and Air Malta, and a lot of new inexperienced officers. What's the first thing we do? We go on strike. And to make it worse we actually went on strike on a Sunday, double time day. Keith Oliver; the Assistant Collector who had Terminal Four as part of his empire; told the Collector that he only needed to take the strike seriously when we downed tools on a Sunday. So we went on strike on a Sunday and lost our double time. In hindsight the whole affair was a debacle. We had agreed to new shift patterns to meet the flight patterns within the new Terminal, but with certain provisos. For example credits for including six o'clock starts. At that time the earliest start was seven o'clock. The credits were agreed by our local managers and the TUS, because they saved the Collector a lot of money by not having to pay for as many night shifts. They, the local managers, were then told by their managers that they couldn't agree to it. As this had national implications our Trade Union got the hump and called a strike. Eventually the credits were agreed and we stopped the industrial action. What a lot of nonsense the whole thing was, on both sides.

**

I was now a pretty senior Officer, and I had trained a lot of the officers, AOs and Officers, who were working in Terminal Four so I was often called upon to advise or act up as Senior Officer. I was still training, which didn't always please Jim, I was unsuccessfully knocking on the door for permanent promotion, so life was quite interesting. Plus it was a tremendous place for seizures as the vast majority of passengers were UK residents and it was much easier to prove intent to defraud when dealing with a UK resident. It was during this period that the fines I took on seized goods reached six figures for the third time.

Some seizures still stand out above others, some for good reasons some not so good. One of the not so good started in the Red Channel on a Friday afternoon. A passenger, let's call him Alex, came into the Red and declared some really awful looking jewellery and he gave a value of about £200, so there was duty to pay as Greece wasn't in the EU at the time. He was also carrying a Yashica camera which I recognised as being a model normally used by professionals. He was a UK resident returning from a short visit to Athens. I examined the camera and then questioned him something like this.

"Where and when did you obtain the camera?"

"I'm not sure. I think it was in this country a couple of years ago"

"Are you sure it was in this country?"

"No I'm not sure"

"The serial number indicates to me that it was probably bought outside of the UK" This being a bluff.

"Well you might be right, as I said I'm not sure"

"Would you be prepared to give me a written declaration about where and when you obtained the camera?"

"No I wouldn't. The more I think about it the more I think you're right. I think I bought it abroad"

"When?"

"I'm not sure"

"Was it on this trip"

"No"

I then searched Alex's baggage. I was convinced that he had bought it this trip. He was being evasive and his body language was not good. Whilst searching his hand baggage I came across the receipt for the jewellery I gave it cursory glance put it to one side and carried on looking for the receipt.

"Now I think about it I'm certain I bought it abroad about eighteen months ago" Alex said.

"Can you remember if you paid duty on it when you returned?"

"I'm really not sure"

"If you did, you would have been given a large pink receipt with all the camera details on it. Does that ring a bell?"

"No not really"

"Do you know where you declared it? Was it here at Heathrow?"

"I'm not sure"

Now Alex is really winding me up now. He is the worst type of passenger. I can see me having to just take the duty or even worse detain the camera and try and establish whether or not the duty has been actually paid. I returned to my search of the baggage. The body language was still not good and I was convinced Alex was up to something. I started to think maybe he had some personal use drugs tucked away so I had him rubbed down; nothing.

I was then idly looking at all the various bits of paper I had on the bench, various receipts, boarding cards, all the usual bits and pieces that people acquire when they travel, when I had another look at the receipt for the jewellery. As I looked at it Alex became very agitated. So I looked at it again. I then realised that the figure on the receipt, 60,000, was US Dollars not Drachmas. That meant the exchange rate was approximately 1.8 to the Pound not three hundred to the Pound. The jewellery was worth in the region of £30,000. I couldn't believe it, it looked like plastic. Apparently it was made by a jeweller who worked in semi precious stones and designed items to order. It was incredible. Alex looked very downcast. It was pure luck on my part.

We retired to an Interview Room and Alex admitted he had reduced the value to evade the duty and VAT he would have to pay. But he was still vague about the camera so I decided to suspend all action until he had time to go home; he lived in Virginia Water which is local to Heathrow; and see if he could find the receipt. About two weeks later Alex came in with his solicitor and admitted to both offences. The jewellery and the camera were both seized and Alex paid a very large fine. He opted not to go before a Magistrate.

So what's "not so good" about that, I hear you ask. Well about a year later I was looking through my incoming mail when I came across a letter from Alex, and in the envelope was a copy of a Duty Slip Receipt showing that he had indeed paid duty on the Yashica on a previous occasion. On the day I spoke to him in the Red Channel he was so pre-occupied with what he was doing in respect of the jewellery, that he really couldn't remember. When he came back with his solicitor as he hadn't found the receipt he just wanted the matter closed, so he admitted to a crime he hadn't committed. I contacted Alex through his solicitor and offered to start the procedure to un-seize the camera and refund the fine he had paid. This wouldn't have been easy but it could be done. But he declined, he was so ashamed of what he had attempted to do, he was more than happy to pay the penalty for something hadn't done. Apparently he only wrote to me because he wanted me to know he wasn't a total liar. For some reason or other my opinion of him meant more to him than the money it had cost him. As they say, "there's nowt so queer as folk".

Now the good end was a massive revenue seizure from an unlikely source. There I was in the Red Channel one day minding my own business, getting ready to cash up and go home. The Singapore, which normally landed very early had gone late and at two o'clock; I was on a seven to three shift, was coming through the channels. A man in his early forties came strolling into the Red and approached my desk. He looked reasonably affluent but nothing special. I remember he was carrying a large Tourister suitcase, which indicated he had a few bob, and a smaller Samsonite. We went through the normal questions and he declared a rather nice watch, a Rolex, not a special model, not precious metal, but still worth a couple of thousand pounds. I asked to see the receipt which he produced .There was something not right about the receipt I'm not sure what. I recognised the name of the shop, the value seemed about right. While we were talking he managed to bring into the conversation that his Company, the one he owned, had the contract for servicing and repairing the HM Customs Cutter fleet. He managed to drop one or two names of people I had heard of but never met. This was not a good sign.

"How did you pay for this?"

"Cash"

"That's unusual, for a sum like this"

"I had Singapore Dollars left and didn't want to bring them home"

This was a reasonable reply, except that as I looked more closely at the receipt there were four little holes where something had been fixed to it.

"What was attached to it?"

The first little hesitation.

"I'm not sure probably the guarantee"

This would be unusual. The guarantees for a Rolex would normally be in the box with all the other bits and pieces. I checked the model against the catalogue I had and the price was about right. I didn't think he was under declaring the Rolex. If he was he had been overcharged.

"Where is the guarantee?"

"I posted it home with a lot of business papers"

"Where's the box" In those days Rolex watches always came in a rather splendid dark green box.

"I threw it away, it was too bulky"

This was unusual. Most people liked the snob value of a genuine Rolex, and the box was proof it was genuine. Also if you wanted to sell it having the box was a definite bonus.

"Where did you stay in Singapore?"

"The Sheraton"

"How did you pay?"

"They're billing me"

Now I was pretty sure that that was a lie. Mr Cutters might have thought he was big wheel but as far hotels like the Singapore Sheraton were concerned he was strictly minor league. I was pretty sure they would have either wanted payment up front or they would have wanted a Credit Card. I was also pretty sure that he didn't want me to see his Credit Card receipts. I had no grounds so far to search his person. I could search his baggage but I was pretty sure that whatever he was hiding if, it was something like a camera, he would be prepared to lie and lie about where he'd bought it. Also there was every possibility that he had posted whatever it was home, or if it was clothing it was being sent home by the tailor. I knew that whatever it was he had I was going to need the receipts and I knew that once I started down the line of anything that seemed like it was heading for an offence he would clam up. So I made a great pretence of looking up the value of the Rolex, all the time leading him to believe that he might have been overcharged and that I would need to rebate the charge accordingly. Absolute rubbish of course but I needed to keep him there. I suspected he had the receipts on his person but I didn't have sufficient grounds to search him.

Eventually, and I'll never understand why, he gave me an in.

"I'll just see if I did pay American Express, it might be amongst my restaurant receipts"

Gotcha.

As he removed his wallet from his inside jacket pocket I could see a wad about half an inch thick of light blue American Express receipts. Now I could ask to see his wallet without it being a search of person, which at that stage I still didn't have grounds for. As casually as I could, just in case he shoved it back into his jacket I said;

"Could I just have a look at your wallet sir?" As I took it from his grasp.

"Er, er, yes, I suppose so"

In the wallet was a wad of light blue American Express counterfoils about half an inch thick. Mr Cutters had spent approximately £80,000 in Singapore excluding his meals and his hotel. Some of it was in the suitcases, but most of it had been sent home. There was jewellery, cameras, another watch, video recorder, suits and silk shirts that were being been sent home by the tailor. Indeed the Tourister itself was new. He sung like a bird. He was so worried he would lose his contract. He was given twenty one days to pay a fine and restoration sum of £47,000. The ironic thing was the price of the Rolex was spot on. Had he left the Amex receipt attached to the receipt he would probably have paid the duty and been on his way.

This was a large amount to find in passengers baggage but not unique. It was 1989 when I didn't top the £100,000 because I was doing so much training. I often think about seizures like this when the politicians are arguing about my non-contributable pension. I feel sure I must have contributed something somewhere down the line. No?

**

These jobs were the exception. A typical seizure straight out of my notebook went as follows:-

"On 7.4.1991 at approximately 07.10 I stopped the person I now know to be Mr B Hall. He was travelling from New York where he had been for one week on holiday. I established that he was a resident of this country. He said he knew he was in the Green Channel and he knew that indicated nothing in excess of his allowances, and he knew these allowances. When asked he said he knew of the £32 limit on other goods. I then explained that the £32 included anything he had either bought or been given. He then declared two ties that he had been given. When asked about previous trips abroad he declared a leather jacket that he had paid duty on. I then questioned him about the camera equipment he was carrying".

Hall. "It was about a year ago in this country"

Nelson; "Where?"

Hall; "Brixton"

Nelson; "Do you know the name of the shop?"

Hall; "No, it belongs to a friend of mine"

I then searched Mr Hall's baggage and found certain items that had not been declared. Total value £112. I again asked Mr Hall if he could remember the name of the shop. He said he couldn't. I then left the Green Channel to consult our records. I returned to the Green Channel and told Hall that it would not be possible to confirm his story as it was Sunday. And that I would require a written declaration. I added that I would detain the camera equipment. He then admitted he had bought it abroad a year ago. At 07.35 I escorted Mr Hall to Interview Room 4 with Mr Matthew Thorne AO.

After being Cautioned Mr Hall later admitted trying to evade the revenue. The undeclared goods were seized by K Farrimond SO and he offered Mr Hall the usual option. He paid a Compromise Penalty of £348 and paid £199 to restore his goods. He left at 08.10.

The whole matter had lasted exactly one hour. The very slight pressure he had been put under resulted in him admitting the offence. But he had tried. He had failed to declare the goods on first importation. He had failed to declare them a second time by going into the Green. He had failed to declare them to me and then he had lied about where he had obtained them. He had been slapped on the wrist. As with most revenue offenders he left thanking me for how he had been treated. And we had it all wrapped up in time for me and Matthew to go and get our breakfast.

I found during my career that most people actually thanked me for how they had been treated, maybe not those involved with drugs so much, but those involved in revenue offences. I always found that it paid to treat people like human beings and talk to them as I would want to be spoken to. In most cases it worked. A lot of people resent the work Customs Officers do in respect of collecting revenue, especially the smokers amongst us. What they fail to appreciate is just how high other taxes would be if import duties were not collected.

**

Swallowers, that is people with internal concealments, were becoming more and more fashionable. I had my first one when I was in Terminal Three but by 1988 they had become almost an epidemic. Most of the swallowers were pitiful pieces of humanity. They were just mules and they were paid on average about £500; this has gone up recently; to risk instant death by carrying half a kilo of cocaine or heroin in their stomachs. The most satisfying swallower case I was ever involved wasn't mine, it was made by a good friend of mine, John Parsons.

John was in the Green Channel one day pulling passengers from the Accra flight. It was a high risk flight and we were being flooded by swallowers who were all carrying about half a kilo of cocaine or heroin wrapped in balloons. The swallowers were all straight out of the jungle and they were being paid about the going rate of £500. Most of them had never worn suits or shoes before and as they came through the Green they stood out like a sore thumb. On some occasions they literally walked out of their shoes. This was especially true of those coming from Columbia. The balloons they were using were just normal balloons that you would use as decorations at a birthday party, they were sealed by tying a knot in the end. Bearing in mind that any seepage would almost certainly have the impact of a massive overdose, it's amazing we didn't have more deaths in custody. In my last year at work we had seven hundred swallowers and we lost three of them because of packages breaking up internally. They were the only deaths we had.

Anyway back to the story. John spotted a woman struggling off of the Ghana Airways flight from Accra. She ticked all the boxes for a swallower. So John stopped her. Her name was Helen Ladiende. While he was talking to Ladiende he noticed another passenger had stopped opposite them in the Green Channel for no apparent reason. John pulled him over and established that he was also coming from Accra, his name was Innocent Garland and although he claimed to be coming here on business John wasn't happy. He thought he was probably Ladiende's minder.

He completed his baggage examination of both of them. From the questioning in the Green John decided he had enough evidence to interview both of them, so he duly arrested then both and had them escorted to two separate interview rooms. He was progressing with his two interviews and as is the way of these situations he was in and out of the box, doing certain checks, tying up loose ends etc. While he was doing this I was in an adjoining interview room dealing with a man with half a kilo of cannabis, who it later turned out, was a schizophrenic. At one point I bumped into John outside the box and asked him what he had got on the second person.

"Well not a lot really, but when I rubbed him down I did find this bit of a blue balloon"

He showed me the torn off neck of a blue balloon.

"Now why would you have a piece of a balloon in your pocket?

At this point we were told by the Duty Senior Officer, Jim Mitson, that we had move to different interview rooms the ones we were in were needed by someone else, probably our Investigation boys. So we moved, John with two prisoners, me with someone who acted like he was two prisoners. This was where for John it got complicated. During the move, which was chaotic, the piece of blue balloon went missing and extensive searches failed to locate it. It was felt at one time that Ladiende might have got his hands on it and swallowed it. But nature eventually disproved that theory. All John had on the minder was a lot of circumstantial evidence plus the fact that a lot of officers, myself included had seen the piece of blue balloon. John who was one of the most professional officers I ever worked with was very down about this and blamed himself for a mistake that was going to let the minder off the hook. He was in fact working with a brand new recruit at the time so that might explain it. But amazingly our Solicitors Office, who weren't renowned for their brave decision making, decided that there was enough evidence to prosecute the minder. The swallower was all wrapped up by now and was just awaiting trial. One note of interest but nothing to do with the case. Ladiende, who was being treated as a potential swallower and was therefore having all his faeces examined, passed an enormous worm. It was at least the size of an earthworm and probably the size of a small snake. It wasn't produced as an exhibit.

The trial of the minder, at Isleworth Crown Court was something very akin to a Brian Rix farce. When it reached the issue of the piece of blue balloon about six of us went into the witness box and swore on oath that on a certain date at a certain time J Parsons, Officer, had shown us a piece of blue balloon that he had found in Mr Garlands jacket pocket. After giving Jim Mitson a really torrid time' including linking him with the IRA because he said he was a Roman Catholic. This because Jim had protested "I'm a practicing Roman Catholic", when he was accused of lying. "So are the IRA", replied the Defending Counsel. So after last one of the blue balloon spotters had finished, the Defending Counsel then got up and addressed the jury as if he was making his closing speech;

"Isn't it amazing members of jury, it would appear every officer who was on duty on this certain date saw the piece of blue balloon" Obviously heavily insinuating a conspiracy on our part.

I was promptly dispatched back to Terminal Four. I located the duty list for the day of the seizure, found anyone I could find who had been on duty that day, and who hadn't seen the piece of blue balloon and told them they would required to attend Isleworth to counteract the inference that the Defending Counsel was making. So next day we had a stream of officers mounting the witness box one after another.

"I was on duty on such a date and I did not see the piece of blue balloon"

"I was on duty on such a date and I did not see the piece of blue balloon"

"I was on duty on such a date and I did not see the piece of blue balloon, indeed I did not see Officer Parsons"

Eventually the Judge called a halt. As I said previously Brian Rix would have been proud of it. The outcome was that jury found the minder guilty much to the delight of all concerned especially our Prosecuting Counsel who was from a lower list than the Defending Counsel, and would therefore have been deemed in legal terms a lesser mortal.

I have always felt that the Defending Counsel won this case for us. By making such an issue of the piece of blue balloon he planted the thought in the mind of the jury that if there was a piece of blue balloon then his client was guilty, and if not he was innocent. The jury obviously believed there was. However had he just accepted Jims and my evidence as the first two witnesses, and moved on the jury may not have found it so relevant to the case. As John freely admitted the rest of the evidence was mainly circumstantial.

For those of you wondering what happened to my schizophrenic, it was confirmed that he was on his way to a clinic in Dublin; he being Irish; so action was limited to seizure of the drugs. It was a strange experience the poor man was obviously battling against the illness and he just couldn't get his thoughts round what was real and what wasn't. At one moment he was perfectly lucid and the next he was totally incoherent. You could see the anguish in his eyes as he tried to make sense of what was going on in his head. Years later when my daughter Claire was studying to be a psychiatric nurse she described exactly what schizophrenia was and it fitted my man exactly. If I'd ever doubted he was genuine she certainly removed that doubt.

On the subject of swallowers, as I said they were like an epidemic, the year I retired we had seven hundred prosecutions of people with internal concealments. The swallowers would carry approximately three hundred packages, normally carrying about half a kilo of heroin or cocaine. The drugs were packaged in anything from condoms tied up with dental floss to balloons tied up like you would tie a balloon you were using as a Christmas decoration. The trouble for us started once we had positively identified someone as a swallower, we then had to watch them every moment of the day and night. Two officers would have to sit outside their cell with the cell door open. The door had to stay open for two reasons.

Firstly they might get in difficulties if the packages burst or seeped. This would give them a massive overdose, and would be fatal. As I said in that last year we had three deaths in custody.

Secondly there was also the possibility that the swallower would pass the packages under his or her blankets and then swallow them again. On one occasion officers from Stansted Airport brought two swallowers in to use our facilities. The Officers were inexperienced and it took them nearly two weeks to finally obtain the packages. The normal time span was three or four days. They had been shutting to cell doors and just looking through the peep hole from time to time. The two swallowers were passing and swallowing happy in the knowledge that all the time they were being held in relative comfort would come off of their sentence when they were finally found guilty.

No doubt about it swallowers were a messy, sordid business.

**

Just before Christmas 1989 we had a fresh arrival in Terminal 4 who was to have a profound effect on the rest of my career. A chap by the name of Ian Denison arrived from VAT and took up the post as Surveyor. Ian was larger than life and twice as visible. He and I were having a drink at the Christmas party, which I was responsible for along with one or two others like Mark Suter, Wicksy, and Martin "Elmo" Elmore, when the issue of his lack of technical knowledge arose. Up until now Ian had spent his whole working life in VAT. I suggested he should have one or two week's one to one training with a Preventive trainer. I also put Joe and John Parsons in the frame for being that trainer. It wasn't until the New Year that Ian came back to me over the idea, but said he would prefer me to be his mentor. This was alright by me, I liked what I'd seen of Ian so far and it was never a bad thing to chalk up a few brownie points with the Surveyor.

Ian had suggested to the Assistant Collector, Keith Oliver, that he do some training but Mr Oliver vetoed the idea, he couldn't see the point.

Or it might have been because it was me. Joe and I had used Keith several times as "resource" on our Induction Courses. Then on one occasion he was late. This wasn't good because the course was all about standards and behaviours. I, a mere Officer, had the unenviable task of telling him, the Assistant Collector, that we wouldn't need him on any future courses. As with the strike issue mentioned earlier in this chapter his judgement didn't always bear scrutiny. So Ian and I had to do the training on the quiet which meant I went to Ian's office each day and we got on with the training. If the phone rang Ian's secretary dealt with it unless it was Keith Oliver. We managed the two weeks of training without Ian being found out, and I even had him in the Green Channel at six o'clock in the morning turning out passengers. And to his credit he actually made a seizure of a watch.

This all worked out well for both of us. Ian actually had some idea what his officers work was all about. The officers respected Ian for putting himself through it, which was a bonus. And me, what did I get out of it. Well Ian had firsthand experience of me as trainer and a manager. It stood me in good stead for future temporary promotions within Terminal 4, it helped with my push towards permanent promotion, and when the opportunity came along it gave Ian the confidence to put me forward as trainer on the Developing Professional Managers (DPM) programme even though I was still an Officer. This wasn't easy to get on, especially bearing in mind that I was an Officer, Band 5, and I would be training Surveyors, Band 9. Joel Farnsworth who I'd last seen on my Induction workshop had put this remarkable management training programme together and he was insistent that only top quality developmental trainers be allowed to train. I didn't make it at the first attempt but Ian put a programme together for me that involved Developmental courses all over the place. One week I was in London, next Southampton, next Bristol, and so on. The importance of getting on the DPM programme was that it gave me a real insight into how people should be led and managed. It also gave me an insight into how not to do it. Once I achieved my Senior Officer promotion I accelerated up through the ranks and I always felt this was because of my DPM training. I didn't always succeed but I always tried to practice what I preached. And when it was pointed out to me that I hadn't I think I was always big enough to admit it.

Terminal Four was very sociable. There was the Christmas party, which was generally accepted as the best on the airport, and which was subsidised by the fruit machine and the pool table that we had in our rest room and which I was responsible for. These parties were famous if not notorious. Although security was nothing like as tight as it is now even then BA would not allow anybody on the premises who wasn't on duty. So we simply opened the back door and allowed in anyone we knew.

We also ran a summer barbecue which as far as HM Customs was concerned was the social event of the year. The first barbecue we held took place in a monsoon and I can still see John Parsons stood outside with his wife Helen drinking their drinks as an overflowing gutter emptied gallons of water on to their umbrella. The barbecues were tremendous occasions, Mark Suter, the same one whose cousin I knocked off in Terminal Three, organised a bar with a chiller so the beers were ice cold. It was an unusual social event for the airport as "other halves" were invited. I organised the food, and most of the male members of Terminal Four took turns in cooking it. We held them at the Admiralty Compass Cricket Pavilion in Langley. We were miles from anywhere so nobody was disturbed. My last memory of the barbecues was watching Brian Nunn, who had left Customs by then, getting out of our taxi on the way home, and holding on to wall of his house as he desperately tried to find the front door without falling over.It was probably organising the Christmas parties and the Barbecues that made me realise the value of delegation. It was a skill I was to call on more and more as I progressed, it was also a skill that as a manger I was always very fond of. Just ask anyone who ever worked for me.

As I've said Terminal Four was very sociable, indeed it was probably the happiest station I ever worked in at that time. Sadly things did change later. I was continually on the move, as I said I started with Jim Mitson's team, and then I was put on a team with a new Senior Officer, Matt Murphy. Matt wasn't new but he had been away for a long time. The rest of the team were all new recruits or promotees. Then I took over from Matt when he moved on, then I moved on to Raj Aiyathurray's team with John Parsons and my very good friends Chris (Wicks) Rowe and Martin Elmore. On top of all this moving about I was continually disappearing to go training. So life was never dull, in fact half the time I didn't know where I was working or who with.

Everyone in Terminal Four had a nickname. There was Clint (Skid) Marks, Tim (Jiff) LeMon, both of whom were on my team when Matt Murphy left. There was Dave (Mother) Hucker, Mark (Bats) Suter, Bill (Bald eagle) Knight, and Neil (Moth) Eaton . There was even a certain Alky Malky.

Like I said I ended up on Raj Aiyathurray's team and this team knew how to socialise. One night we had a Caribbean night, as you might guess it involved drinking a lot of rum, mainly Cockspurs. Another night it was a shorts and shades party. I can still see Wicksy stood on the pool table playing "air guitar" to the sound of Steve Harley and Cockney Rebel, singing Come Up and See Me, Make Me Smile. It was the team anthem. To use the old adage, we played hard and worked hard. Sometimes it might have gone a little bit too far, on one occasion an Officer who was either asleep or unconscious was carefully picked up

The author relaxing on nights on Raj's team in Terminal Four

and lovingly placed in the deep freeze along with all the seized meat. He was walking around all morning dripping wet. On another Charlotte managed to remove every button on the SOs shirt with one tug. I don't know what she was trying to do, something to do with him displaying his hairy chest, but it obviously seemed like a good idea at the time. I'll spare the SOs blushes but just for the record it wasn't Raj. We then spent the rest of the night watch searching for his buttons so they could be sewn back on. Raj's team was responsible for more drugs seizures than any other team in Terminal Four. The socialising only took place after the hard work was done. Much as some people felt we weren't paid to socialise we were paid to work, nobody socialised while there was work to do. Yes we could have "found" things to do. We could have wandered round the airport carrying out pointless checks. But the Team Building that went on more than outweighed any advantage HM Customs would have gained from that.

**

The highest risk drugs flight we had in Terminal Four was the BA262 from Kingston Jamaica. It was a constant source of cocaine and cannabis jobs. There were two flights a week and the most popular one was the Sunday flight. It was like a madhouse. Virtually every passenger was turned out because if they didn't have drugs they would certainly have too much over proof rum.

The concealments ranged from bags full, to internal concealments, i.e. swallowers. For a long time wigs were very popular with Jamaican ladies, half a kilo of cocaine could be concealed under a wig. On one occasion I was nearly hit on the head by a wig that had been thrown over the top of a search box. The lady concerned had literally torn it off of her head and thrown it out of the room, there being no ceiling. When I say torn it, I mean torn it, as the wig was sewn on to her real hair.

There she was with little rivulets of blood running down her face. Anything that could be hollowed out was used to contain drugs. Any container, talcum powder tins, shampoo bottles, toothpaste tubes, tinned goods, suitcases with false sides, tops and bottoms. An average sized suitcase with a false top and bottom could conceal up to 10 kilos of cocaine. Factory sealed tins of fruit and factory sealed bottles of gold rum could contain cocaine in solution. Sometimes a single suitcase would contain several different concealments; it would be like a training exercise. Books with thick covers, photograph albums might contain cannabis oil. At one time we were inundated with concealments of cocaine inside coconuts. The coconuts were cracked in half the flesh was scooped out and they were filled with cocaine. The two halves were then glued back together and because of the fibre on the outside of the coconut, to quote Ernie Wise, you couldn't see the join. The more sophisticated smuggler would put in a small plastic phial containing water so that if the unsuspecting Customs officer shook it he, or she, would hear the "coconut milk" sloshing about inside.

On one occasion Garth Powell, the same Garth who had saved my blushes when he stopped Derek sniffing the cocaine on their training course, was searching the baggage of a young lady from Jamaica. He was convinced she had something, and he was convinced it was in a large box of coconuts that she was bringing back with her. It was the end of the flight and everyone was watching Garths meticulous examination of her baggage, and hoping that they would soon be witnessing a nice cocaine seizure. It was like a training exercise. Eventually he came to the box of coconuts. Playing to the gallery he picked up one of the coconuts. Spoke to the young lady. She shrugged. He shook the coconut and spoke to her again. She shrugged again. Then, fully aware of the dramatic affect, he held the coconut at arms length, and spoke to her for a third time. She, as with the two previous occasions, simply looked him in the eye and shrugged. She wasn't saying a lot. He then let the coconut fall from his hand on to the hard tiled floor, where it smashed into several pieces and covered his feet, his uniform trousers, her feet, her legs, and the floor all around them in:-

Coconut milk!

The young lady didn't flinch. She didn't even look down at her feet. She just continued to stare Garth straight in the face.

Very unprofessionally the gallery roared with laughter, and to his credit even Garth managed a smile as he made his apologies. Garth was an excellent seizing Officer who made many a good drugs job, he was probably one of the best officers I ever trained, and was even the focus of a "fly on the wall" documentary on the television. But this was one he got wrong, which just goes to show that you can't win them all.

**

I was now doing more and more DPM's. Much to the amazement of my co-trainer, a lovely lady by the name of Ina Elliott I actually did the first two days of my first course without a training module. I loved the DPMs; the only sad thing was that I was no longer training with Joe as he hadn't become involved in DPM. I'm not sure why, but he was now a Magistrate and as DPM meant whole weeks away at any given time he probably couldn't fit them in.

Doing more DPMs obviously meant I was working less at the airport and because of this I found myself in a bit of a predicament. The Review of Anti Smuggling Controls (RASC) was looming large on the horizon. This ill conceived initiative, which I'm happy to say I had a major part in reversing at Heathrow in later years, was aimed at splitting the work of

Customs officers between those who worked at catching smugglers, and those who did everything else. For instance the officers who worked in the Red channel would no longer be expected to catch smugglers, and those who caught smugglers would no longer be expected to take duty and VAT in the Red Channel. The implementation process was amazing for many reasons but mainly for the duplicity of the Implementation Team. The recommendations contained within RASC had mainly been based on the system at Heathrow. The decision was taken by the Collection Management Group (CMG) to turn this on its head. It was obviously going to be very unpopular with the staff. To try and sell it to the staff the Implementation Team, or the Scottish Mafia as they were known, decided to hold a series of meetings in the Terminals. They held one in Terminal Four where we let them know in no uncertain terms that we weren't happy. They then went off to Terminal Three. About an hour later I picked up the telephone in the General Office and I was immediately verbally assaulted by Claudette Knox an Officer in Terminal Three, just why had we agreed to all the proposals she wanted to know. I then informed her that the proposals had all gone down like a lead balloon in T4. Well that wasn't what the Scottish Mafia had told them, they'd told T3 that the officers in T4 were all quite happy with proposals. Talk about divide and rule. They obviously didn't realise that we actually spoke to each other. They must have been judging us by their own standards. I wasn't unduly surprised at the way Charles Haughey and Ian Watson were behaving. Haughey would later show his penchant for bullying those who disagreed with him; this despite being a most generous man, and Ian was Ian, desperately trying to climb the tree. Ian and I had been colleagues on the bench and had played football together so I knew exactly what to expect from him. But Eric Heron had amazed me. Eric, along with Ron Farnworth, formed the best Deputy Collector team that we ever had at Heathrow. He was a dynamic, straight talking man who always let you know just what he did and didn't like. And he didn't dress it up, if he thought something was rubbish then that's exactly what he told you, hence my amazement.

As a trainer RASC would mean that I was going to be unwelcome wherever I opted to go. The Anti-Smuggling AC, Mr Charles Haughey had stated that he wanted a highly trained professional Division. But he was unwilling to release officers to be trainers. Quite how he was going to get highly trained officers without releasing trainers to train them he never actually explained. So that didn't look good. And the Passenger Services Division was so short of numbers that my release for training would be extremely difficult. In the end I opted for Anti-Smuggling partly to beard the lion in his den and partly because that was where my heart was.

**

My last memory of Terminal Four was dealing with MP David Mellor and his wife in the VIP Lounge. Mr Mellor was the Arts Minister at the time and he and his wife were returning from a short trip to New York. Normally a trip to the VIP Lounge just meant showing the flag, establishing the VIP had nothing to declare and disappearing again. However on this occasion Mr Mellor had an extra carton of KSF cigarettes and even in 1990 the duty and tax on 200 cigarettes was over £20. I knew he wasn't going to be happy, he wasn't in a good mood anyway. The conversation went something like this.

"The duty and tax uplift will be £25 Mr Mellor"

"How much"

"It's £25 I'm afraid"

"Are you sure"

"Yes I am it's £25"

"I can't believe it. That seems to be an extortionate amount of money"

As someone who had been involved in voting in several budgets since 1979 all of which had included increases in the tax on cigarettes, I was amazed that he was amazed. I made a pretence of checking my figures.

"No I'm afraid the duty and tax amount to £25"

"Well I really find it quite inconceivable etc etc etc etc"

At this point Mrs Mellor entered the fray. "Look, if you don't like it why don't you have a word with your Chancellor and see if he can do something about it in the next Budget"

At which point the Minister gave her what can only be described as a withering look and said.

"Well at least under my Chancellor I can still afford to pay it. God knows how much it would be under yours"

Mrs Mellor looked at me gave me a charming smile and said.

"My husband's never forgiven me for voting Liberal Democrat at the last election"

Mr and Mrs Mellor were daggers drawn across the coffee table, so I took the money. And having stirred up a hornets' nest, just like the tabloid newspaper reporter, I made my excuses and left.

**

Again just like Terminal Three it was the characters that made Terminal Four such a fabulous place to work.

John Parsons; he of the blue balloon case, never knowingly beaten in an argument.

Mark Suter; not only did Mark run the bar at all out various social gatherings, a bar complete with chiller for the lager. He is also famous for his jamming sessions with Eric Clapton in the locker room. I don't know what hold Mark had over Eric but he seemed quite happy to sit and play guitar for hours at the end of a long flight.

Then there was Paul Rarity. Now Paul was not only named Rarity. He was a rarity. In fact he was the only Officer I ever knew who took a blood test to actually prove that he had been drinking. During one of my spells acting up as SO I sent him home after one night watch when I considered he was too drunk to carry out his duties. Paul was convinced he was being victimised so he went straight to the Middlesex Hospital and paid to have his blood tested. He then produced the positive result as proof of his innocence. Eventually Derek Matthews the Trade Union rep managed to explain to Paul that he had just proved his own guilt. He explained to him that although the test showed he was below the legal limit to drive, the fact that he had been drinking at all meant that he was guilty of drinking on duty. Paul was nicknamed "Mac the Knife", partly because he was Scottish and partly because he was rumoured to have threatened a fellow officer with a knife when he worked at Portsmouth.

My great pal Chris Rowe, Wicksy, as he was known because of his success with the ladies. Always up to something always involved in something, very sadly a diehard Plymouth supporter. And even more sadly he actually dragged me along to a couple of their games.

My old friend Chak, who by now had reached the dizzy heights of Admin SO.

Garth Powell, he of the coconuts and the man who saved my career by stopping Derek Bowen from sniffing the coke.

Rob Hastings-Trew; HT as he was known, a real gent, a bon viveur of the highest calibre. Sadly HT is no longer with us having succumbed to the ravages of cancer of the oesophagus.

John Dunne SO; John who ran the National football team and spent most of his time talking about it. Famous for buying double time Sundays to boost his pension, famous for his amazing rudeness to women, how he was never disciplined I'll never know, and famous for the bobble hat that he insisted on wearing. He also succeeded in causing me acute embarrassment on one occasion when he tried to rent out his villa in the Algarve to an offender I was in the process of knocking off. John never did the job as an officer on the bench and didn't really understand the protocols.

Ian Denison; Ian the man at the top of Terminal Four along with Mike Tabb his co-Surveyor. Ian to whom I owe an awful lot, the best manager I ever worked for. I was blessed by having many good managers during my career but Ian was top of the pile. Tabby, one of the old school, a fantastic character who sadly died shortly after his retirement in his beloved Greece.

Charlotte; the best Assistant Officer I ever managed. And the only one I know who managed to remove all the buttons on her SOs shirt in one tug on one night shift.

Pete Lawley; nicknamed "lurker" because of his habit of lurking about apparently doing nothing. Pete worked on one of the Information teams and spent a lot of his time talking to airport workers, working with Special Branch and generally lurking about. It paid off though and in 1990 Pete was heavily involved with one of the most infamous drug cases that came out of T4. Two young girls, Ms Cahill and Ms Smith appeared at the KLM ticket desk one Sunday evening. A dark looking gentleman purchased tickets for them to Bangkok. He paid cash. Now the young lady at the KLM desk was one of Pete's contacts, because of this she knew the relevance of cash paid tickets, and duly passed this information on to Pete. Pete checked out the two girls when they departed the next day and forwarded the information on to our Central Intelligence Division who liaised with the Thai authorities. They then tracked their movements in Thailand where they did none of the usual things a tourist would do. Eventually they were stopped as they were about to board a flight for Amsterdam where they were to board another flight for the Gambia. In their baggage they found thirty two kilos of heroin hidden in shampoo bottles, and tins of coffee and biscuits. The girls claimed that they didn't know what was in the packets they thought they were sweets. One can't help but wonder why they thought people would go to all that trouble to send sweets from Thailand to the Gambia. They were sentenced to life in prison and were residing in the notorious "Bangkok Hilton" when in 1993 after a lot of tabloid and TV pressure, John Major's Government was instrumental in obtaining a Royal pardon for the two little innocents!

John Miller. Wind as he was known to his friends and that had nothing to do with the normal "Windy Miller" nickname. John was an excellent drugs seizing officer who was more effective with his one arm than the vast majority of officers were with two. I can still see John doing his unicorn impression with his arm strapped to his forehead. I also remember the first time he literally threw his arm in when he was losing on the pool table.

Last and by no means least my long suffering boss Jim Mitson. It was a sort of love hate relationship between the two of us. I thought I was a "Well Fitted" for promotion on my Staff Report, Jim never saw me as anything above a "Fitted". I got him results and took on any extra work that needed doing, and in return I expected a bit of flexibility. Jim's mission was to make sure that flexibility stayed within limits. I'm still not sure who won.

**

The camaraderie and the friendship that was obvious through Terminal Four was exemplified by an incident on Remembrance Sunday 1989. At that time the Airport authorities gave no cognisance to the one minutes silence. On that Sunday the Officers in the Green Channel decided we would observe the silence and at 11.00 we stood still, explained to the passengers what was happening, they stood still. Passengers moving from the Red Channel towards the exit were told to stop and why. They stopped. It was to the best of my knowledge the first time the minutes silence was observed in a public area within Heathrow Airport. It is now observed across the Airport.

I don't think any other group of officers I worked with would have been prepared to go out on a limb quite like that. But we all knew that if there were any consequences, and remember BAA's attitude when I shut the Channels in Terminal Three, we would all be in it together.

**

During my time in T4 we lost both of our dads.

My eldest, Mark, was by now living in Fulham with Carol's dad Arthur, Pop as he was known by everybody. On the 24th of February 1989 he came home to find Pop had fallen out of bed and was dead on the bedroom floor. He had died of a heart attack. It was sudden but not unexpected. Pop had never recovered from the death of his beloved Chum eight years before and despite having heart attacks previously, he didn't look after himself. It was as if he didn't really care. And maybe he didn't. He had a lot to bear and I don't think any of us would have wanted to walk a mile in his shoes.

Sadly Mark had even more to cope with just over a year later. Walter Nelson, the man behind the whole forty years, died suddenly of heart failure on the 23rd of June 1990. I say suddenly because although he had suffered with a dodgy heart for a number of years, on this occasion we knew he had a chest infection, but we hadn't been warned it could be terminal. And as a consequence both Valerie and I were out of the country on holiday when it happened. The two eldest grandsons Mark and my nephew, and godson, Andrew, had to manage the immediate aftermath, and look after mum. I was very proud at the way they coped. Losing dad was something I just wasn't prepared for, you never realise how much you miss something or someone until they're not there.

However it wasn't all bad news. Mark was beginning to make an impact in the music business, a career that would lead to him and his band, the Young Disciples, having a record voted the best record of all time by Kiss FM listeners. Claire was growing into a lovely young lady, despite giving us all the usual problems associated with the teenage years. And on the 6th of April 1992 James's partner Lisa presented us with a beautiful granddaughter, Neoma Mary. She was and is the light of our lives. As I write she is preparing for University and we couldn't be more proud.

**

5. The Russian experience.

Just before I was promoted in 1992 I was sent to St Petersburg in Russia to train ex members of the KGB how to become Customs Officers. It was a short but eventful interlude in my forty years. I was training with a chap by the name of Peter Sokhi who at that time was based in Dover but who went on to work all over the world training and working for the EU. We met up again later in our careers when Peter was running the programme to get Malta ready to join the EU. The whole experience was an eye opener. Russia was coming out from under its Communist cloud, there were shortages everywhere, but the people were fantastically welcoming and generous.

We were housed in the Pribaltiskaya Hotel and enormous modern looking hotel. The rooms were comfortable and the food was cheap, although getting into a restaurant wasn't all that easy, but more of that later. The hotel itself was more than adequate but it did have one major drawback. The Russians had embraced free enterprise and as a result it was absolutely running alive with prostitutes. They were in the foyer, in the night club, in the bars, in restaurants, everywhere. And they didn't wait to be approached, they would come up to you at the bar.

"I come to your room, we have a nice time: only fifty dollars"

At first we were quite amused, the girls were all young and attractive, and when you said no thanks they moved on to the next potential client. Then the next one would come up with the same offer, then the next one, and then the next, and so on and so on. You couldn't have a drink or a conversation without continuous interruptions. Every time you came out of the lift into the foyer they would descend upon you. It wouldn't have been all bad but our expenses didn't cover the fifty dollars. After the second day Pete and I had had enough, we had a council of war and Pete came up with a brilliant idea.

So on the third morning Pete and I were in the lift descending from the sixteenth floor. When we reached the ground floor and the doors opened, the girls descended upon us as usual. But this time Pete and I stepped out of the lift holding hands and looking lovingly into each other's eyes. It worked amazingly well, we were left completely alone for the rest of our stay. These were early days after Perestroika and our ruse worked, my cynical mind suggests that nowadays we would probably have a procession of young boys or men offering their services.

Our training was taking place in an enormous room that was lit by an equally enormous chandelier. It looked like it was left over from the time of the last Tsar and somehow or other it had survived the revolution and the Second World War. And we were training a mixture of ranks from the ex KGB. The trainees ranged from the equivalent of our Assistant Officers to the equivalent of our Collector. They were from as far apart as Riga in Latvia and Murmansk in the far north of the country. So it was a real mixture. We were also doing all the training through interpreters. So you can imagine it was quite a challenge. When we explained to our hosts the methodology, that is lots of syndicates, brainstorms, self learning, etc, in fact virtually anything but chalk and talk, they were horrified. The only trainers they'd seen so far came from the USA, to be exact from the Drugs Enforcement Agency, and these people obviously weren't real trainers. They had simply stood in front of large classes and talked and showed them colour slides. I'm pleased to say that out methods were light years ahead. Eventually they agreed and they were amazed at how well the trainees took to it, like ducks to water is the best way I can explain it. What amazed us was seeing syndicates of mixed ranks, from the highest to the lowest operating so democratically. We couldn't understand a word they were saying but it was so obvious that everyone had a fair say and nobody counted above anyone else. In an ironic sort of way it was probably communism in its purest form, and working just how Karl Marx saw it working.

**

Being ex KGB of course our main problem apart from the" working girls" and the language barrier, was their feeling that all that had to do was shout and act threateningly and people, that is passengers, would immediately knuckle their foreheads and admit to having broken the rules.

This was particularly evident when we were doing practical training at the airport. I was working at one end of the bench near the x-ray machine, when I became aware of furore breaking out at the other end of the bench. By the time I reached the passenger there were three burly ex KGB officers threatening a most perplexed passenger with physical violence unless he admitted to lying and making a false declaration. Now bearing in mind that I'm getting this all through an interpreter you can imagine my horror when I deduced that at this point nobody has actually found anything.

What had happened was that one of the trainees, Igor, yes he really was called Igor, had stopped a passenger because he had three large suitcases. Now this was a large amount of baggage for a passenger who was coming back from a holiday in Turkey, so there were grounds to suspect that maybe he had purchases that should be declared; so far so good. On the face of it this was a good interception, but this was when it went downhill. Igor, the trainee, asked what he had to declare. The passenger said he had nothing to declare. Igor then asked why he was carrying so much baggage. The passenger said they were just personal goods, clothes, etc.

This was very likely to be a lie. Not many people need three suitcases, one of which looked new, when going on a beach holiday. Plus the fact that clothing was very cheap in Turkey and very very expensive in Russia. At this point Igor should have asked to look in the suitcases. Instead he reverted to his old KGB style. He shouted. When that didn't work he called in one of his colleagues. Then they both shouted. Then one of them started to manhandle the passenger. Then just in case they couldn't manage it between them a third trainee joined and he shouted and manhandled the passenger.

At this point enter stage left yours truly. It was all calmed down very amicably. The passenger was dusted down and his clothes were straightened, and it was decided to let him go without being searched. We were very aware that we were being watched extremely closely, and we really didn't want a political incident.

**

Pete had this obsession about wanting to see a real Russian pub. Our hosts didn't think it was a good idea. But Pete went on and on and eventually they gave in. It was unlike any pub I had ever been in anywhere else in the world. It was absolutely packed, it was filthy, everybody but everybody was drunk or semi drunk, there was a horrendous stench of unwashed bodies, and it only sold beer. When I say beer, it was a sort of lager with all sorts of bits floating about in it.

Having fought our way in my first instinct was to fight my way out again, and I don't often think that when I'm in a pub. But it was too late we had been spotted. It looked very threatening, there we were dressed up in our suits looking like we were worth a few bob, surrounded by the great unwashed all in a state of inebriation. Suddenly we were penned in. I could see by the looks on our hosts faces that they we also very worried. Then in an instance it all changed. There was a shouted conversation between our hosts and the bar manager. This was followed by a bellowed conversation between the manager and his clientele. And in an instant it was all smiles. We were everybody's friend, the manager ushered us into a side room, and beers were produced. Very dubiously we started to drink. Then more beers were produced. Everyone wanted to come in and say hallo. Everyone wanted to buy us a drink. Someone went to the shop next door and bought a bottle of vodka. The little room was packed. An amazing number of the people could actually speak a fair bit of English. We ascertained very quickly that they were incredibly pro British. Our hosts had no need to have worried. We found out later that the reason they were worried was that until Pete and I turned up they had only dealt with Americans and the residents of St Petersburg were as anti American as they were pro British.

It was an amazing experience. I will always remember the amazing generosity of people who had nothing. Everyone wanted to give us memento to remember them by. I will also remember their sense of humour. Our stereo type image of the dour Russian couldn't have been further from the truth, and surprisingly it was a very British type of humour; lots of sarcasm and cynicism. I will also remember the stomach ache I had the next day no doubt the result of all those little bits floating around in the beer.

Life was full of surprises. When I'd found out I was going to Russia I had to take all the jokes about eating nothing but cabbage. The reality was that there was a cabbage shortage at the time. We were invited to Alexander's; one our hosts, home; for a traditional Russian meal. The main course was pelmini, which is a dumpling with minced beef or pork, and cabbage or onions in a sauce in it. Sadly because of the shortage of vegetable we had it with just the minced beef. It was also surprising that Alexander's flat was protected by a solid steel inner door, and two very large Alsatian dogs.

It was also a culture shock to be travelling around the town and to hear on the radio that a certain cafe had cakes for sale. Off we would go at full speed. Cakes were a rarity. Then when you got there the cakes were all gone. But you would join the Russian St Petersburg housewives while they had their mid morning or mid afternoon vodka.

St Petersburg was a beautiful city, full of beautiful buildings that had miraculously survived the German bombardment during the war. St Isaacs with its gold dome, the Hermitage gallery, in which each room had a person employed with the sole duty of turning the lights on and off as people moved in and out, the Peter Paul Fortress, the Winter palace; with all the history of the Tsars; a beautiful and fascinating city.

**

We usually ate in one of the hotels restaurants and this in itself was an experience. We would always book a table otherwise we had no chance of getting in. Every evening we went through the same pantomime. We would arrive almost as soon as the restaurant opened. We would approach the head waiter and ask for a table. He would shake his head very sadly. The restaurant is completely empty we are the first people there.

"We have booked", we would say.

He would then look at his reservations book and shake his head. He hasn't even asked out names at this stage so quite how he knows we're not there is a mystery.

"We have booked on the name of Nelson or Sokhi", we say.

He then looks at his book and shakes his head again and tell us he has no reservation in that name. We then look at the book and see our names in large print.

"Look there are our names", we say.

He looks amazed. He then looks around the restaurant as if he is trying to find a table for us. It is a large restaurant with at least thirty tables none of which are occupied. He scratches his head. He looks perplexed. By the end of the first week we know that he isn't looking for a table. He's looking for something a lot more useful. Yes he's looking for a tip.

We take the decision out of his hands and tell him where we are going to sit. He looks disappointed and shrugs his shoulders. Then we go through the pantomime of ordering our meals. There isn't a lot of choice. There's pink caviar or soup to start and chicken escallops or fish for the main course. The pink caviar sounds great but it is almost tasteless.

"We'll have two soups please", we say.

"Soup is off ", says the waiter.

"It can't be off. We are the first people in here. If it's off it shouldn't be on the menu"

"Soup is off"

"Get the head waiter"

Over trots the head waiter, he tells us the soup is off. We tell him we want to talk to the restaurant manager. There is a muttered conversation between the waiter and the head waiter.

"Two soups", says the waiter as he writes it down.

The reason for this little charade is that soup is a speciality and the waiter wants a tip part of which he will be expected to give to the head waiter. This happens every night. The main course is fine and by now we are not having any trouble. The chicken is a little worrying because there are lots of chicken escallops but you never see any legs or wings. Makes you wonder if the Russians have managed to breed a wingless, legless chicken. The legless part wouldn't be too difficult they'd just need to copy half the population. The other solution of course could be that the chickens were bred in Chernobyl.

So why do we have to go through this every evening? Well we soon realise that it's all to do with the "working girls". The head waiter is taking a bung from the girls who occupied the tables with their clients. He was being tipped by the punters who accompanied the girls. And he was taking a rake off from the waiters. On top of that we were paying in Roubles whereas most of the girl's clients were paying in US Dollars. No wonder he hated the sight of Pete and me and did his best to keep us out of his private gold mine. By the end of our time there Pete and I were exhausted. The training was hard work, the dining was hard work, and our hosts seemed to think they weren't doing their job properly unless they were plying us with vodka or Armenian brandy, which I have to say, was of remarkably good quality. On one occasion Pete's wife got through to him in his room, all the rooms had direct lines, but Pete was unable to speak coherently. So very sensibly he put the phone down and disconnected it. Later that evening he called his wife. She immediately told him that she had tried to speak to him earlier but she had got through to someone speaking a foreign language. She was right of course, it was language called "drunk" or maybe it was "gibberish".

It was a thoroughly exhilarating experience, and one which I count myself very lucky to have taken part in. The generosity of out hosts was amazing we had gone laden with things to give people. Things that we knew were in short supply in Russia, nothing fancy, things like mars bars. But the problem was every time we gave anybody anything or paid for a meal or a drink they felt obliged to reciprocate. We bought Alexander's son a toy car from the shop in our hotel. The next day Alexander turned up with two mink fur hats. Fur garments being one of the few things there were plenty of and they were comparatively cheap.

As we flew out of St Petersburg the first heavy snow of the winter was falling. It was a very poignant moment.

6. An insight into how Customs get their man "or woman"

So what makes Customs officer select a particular passenger? Why do we pick him and not him? Is it intuition, is a sixth sense, is it an ability to look into people's eyes and just know? Sadly it's none of these. A lot of officers will say, "There was just something about him"

It was a Thursday afternoon in the mid Seventies. An officer was stood in the Green Channel Terminal Three watching the Kenya Airways flight from Mombasa go through. He wasn't actually there for that flight but it happened to be coming up opposite the entrance to the Green Channel. He noticed a bright pink Samsonite suitcase go round on the baggage carousel. That's a bit odd he thought, you don't see many suitcases that colour. Then as he was still watching another bright pink suitcase appeared and proceeded to bobble along the belt. He stood there watching these suitcases. Then as the passengers started to come down the stairs from the Immigration Hall he noticed a shifty little chap appear. He looked a bit like a certain Derek Trotter of Peckham, a bit of a spiv. What is more he looked out of place, he just didn't look right for the Mombasa.

The Officer was now watching two pink Samsonite suitcases and a dodgy looking character who was looking more and more suspicious with every passing second. The only thing he couldn't understand was that he looked to be about seventy years old. Then as the Officer was trying to make up his mind whether or not to stop the suitcases or the dodgy pensioner his prayers were answered. The dodgy passenger picked up the dodgy suitcases and headed for the Green Channel.

The Officer stopped the Del Boy lookalike; he established he was a UK resident, from a place called Harold Hill, near Romford in Essex. He was indeed seventy two years old; he had a CRO, that is he'd been inside. The two suitcases were completely full of compressed herbal cannabis, nothing else but cannabis. To give it its technical expression;" a bagful". No clothes, toiletries or souvenirs; nothing but cannabis, two bagsful.

He, the passenger, was so surprised. In fact he was amazed. He didn't know what was in the suitcases. He'd been asked to bring them over for someone. No, he didn't know who they were for. Someone would just come and collect them from his house. And being an old lag he wouldn't budge from his story. So he was charged and as he was an OAP, it was felt by the Magistrate that was unlikely to abscond, so he was bailed and sent back the Harold Hill.

End of story, not quite. Two weeks later I was in the Green Channel with the rest of the team. We were watching the bags from the Mombasa come up onto the carousel when all of a sudden a bright pink Samsonite appeared, then another. We were nudging each other and nodding in the direction of the suitcases when a Del Boy lookalike appeared at the top of the stairs. Down the stairs he came, straight up to the carousel, picked up the two bright pink suitcases and headed for the Green Channel .I know those of you who travel abroad will find it incredible that the suitcases were there before the passenger, and I know this might make you question the veracity of the author. But it is true, in those days the suitcases did sometimes arrive before the passenger. However once the baggage handlers realised how much the passengers appreciated this they soon put a stop to it.

Anyway there was our Del Boy lookalike, pink suitcases in hand heading straight for the Green Channel. He just about reached the line between the Reclaim Area and the Green Channel when he descended upon by one of my teammates. Same story, an OAP, from Romford, been to Mombasa, criminal record, two suitcases full of compressed herbal cannabis. He also didn't know it was there, he also had just been asked to bring them back, take them home, and somebody would come and collect them. He was duly charged with an offence against the Misuse of Drugs Act and the Customs and Excise Management Act. He was then given bail and disappeared back to Romford.

Three months this went on for, every other Thursday two pink Samsonite suitcases full of compressed herbal cannabis. What colour they were using on the other Thursdays we never discovered.

This story gives us three of the most important reason why an officer stops a passenger;

Firstly, there's something a bit odd, something's not quite right. The bright pink suitcases were unusual, they are freely available via the Internet now but they weren't then. The passenger did not look like he'd been on holiday in Mombasa, he didn't look like he was returning business man, he didn't look like he was Kenyan resident visiting this country, and he didn't look like a holiday maker.

Secondly, subsequent to the first detection we were acting on information about a previous seizure. So when we saw the pink suitcases we were already alerted to the fact that there was a potential importation of compressed herbal cannabis.

Thirdly this importation became a trend or a profile.

Just to complete this story I actually had the pleasure of interviewing the organiser of this little scam. He was about thirty, and yes he came from Essex. He had deliberately selected old lags because he knew they would keep their mouths shut. However eventually one did speak and we got to speak to the organiser. He was so sincere. I can see him now as he leant across the desk looked me in the eye and said to me. "I juss dan unnerstan ow you kep nickin my boys." I do apologise for the dreadful attempt to put the low life Romford accent into words.

At first I thought he was winding me up. But when I saw he was serious I didn't have the heart to tell him it was like shooting fish in a barrel. I also didn't like to point out that his "BOYS" as he put it were all old enough to be his grandfather. Why did he keep going with bright pink suitcases when we kept picking them up. We never found out. Perhaps the OAPs were sacrificial lambs and he was bringing in ten kilos of heroin on the same flights, but I doubt it. They might have been over seventy but he would have been risking some severe rearrangement of his facial features if they'd ever found out. And why not make it just one suitcase if you're planning to lose it anyway. He had probably bought a complete consignment and the money was paid up front so he had nothing to lose by letting "his boys" do these suicide runs.

The Sheffield whores. Similar to the pink Samsonites, an Officer in T3, Frank Munoz, was watching a Caribbean flight. The BA262 from Kingston was high risk flight. It was the usual mixture of Jamaicans and returning UK holiday makers. The he noticed two ladies who not only didn't look quite right they looked completely wrong. Most white women of their age, they were in their early thirties, were returning holiday makers. They would be wearing cut down jeans, t-shirts, hair very casual, very little make-up, flip flops on their feet, with a bit of a red coloured sun tan. These two girls were in high heels, they had short skirts, long sleeved tops with a plunging neck line, lots of make-up, although they appeared to have little or no suntan, and their hair permed. To complete the picture one of them was chewing. If they had had a lamp post to lean against they might have done some business. They came through together and when the Officer stopped them he established that they were from Sheffield and had been to Jamaica for one week's holiday. They had cash paid tickets and they had stayed in

Kingston for the whole week, which is not the ideal place for two white women unless it was a "working holiday".

He found nothing in their baggage. They had nothing on their persons. They were both carrying a sealed down duty free box containing to commercially intact bottles of gold Jamaican rum. There was nothing to indicate that either the box or the bottles had been tampered with. In fact they hadn't. The bottles were factory sealed and the boxes were genuine Duty Free Shop boxes. Eventually he opened one of the bottles and tested it for cannabis and cocaine and much to his surprise it proved positive for cocaine. There was half a kilo of cocaine in solution in each bottle. In all there was cocaine worth about £102,000 on the streets. This started a run of seizures from white prostitutes from the Sheffield part of Yorkshire. This eventually dried up when the ponce for one of the working girls was put in the frame.

Here we have the same sequence of events. Firstly the Officer observes something that is not quite right, i.e. their appearance. Information is given to officers for future flights. This then establishes a trend or a profile.

**

It was the late seventies and I stopped a young Texan on his way from New York. Why did I stop him? He just looked out of place. It was first thing in the morning and he had just landed on the "red eye". The "red eye" so named because the vast majority of passengers were business men on their way to meetings. They worked all the way over and as it was overnight they arrived red and bleary eyed. Gary was obviously not a business man. He looked like he was coming from San Francisco or Los Angeles. Dirty jeans and t-shirt with a knap sack over his shoulder. He had almost no money on him and he had no credit cards. It's amazing that HM Immigration had allowed him in, but they tended to be very lenient towards Americans. His ticket was cash paid. He was coming here for a short holiday and I suspected that he was funding his trip by bringing drugs. At that time all drugs were much, much, cheaper in New York than they were over here. He had no hotel booking and claimed that he didn't know anyone here. He was going to try and get some casual bar work to fund his trip. I rubbed him down; nothing. Frank O'Neil the SO agreed to a urine test; this showed positive to cannabis.

Now cannabis was unusual for a swallower even in those days. Gary admitted that he'd used cannabis before the flight. He was also looking worse and worse the longer I kept him. By now we were in an interview room. He suddenly asked to see a doctor and in the same breath admitted to having swallowed thirty packages of cannabis. We kept Gary for seven days before his packages finally passed through. After I'd charged him I found out why it had taken so long for the packages to pass through him, and why he looked so ill.

Apparently just as his flight was about to touch down he suddenly felt very sick. He dashed to the toilet, or the "can" as he put it, threw up into the sink. Having had the presence of mind to put the "stopper" in the sink, he then swallowed them again. This was why he looked so ill and why nature had taken so long. We had been calculating that he had swallowed them about twenty four hours before he landed here, so that plus the three to four days that was the normal period we had to wait, plus the delay caused by the trauma to his digestive system all added up to seven days.

So why was Gary stopped? Firstly because he looked out of place, if he'd been on the San Francisco flight or better still if he'd been on a flight out of India or Pakistan with all the other hippies and back packers then he wouldn't have stood out like a sore thumb. Secondly he also fitted the profile of small time user dealer.

The vast majority of swallowers were illiterate mules who were dispensable to the drug organisation. Some like the Columbians were literally straight out of the jungle. In those days they were paid about £500 but now with inflation I'm told it is more like £1500. The weak link in their armour was their stories which could be pulled apart so easily. My second swallower a Mr James Harris of Kingston town was typical of this.

He was coming here for a week to go to his aunts wedding. He hadn't seen his aunt for at least twenty years yet he had paid approximately a third of his annual salary on his ticket. He knew she lived in Brixton but he didn't have an exact address. Someone was going to meet him but he wasn't sure who, and he didn't know where he was going to stay. A urine test proved positive to cocaine, which strangely he said he hadn't used. Most swallowers say they've used the drug they're carrying to explain the positive test.

All the alarm bells were ringing so Mr Harris was arrested and taken to an interview room. The interview was short and sweet because as soon as we got in there he had to use the toilet, so we soon had some very positive evidence to use against him.

Why was he stopped? He fitted the classical swallower profile. He was travelling alone carrying very little baggage, and he was coming from a high risk area.

**

Mr Nosiru, the man with the television that contained half a kilo of heroin coming from Lagos. Why was he stopped? He looked absolutely normal. He looked like a Nigerian. There was nothing exceptional about his appearance. But he was coming from a high risk area and he was carrying an enormous cardboard box. This is why he was stopped. Then we found out he had a television in the box. Just ask yourself. Why would anyone bring an old television all the way from Lagos to London?

Exactly: It didn't make sense.

Look at the Reverend R the passenger with the Church Army uniforms. He looked normal enough, and he was in the Red Channel. But he was carrying ten pieces of baggage and he'd only been away a few days. He had to have obtained something while he was away. And what can you buy that will fill ten pieces of baggage but still be worth less than £28. Plastic spoons maybe.

Catherine Madeke had the biggest suitcase I've ever seen. It was big enough to carry forty two kilos of compressed herbal cannabis. She was acting suspiciously by not picking up her suitcase, but she would have been stopped anyway just because of the size of the suitcase.

On one occasion in the Green Channel T3, a certain Mr Brown was pushing his trolley through with six cardboard boxes on it, nothing else but six cardboard boxes. The boxes had the name "Wray and Nephew" printed on the side. This white over proof rum is a favourite with Jamaicans. We all looked at each other, you could see everyone thinking,"Surely they can't really be full of rum". I moved faster than everyone else. It was still the days of seizure rewards. Sure enough Mr Brown was walking through with seventy two bottles of rum. He paid over a thousand pounds for his cheek, and lost the rum.

So it's not necessarily the person who causes the suspicion it may be excessive or unusual baggage.

There are of course occasions when passengers bring the most ridiculous things for no apparent reason. I have literally had the kitchen sink declared to me in the Red Channel. I also had a bizarre incident with a Mr Omar, a Bangladeshi who lived in this country and was returning from Dacca where he had been on holiday to visit his broader family. Mr Omar was travelling with his wife and his two young children. He came into the Green Channel, T3. His wife had control of his two children and a trolley piled high with their suitcases. Mr Omar was pushing a further three trolleys that had on them four items of bedroom furniture. He had a wardrobe, a dressing table, and two bedside tables. They were all made up, and they were rubbish. To put it mildly they made MFI look good. They looked like they were made out of packing cases. I estimated the value was within the £28 other goods allowance, they were that bad. As far as I could ascertain; Mr Omar did not speak good English; they were either given to him by an aunt or he was bringing them for an aunt. I couldn't believe that anyone would pay excess baggage to bring over such rubbish.

I decided to turn them out. I called in a friend, Jim Pressley; he agreed there had to be a reason why anyone would bring all this second rate furniture all the way from Bangladesh.

So we searched the baggage: Nothing.

We disassembled the furniture: Nothing.

We sawed some of the wood in half: Nothing.

We tested some of the wood to make sure it wasn't saturated with a cocaine or heroin solution: Nothing.

We had Mr and Mrs Omar rubbed down: Nothing.

What was making it worse Mr Omar remained totally calm and placid throughout the whole operation. Most innocent people would have been kicking up a fuss.

We cut up a few more pieces of the wood: Nothing.

After about an hour of futile examination Jim and I decided there really was nothing there. Everyone else of course thought the whole thing was hilarious; I thought Joe was going to burst with suppressed laughter.

So we put all the wood on to one of the trolleys, it was now flat pack, there was no way we could reassemble it. We placed the "How to Complain about Customs" leaflet on top of the wood, and we placed the "How to Claim Compensation" leaflet on top of that. The only positive thing as far as Mr Omar was concerned was that he and his wife now had only one trolley each to push. He never did complain, but he did claim compensation.

There were so many theories going around about what Mr Omar was up to, was it a diversion, were the children carrying something, was he mentally unstable. Then one day I was sat down assessing the value of the furniture, for the compensation claim, and I was using an MFI catalogue. A colleague of mine, Lesley Husher, looked over my shoulder.

"That's what it was all about".

"What is, what it was all about?"

I'd had enough by then. I'd been on the wrong end of a lot of mickey taking.

"That's what he was up to"

"What was he up to?"

"It was gigantic scam to get money out of Customs and Excise, so he could buy some nice bedroom furniture from MFI"

How devious can you get. I hadn't known Lesley long at that time but later on we were to work very closely together in Passenger Services Division. She was, in my opinion, one of the best SO's never to reach the rank of Surveyor. But I never forgot just what a devious mind she had. Or is that just women.

**

There is of course beginner's luck, which by its very nature you can't rely on for very long. For instance a very fine officer by the name of Dick Fielding was in the Green Channel T3 on his very first day on duty. The Kingston was going through. He stopped the first person he saw just to get his questioning going. He opened the suitcase and lo and behold a bag full of herbal cannabis. Now I never had a bag full in my whole career. Catherine Madeke with her plantains was as close as I got. Then there was the trainee who pulled a little old lady in the Green Channel Terminal Two. She was coming from Tenerife on a bucket and spader, this is a flight full of package tour holiday makers. Lo and behold ten kilos of heroin. This was a particularly good job as we nabbed the minder as well.

Another new boy, first week on duty in the Red Channel, T3. A Business Class passenger from Singapore declares an extra bottle of Scotch. The Officer decides to look in his brief case. Lo and behold five kilos of heroin. That passenger had been visiting this country every other month for at least two years, but of course this was the first time he had tried to import any heroin. This smuggler didn't look out of place he looked like a successful business man, and he undoubtedly was!

To summarise then. There are three things that go towards an officer stopping a passenger they suspect of having drugs;

Something's not right about the appearance of either the person or the baggage, there's information pointing in that person's direction or the passenger fits a profile or a trend.

For revenue goods add signs of obvious wealth and signs that purchases have been made abroad. For instance a footballer called John wearing a fur coat.

**

On top of all of this, when you have stopped someone the body language is vitally important in deciding just how far you are going to take the examination.

One day in T3 Green Channel , Ian Richardson, an Officer I had worked with in London Port, called me over and asked me to stand close, as he put it;

"I think chummy might kick off"

How right he was.

Just as I reached the end of the bench where the suitcase, still closed, was sitting, Ian opened it. As soon as he did chummy's hand shot into the case and went straight up to his mouth. Ian a large man leapt over the bench and pinned the man down. He had his hand round his throat so he couldn't swallow and was laying on him. I sat on chummy's legs to stop him kicking the life out of Ian. We were in a stalemate situation. After what seemed an eternity, although it was probably only about a minute, Ian muttered in his broad Scottish accent;

"I'll tell you what we'll do. I'll squeeze his throat a bit tighter and when his mouth pops open you stick your hand in and get whatever it is he's got in there"

My reply ended in "off". I had a better idea.

"If I get off and let him kick you for a few seconds I can squeeze his throat and hold his nose at the same time. He will have to open his mouth sooner or later".

Ian agreed, and that is what we did. Two or three minutes later we had a very red and very short of breath passenger. But most importantly we also had a small piece of tin foil containing approximately eight grams of opium.

Ian had assessed chummy's body language perfectly. He went from calm to twitchy in a very short period of time. Ian called me in at exactly the right time, and between the two of us we had secured the goods without having to wait for nature to take its course.

**

The last reason I will cover involves what I might term obvious diversionary tactics. For instance the passenger who has a very loud conversation with a fellow passenger across the Green Channel, like the lady with the fur coat who lived in the castle, or more often, the screaming child.

The Hong Kong was going through the Green in T4 when a family of Hong Kong Chinese appeared pushing a trolley piled high with the blue and white striped bags that they love. There was mum, dad, and two children. The youngest child was to put it mildly "screaming his bleeding head off". And surprisingly neither parent appeared to be in the least bit interested. I called them over to the bench and began to question them. Their little darling was still screaming on full volume, and still neither of them seemed in the least bit interested. This was strange because the mother was stood right beside the little darling and could easily have comforted him or told him off. Eventually I'd had enough and I decided to lift him up and sit him on the ledge at the front of the x-ray machine where the suitcases are loaded as they're being fed into it. As I did it I said, "Now you sit there where you can see exactly what's going on" What made me think this would shut him up I will never know, but for some reason or other it did. I smiled at mum and dad who both stared blankly back at me, and I continued my questioning.

Unbeknown to me an Officer, I think it was Windy Miller although he denies it, had a suitcase in the x-ray at the time. He then decided he had nothing so he pressed the button to bring the suitcase out of the machine. The machine started with a jolt, the little boy toppled backwards, and disappeared into the machine. All hell was let loose. The parents ran around screaming and rushed to the other end of the x-ray, and the little boy could be heard wailing from within the machine. The Officer hearing all the noise looked up to see what was happening, and when he looked down again he had the perfect picture of a child's skeleton on his screen. Forgetting that when the picture comes up the object has already had its dose of x-rays, he immediately hit the reverse button. The little boy was then sent back through for another dose of radiation. I fully expected him to pop out glowing green.

Eventually calm was restored. The little boy was really quiet now, he probably didn't fancy being put back through the x-ray. The parents were very unhappy about what had happened, but they didn't formally complain. It might have had something to do with the Gold Rolex and the solitaire diamond ring they had forgotten to tell me about. George Duncan the SO did ask them if they wanted to make a formal complaint.

But no they just wanted to pay up and go home to their Chinese Restaurant in Oban. They never could explain just why he was screaming so much.

**

7. Promotion again and again

It was 1992 and the Review of Anti-Smuggling Controls (RASC) was duly implemented and I was placed on an Anti-Smuggling team with Frank Bali as the Senior Officer. Frank was a real gentleman and I felt very sorry for him being lumbered with me. Not that I was a problem regarding the work, I was in fact his most experienced officer. It was the training issue. I was constantly asking to be released and the AC was anti training. It was a battle but I'm pleased to say it didn't last long, as my long overdue, in my opinion, promotion was not far away.

**

Within a few months I learnt that I was on the list for promotion to Senior Officer. And miracle of miracles the system had been changed, which meant I could apply to take up my promotion at Heathrow. Prior to this promotion invariably meant that you had to take up a post in either VAT or Headquarters. Both of which were not only boring but resulted in a drop in money because there was no shift pay or overtime. My luck continued when I found out I was one of the top two on the list and there were two vacancies at Heathrow. The other person on top of that list was my friend Ken Joy my doughty witness in the case of the Reverend R. There was one vacancy in Anti-Smuggling and one in Passenger Services Division (PSD). For some reason or other I had first choice, and I think I astounded Ken when I opted for PSD. There was however a method in my madness. The work obviously wasn't going to be quite as interesting. The money was more or less the same, and so was the shift work. But I was now looking for my next promotion. I had spent a lot of time acting up as SO and a lot of time training managers to manage. Therefore I was ready to push for promotion to Surveyor.

So why did I select PSD? Quite simply because I assessed there would be less competition when it came to temporary promotions and this would give me more chance to show I was fit for the next grade up. When I say there was less competition this wasn't because the SOs in PSD were of a lower calibre, indeed the general standard was very high. But very few of them were interested in moving up. Most of them had reached a level where they were content to finish their careers. I have to say my assessment of the situation was perfect, I was acting up within six months and I was promoted permanently within two years.

My first and only post as a Senior Officer was back to my old hunting ground in Terminal Three managing a team in Passenger Services Division. The Terminal Manager was my old boss from T4 Ian Denison, so it was like home from home. I then had an enormous bit of luck. I was heading a brand new team so the other SOs had to nominate members of their teams to move to my team. Normally this kind of manoeuvre gave SOs a chance to unload any dead wood that they had on their teams. But on this occasion I was given some really top class officers. Derek Riley moved Pauline Hastings, later to become Pauline Sankar, and Glen Sankar. They proved to be two of the very best Officers I ever had the pleasure of managing. I also picked up again with Inder Alagh the chap who had nearly given the game away when I was trying to convince two Asian passengers that we could carry out a test to prove the age of their jewellery. The team was like the United Nations, it was like an equal opportunities training exercise. The average member of staff in HM Customs at the time was a white male. Out of a team of twelve I only had one white male, myself excluded, and even he was an Arsenal supporter so he didn't really count. However they were a brilliant team to manage. I was able to put into practice all the theory that I'd been advocating on my DPM courses, and they responded magnificently. Pauline and Glen just didn't know what had hit them. Delegation and development was the name of the game, and I was determined to make sure that everyone had their chance to make the most of themselves. I knew I was getting somewhere when one of my AO's, a young Asian girl called Affiah, had the confidence to tell me that I was the best SO she'd ever worked for and that one day I would be Collector. At this time I was giving her so much to do and she loved the opportunity. It wasn't just the compliments that I liked, it was the confidence she displayed in actually telling me, it was just what I was hoping for.

The other SOs were Gordon Addison, Bob Sainty, and Derek Riley. I think they tolerated me with a great deal of benevolent amusement. They were all much more experienced than I was and they had seen it all before. It was a good team of SOs because I could feed off of their experience and they could let me take on all the jobs that they didn't want. I also forged a friendship with Derek that was to last the rest of my career. On one occasion we were suddenly given a massive list of staff risks to assist us in our management of our teams. It was really daunting and if you'd been daft enough to try and cover all of them then your whole working life would have been taken up with it. This was always happening. Some bright spark in HQ with nothing better to do and no staff to manage would come up with an initiative that would make life unbearable. Anyway, having decided that it was something that couldn't be ignored and it was something that couldn't be managed in its present state. I set about grading the risks. I had those in Green that were so low as to be not worth worrying about, some in amber that were low but needed keeping an eye on, and some in red that were genuine risks for my staff. This reduced the work to about 10% of what it would have been. As I was doing this I noticed lots of tolerant smiles from my fellow SO's. New boy, he'll learn etc, etc. However the next thing was Derek asked me what I had done, then

Gordon, then Bob. This was positive feedback of the best kind. Without me knowing it that graded risk assessment became the risk assessment for the whole of PSD, and I didn't find out until I was acting up as AC.

**

I hadn't been there long when I was in the Red Channel one day just talking to one of the team and watching them work when I noticed that none of the officers were looking in suitcases. They were just accepting the declarations, working out the duty and sending the passengers on their way. When I asked why I was told that PSD officers were not allowed to look in bags. I couldn't believe my ears. It sounded like the lunatics had finally taken over the asylum. Apparently what had happened was the Anti-Smuggling Assistant Collector, Pat Haughey, had issued an edict preventing PSD officers from looking baggage because it wasn't their job to make seizures. This had been challenged, in particular by Gordon Addison, but he had been threatened with disciplinary action if he continued. This never happened because Gordon took legal advice and threatened to go to the House of Lords if necessary. However the result was that PSD officers didn't look in bags.

This gave me a major problem because I just couldn't countenance even a tacit agreement for this ridiculous edict. The negotiations for the implementation of RASC had been bad enough with the negotiating team proving totally untrustworthy in how they managed it, but this post implementation activity was even worse.

However in my experience there's always more than one way to skin a rabbit. I instructed my team to follow the Red Channel guidelines. Nobody could criticise me or threaten me or them with disciplinary action for that. These instructions instructed Officers to view any declared items to establish if the value was correct. This instruction was in place not only to make sure goods weren't being under declared, but also to make sure officers weren't charging duty on unrealistic values. To do this bags and suitcases would obviously have to be opened. If during the viewing of these items other undeclared items were discovered or it became obvious that the goods had been under declared they should report the matter to me. I would then offer the seizure to any anti smugglers who were present and if they were unwilling to progress the seizure, which nine times out of ten they would be, we would deal with it ourselves. If challenged, the officers were only following the Red Channel guidelines.

This seemed to be working even though it wasn't official policy. My officers loved it, and I suddenly found that the keener Officers such as Charlie Murray and Val Taylor were swopping on to my team as much as they could. Then out of the blue a meeting was arranged between Passenger Services Division (PSD) and Anti-Smuggling (AS) to sort out this very issue. AS had a new Assistant Collector, Derek Braden, who I'd worked with as an Officer many years ago in T3. He and Geoff Newman, the PSD Assistant Collector, had recognised the ridiculous position we were in and they were looking for a way out of it. Fortunately I was selected as one of the PSD representatives, and we ended up with an agreement that allowed us to do almost exactly what we were already doing; which was nice.

Things moved on very fast in T3. I hadn't been there long when Ian was replaced by Libby Munroe as the Surveyor. The day we heard the news must have been the worst days of Gordon's life. He was a misogynist who was also a very devout church goer. The Church of England was one of the pillars of his existence. Within half an hour on that day Gordon heard that his new Surveyor was to be a woman, and if that wasn't bad enough, the Church of England announced its intention to allow women to be ordained as ministers. He was inconsolable.

Libby was very upwardly mobile and as a consequence was often not there. This was when I had my first taste of managing a whole Terminal. I loved it. Pauline acted up in my place and she and Glen were inundated with delegated work. As Glen later told me; "We just never knew what we would be picking up, every time we opened our pigeon holes there was a new job, a new challenge" Then I had my first chance to be involved in real change within PSD. Libby was asked to head a team looking at how in PSD we could manage our resources more effectively. She asked me to join her, and Jim Mitson was brought over from T4 to act up in Libby's place. Pauline took over from me again leading my team. This was virtually the end of my time leading that team. It was a shame because it was a great team; we were such a mixture of different types of people. As a parting gift, although I didn't know it at the time I introduced them all to the delights of "brandy sours". On one night shift, before the no alcohol policy I hasten to add, I brought in the constituent parts, and proceeded with the indoctrination. It reminded me of Dennis Fowler all those years ago with the gin and bitter lemon. Pauline, and Chloe Pinnell went a sort of luminous pink in a matter of minutes, Glen at one point seemed to lose the power of speech, but the star of the show was Phil Baldwin. Phil was a friend and fellow Spurs supporter, as is Glen, he was and he is also a very big bloke. The brandy sours made him emotional. In fact he was as emotional as a newt, and as he was walking into the gent's toilet his legs collapsed beneath him and he managed to destroy the complete set of brooms and mops that belonged to the cleaners. Somehow as he fell against them; they were propped up against the wall; he managed to snap every one of them clean, no pun intended, in half. And at least two of them were metal.

The London Airport Services Review (LASER) took three months to complete and it's fair to say it revolutionised staff deployment at

London Airport. Until then we had operated on a fixed Terminal basis. Terminal One staff only worked in Terminal One etc. LASER brought in a system where although staff had fixed stations they could be moved around from Terminal to Terminal as the demands of the work required. It also introduced a system where stations could be left unattended at times of expected low activity. A system of helpline telephones were brought in to provide response if there was nobody there. It made sense because we simply didn't have enough staff to cover every control post all the time. Those of us involved weren't very popular because we were seen as slaughtering the holy cow. It even brought me into direct conflict with my good friend Chak who by then was the Surveyor in charge of Terminal One.

Looking back it's hard to believe how revolutionary it was seen as. In no time at all it was recognised that it was the only way to operate and it was adopted throughout the UK. It also shows how far ahead we were. This was 1994, now Customs have combined with HM Immigration as the UK Border Agency, and we find that Immigration still operates on a fixed Terminal basis. So if there's enormous queue in Terminal Two and there are Immigration officers with nothing to do in Terminal Three, they have no mechanism to move Officers to deal with the queue. As I said, it shows just how far ahead we were.

This also demonstrated Geoff Newman's skill as a Senior Manager. About six months later we had directive arrive from HQ instructing us to inform them what plans we had to implement flexible working patterns. Geoff just sent them a copy of the LASER report. He had friends in very high places, he was also a networker supreme, and as a result he was always one step ahead of the game.

**

It was shortly after the LASER review was completed, in 1994, that I was given my first formal spell of temporary promotion. Alec McNally retired from PSD5. This District didn't operate within a Terminal it was mainly concerned with processing airline crews, VIPs, anything that happened on the Tarmac area, and all the small airfields in the London Airports Collection including Northolt. It was seen as bit of a poisoned chalice. The officers were anti management in almost every shape or form. Or so I was told. Alec had been happy not to rock the boat in his last couple of years, and who can blame him, so there was a lot that needed doing to bring PSD5 into line with the rest of PSD. I was now based in the Custom House, within the corridors of power. My boss Geoff Newman was a couple of doors away and the Collector Doug Tweddle a bit further along. It was the first time since 1972 that I'd been based outside of the Terminals and it did seem strange.

My main job was to try and get the officers in PSD5 to recognise that they were part of PSD and as such would be required on occasion to support their colleagues in the Terminals. My first job was to persuade the SOs, and this wasn't easy. I have to confess here to a slight piece of deviousness to get these changes accepted. One of my SOs, John Knapman, was close to retirement and really wasn't interested. He was a smashing chap, with a sharp brain and lovely sense of humour. But he simply wasn't interested in any form of change. I don't know how this happened but by "pure coincidence", every SO meeting, and every District meeting I arranged just happened to fall on John's days off. It was just bad luck I guess! But it certainly made the meetings a lot easier, and the acceptance of the changes a lot smoother. It wasn't in any management manual but it certainly helped.

It was a battle, but the advantage I had over most managers was that I had actually done the job. The constant gripe from the officers; "What does he know about it he never did the job", just didn't hold water.

Because at some time or other I had done virtually every job there was for an Officer to do at the airport. At one time I was even the Accounts Officer in Terminal Three. I have to say that despite the battles I made good friends in PSD5, people such as Dorothy Watson, Tony Rapley and Neil Stone. These were Officers who would moan and moan about what they saw as my next crackpot scheme. But they were professional ,and after they'd had their say they would always get on and do whatever it was to the best of their ability. A manager couldn't ask for more.

**

However this role didn't last too long as the vacancy I was filling was advertised and the promotion process went into action. Eventually it was whittled down to four of us and we had to undergo an interview by a panel that was headed by Doug Tweddle. I was by far the most junior of the applicants and as such I was the outsider. But I had been filling the post so my answers could all be related to the actual post they were trying to fill. This obviously worked because amazingly I got the nod.

Although the post I was promoted into was Surveyor, PSD5, Geoff Newman the AC, almost immediately shuffled his pack and we all moved round. When the music stopped on this occasion I found I was back in T4, I was taking over from Miles Crook who was going to one of the other Terminals. It was 1996 and I was back in the Terminal where four years previously I had been an Officer. It was tricky because I was now managing people like Jim Mitson who previously managed me. It's a tribute to their professionalism that it never proved to be a problem. It was ironic that during this period I had to introduce the "No Alcohol" policy that was adopted by HM Customs and Excise. I can imagine some of those old POs from West India Dock turning in their graves.

However I was lucky in T4 as I was one of the few Surveyors who still had a Surveyors Clerk. This post was gradually being done away with but I had Fatima Bahrwanni, my clerk, and Padma my Admin Officer, to organise me and keep me from turning my office into paper chase. Fatima had organised for Miles a superb filing system that worked perfectly. Fatima was a very devout Muslim and represented everything that is good about that religion.

It wasn't all plain sailing in T4, apart from the No Alcohol Policy, there were so many changes going on and the staff failed to see the value of many of them. The implementation of RASC had left many rough edges and in PSD we were forever trying to find a system that would enable us to carry out the work with an ever reducing workforce. LASER had helped to plug the holes in the dam, but it wasn't the complete answer as every year we were being allocated fewer and fewer staff years. The problem stemmed from the fact that very few Officers who worked in uniform were interested in promotion, and as consequence very few of them moved to HQ. This resulted in a lack of representation when the people in HQ were making the decisions on how to allocate resources. In addition they saw our work as very low priority, so they allocated accordingly. Of course when the s*** hit the fan, then it was down to the local managers to explain what had gone wrong.

As I said previously there were many officers who I had worked side by side with as an Officer not that long ago. And when the changes being proposed were actually costing them money it wasn't always easy to convince them. I do remember that on one occasion Derek Matthews, the Trade Union rep, asked me how I lived with myself. It was at a time when we were proposing changes to the roster that were going to reduce the number of nights that officers worked and as a consequence their shift pay would go down. Now Derek and I got on well enough even though he had nicknamed me "bullhead" behind my back. This was quite polite for Derek, and apparently the reason for the name was because of the way I approached any problem, that is head on, not looking for a way of putting it to one side. I had obviously changed from when I was dealing with John Knappman only a few months before. Anyway I took it as a compliment, although I'm not sure it was meant as one. When I was asked how I lived with myself, which Derek did in my office in front of my SO team, I was able to quote my dad. He used to say , "Don't think you're always right, but always think you're doing the right thing". It was something I always tried to live up to. Derek was bemused to think that a drop in take home pay could be the right thing. But as I pointed out to him, without the proposed changes, and the consequential savings, we were looking at losing even more staff posts. So better a little pain for everyone, rather than a lot of pain for a few. I'm not sure if Derek agreed as he was one of the people bearing the little pain.

While I was in charge in T4 I did a really silly thing. I volunteered to run the Collection Conference. I'd attended two of them by now, one when I was acting up and one after I was promoted and they seemed to represent the biggest example of missed opportunities imaginable. The only thing I could remember from either of them was the sight of Eric Heron, one of the DC's, telling Malcolm Clark; one of my fellow PSD Surveyors; at three in the morning in the bar, he was sacked. All because he didn't agree with something Malcolm was saying. It really was very funny as Eric was about five foot two and Malcolm about twelve inches taller. The Collector by then was Martin Peach, Doug had gone off to be head of the World Customs Organisation, and he, Martin, was very keen that the Conference should be a springboard for the sort of initiative that would change the culture in London Airports. It was one of the hardest tasks I ever took on. Mainly because nobody really liked the Collection Conference and it was just seen as a good excuse for "networking". Nobody really wanted to do anything positive, certainly nothing that hinted at hard work. So there was I the most junior of all the Surveyors trying to get everybody involved. I know I ruffled a lot of feathers but as I had the backing of the Collector no-one was going to complain too loudly. The two days went quite well and we ended up with lots of working groups to follow up the issues that had been identified. If nothing else these groups did actually enhance the communications within London Airports, so at least something could be shown to have been achieved.

The other thing I became involved in at this time was the PSD application for a Charter Mark. It was in the grand scheme of things probably one of my greatest achievements in my forty years. Certainly Martin Peach described it as the single most important achievement in his tenure as Collector.

Now the idea was Geoff's. No part of Customs had ever been awarded a Charter Mark. A couple of VAT Districts had, but then their work was more service orientated so it wasn't that surprising. It was of course a monumental challenge, Customs officers just didn't see themselves as service providers and of course much of the work they carried out wasn't a service, it was making sure that the public abided by the laws as laid down by the Government. But I figured that if HM Prison Parkhurst, on the Isle of Wight could convince the Cabinet Office that they merited a Charter Mark, then so could we. This was another example of Geoff's remarkable antennae, from somewhere or other he had picked up on the fact that Valerie Strachan the then Chairman of the Board of Customs and Excise, was keen that all sections of her department should be actively looking at service delivery. For us to be the first front line Customs Division to be awarded the Charter Mark would be a major feather in his cap. Unfortunately for him it was a long, drawn out process and he had retired before we could achieve it.

**

Then before the Charter Mark application could be completed I was off again. It was 1998 and Geoff had retired and I was acting up as Assistant Collector in his place, I'd already filled in for him a couple of times for leave and things like that. Libby his natural successor had been promoted and Ian Denison the other option was away with the Territorial Army so much he wasn't considered. So to everyone's surprise there was Malcolm Nelson, six years ago an Anti-Smuggling Officer, now Assistant Collector for Passenger Services Division. This was big step up and the workload was considerable. It not only included all the Passenger Services work at Heathrow, it also included the Passenger Services work in the two Terminals at Gatwick. I became very knowledgeable on the workings of the M25. Altogether I had about 300 staff in my Division. This first spell only lasted about four months and unfortunately during this time the Charter Mark application was put on hold. Quite simply there just wasn't the time.

There was also another minor incident during this period that left me slightly confused. Nothing strange there I hear you say. Mark my eldest, who was in a band at this time, called me to say that on his way through Terminal One the previous evening he had been stripped searched. Fair enough, Bands were always fair game.

"Why was that?" I asked.

"Gareth had some weed in his pocket"

There were nine members of the Band, Mark and Gareth were the only white members.

"Was everybody searched?" I asked.

"No, just me and Gareth, I told them my dad was the Customs Manager in Terminal Four".

"Was it just a rub down?"

"No full strip, cheeks apart and everything".

"Was that after you told them I was your dad?"

"Yes"

Now I'm really p***** off. Not because he's my son and I think he's above the law. There's nine lads. One has some weed in his pocket and he's white. So let's pick on the other white lad. Sounds logical doesn't it. Then he mentions that his dad is the Surveyor in Terminal Four. So let's really put him through it. I'm not happy, not just because it's my boy but because it makes no sense and it's so unprofessional. Still no rules have been broken.

"Leave it Mark", I said.

The next morning a Senior Officer from Terminal One, where the search took place rings me. It's Mike Nolan a personal friend of mine. He asks me if I heard about the incident with Mark the night before. I told him I had. He apologises. No need for that I say. As long as they had grounds for what they did. If they didn't, then they really need to look out. It then turns out that the Officer involved is a top rank idiot. I don't need to sort him out, he's quite capable of doing that for himself. And he does. He goes long term sick. Then while he's sick he manages to break his leg skiing.

What a plonker!!

Don't get me wrong. Mark isn't entitled to special treatment because he's my son. But he is entitled to be treated according to the rule of law. Were there grounds for a rub down? Probably. Were there grounds for a full strip search and parting the cheeks. Never in a million years. Officer Plonker obviously didn't understand this. Like I said: "What a plonker".

**

It was also in 1998 that Claire made us so very proud by gaining a Nursing degree at the Royal Berkshire Hospital. She had worked so hard and thoroughly deserved it. We threw a barbecue in our garden for the whole of her year and their parent's on graduation day. It was a day to remember, everybody had too much to drink, and in fact the parents were worse than the students. This included mum, the last remaining grandparent. She had three grandchildren plying her with gin and tonics all night long. She was eighty four but she retained her ability to consume large quantities of gin. By the time a friend of ours, John Casey, helped me push her round the corner to the Nursing Home she was staying in, she had slipped into such a deep sleep we weren't sure if we were going to be arrested for being drunk in charge of a wheelchair with a dead body in it.

By the year 2000 Carol was working for herself from home as a Travel Agent after years of working for the high street travel companies. James, sadly, had separated from Lisa but we still saw lots of Neoma. And Mark was becoming ever more successful in his music career, and actually got to play solo at the Albert Hall

**

Just as I was feeling settled and feeling that I could get to like the job, along came Tony Walker, and I was off to Terminal Four again. Tony had spent a lot of time in East Africa and came along with a whole different way of working. Whereas Geoff had been very hands off Tony wanted everything and I mean everything channelled through him. Tony was also a workaholic, something we could never accuse Geoff of. I was back in T4 and the Charter Mark work was going full ahead. To help me we managed to drag a Senior Officer, Chris Senior, yelling and screaming from Staines VAT. Chris and I had known each other for a long time, he was ex Heathrow and ex Cutters he was also very computer literate which was lucky because I wasn't. Most importantly he owed me a huge favour as I'd been on the selection panel that got him out of VAT and back to Heathrow.

The pace we were working at was absolutely manic. Tony was a perfectionist and as Application Day approached we drafted and re-drafted. The Charter Mark application was extremely restricted. For every one of the six criteria we were only allowed one A4 page of written evidence. The supplementary evidence was unlimited but the original application was the chance to paint the picture you wanted the Cabinet Office to see. On the evening before the application was due to be delivered we were still re-drafting. Chris and I were in T4 and Tony was in the Custom House. The wires in between were red hot. Tony was at his most pedantic, Chris and I were tearing our hair out, and neither of us had that much to spare. Eventually we got him to agree the final draft for the "Value for Money" criteria; this had been the sticking point. There was something that Tony was insistent should be included and at last we managed to squeeze it into the last paragraph on the page. Eureka! Everyone was happy. We had agreed that Chris would print the final version on his printer at home. It was far superior to the official printers and it did colour beautifully. The ironic thing was that, after Chris had included page numbers, the paragraph Tony was so insistent was included didn't fit on the page. At midnight Chris was on the phone to me seeking a way out. Publish and be dammed I told him. We were delivering the final version to the Cabinet Office the next morning by hand, so nobody except Chris and I would see it before then. And do you know, I don't know how, but somehow or other I completely forgot to tell Tony about the little glitch we had experienced the night before. I don't know how that happened, but it didn't matter. Tony never noticed and we were duly accredited so everyone was happy.

Martin Peach actually wrote to me saying that it was the single most important achievement during his tenure as Collector of London Airports. Martin decided to print the letter for general consumption. To say that this got up the nose of the Anti-Smugglers was putting it mildly and unfortunately some of the angst directed at Martin rubbed off on me. But by then I had learnt a lot from Geoff Newman, the Teflon man, so it was water off a ducks back.

Tony's term as AC was remarkable for re-organisations, re-structures, etc. We seemed to spend our whole time in negotiation the Trade Union Side (TUS). Tony was so meticulous in his preparation that once he had decided on a course of action it was almost impossible to change his mind. But I was learning quickly in this world of politics and I remember one occasion Paul Stephenson; he was Surveyor T3 at the time; and I, realising we needed to make sure our point of view was the one that prevailed on a particular subject, devised a cunning plan. We had been called for a meeting by Tony and we had a pretty good idea the way he was thinking. So Paul and I got together before the meeting and mapped out our whole argument. I actually put it onto newsprint and arranged for a meeting room that had presentational facilities. It was the shortest meeting I ever experienced with Tony. He left the meeting after agreeing to our point of view, shaking his head in disbelief, and muttering about being ambushed. He then put out an e-mail suggesting that in future we should share our thoughts as they occur, so as to be better prepared, rather than putting them on the table, or as in this on newsprint, at the last moment.

Tony's Divisional meetings were infamous for the length of time they lasted. I developed the habit of finding excuses to leave them early. I found out later that the admin staff used to run a sweepstake on firstly how long the meeting would last, and secondly how long I would last. Despite all of this I thoroughly enjoyed Tony's time as AC. He worked hard but he was also a great socialiser and I can directly relate two of the worst hangovers I ever had to his style of Christmas party. As a boss the only complaint I had was that he didn't realise how hard he was driving people. As I said before having worked for Geoff it was water off of a duck's back to me. But to some; people like Paul Richardson, a friend who was on Temporary Promotion as Surveyor; were literally ground into the dust. Paul eventually resigned, and I'm sure the pressure he was put under was a major contributory factor.

The last incident of note during Tony's time was a National Audit of the Red Channels. Chak was working on the Audit team and eventually we had to appear before the Public Accounts Committee (PAC) to try and explain the huge drop in Red Channel takings. It really wasn't rocket science, although maybe it was a bit complicated for a group of MPs. Firstly we had the introduction of a little thing called the Single Market in January 1993. Then we had RASC which succeeded in de-skilling a whole raft of Anti-Smuggling officers, to the extent that they wouldn't know how to take duty on items such as cameras, should they ever stumble across them in the Green Channel. Then on top of that we had the continual reduction in staff. Takings in the Red are down! Amazing isn't it? What I found really sad was how little the MPs on the PAC knew about the workings of HM Customs. Here were the people who were supposed to be the guardians of the national finances and they didn't have even the basic information about how the Red Channel operated. There were questions such as:-

"If a person goes into the Red Channel and there isn't an officer in attendance is the passenger entitled to walk through without paying?"

"No they should use the Helpline telephone"

"But if they do walk straight through will those goods still be liable to duty and tax or will they have got away with it?"

"The goods will still be liable and the person will be deemed to have evaded the duty and tax"

"So if they took them abroad again and came back through they would have to declare them"

"Yes"

"So even though they've got away with it once they are still liable to duty"

"Yes"

These are questions I would expect from a layman but not from a Member of Parliament whose specific role is to guard the public finances. But in hindsight, especially in view of the MP's Expenses debacle, why am I surprised?

**

Then in December 1998 a tragedy hit us in Terminal Four. One of my AOs, Surgit Athwal, a bright vivacious Sikh girl disappeared. It was suspected right from the beginning that she had been murdered, and in 2007 her husband and her mother-in-law were found guilty of her murder. She had two young children but she was unhappy in her marriage, and it was widely known that she was having an affair with another officer at Heathrow. She went on leave on the thirteenth of December 1998, ostensibly to attend a family wedding back in India, and we never saw her again. It was Boxing Day when one of my Senior Officers, Dave Twynholm, rang me to say that Surgit hadn't returned from leave and the Police were concerned about her non-appearance. Apparently her brother had reported her missing. Not her husband, her brother. We promptly detained all CCTV footage from the day she was known to have travelled. These tapes established that she had travelled with her mother-in-law in the middle of December. From this Police the ruled out the possibility that she was buried under the drive of the family home in Hayes. The drive was newly laid and the Police were on the point of digging it up when we were able to prove she had left the country, and there was no record of her returning. It was deeply upsetting for everyone in the Terminal, but at least some of us had the satisfaction of giving evidence at the trial, and seeing the husband and mother-in-law found guilty of murder. The main plank of the defence was that the marriage had been a happy one so where was the motive? Why would the husband want to kill his wife if they were a happily married couple? I and several other officers were able to give evidence in 2007 at the Old Bailey that directly contradicted this defence. There had been occasions when the husband had come into the Green Channel looking for Surgit because he was suspicious of her whereabouts. There was also the telling point that I, as the manager of the Terminal, knew what was going on. And as we all know the manager is the last to know anything. The Prosecutions point was that if I knew, it was certain that the husband knew, as I said the manager is always the last to know. It was all very, very sad, and something that a small community, like Customs in Terminal Four, really struggles to come to terms with.

**

It was during this time that Glen Sankar began to show his true colours. We had stayed good friends after I left the team in T3. He had shown very little interest in management but the more and more he was used, especially by me, working on rosters and facts and figures the more he was drawn into the web. And in 2000 he made the jump to Higher Executive Officer (HEO) the equivalent of Senior Officer.

Just as it appeared that there might be some stability in my working life my upwardly mobile boss, Tony, departed on promotion to HQ and there was I AC again. Lesley Husher, who had so wickedly suggested the reason for bringing in the rubbishy furniture mentioned in Chapter 7, took over from me. She took over a District with the heaviest workload in the whole of Heathrow, one that the other Surveyors had decided I was the best man for, which was nice of them, and she did a magnificent job during a difficult time. I will never know how she failed to get her substantive Surveyor post; she retired as probably the most effective and accomplished SO, in terms of management skills, who ever worked for me.

This time things were a little different. Martin Peach had departed and the new Collector was Mike Hill a very personable guy who had in his youth been a footballer on the books of Bristol Rovers. This was a long stretch of Temporary Promotion and during it there were some very significant changes. The folly of RASC some ten years earlier was recognised but never owned up to. Sir Richard Broadbent the new Chairman of the Board, does sound like a band doesn't it, decided to shake the whole department up. And Mike set in motion the move to merge the Anti-Smuggling and Passenger Services Divisions, and to form Detection. It was a big job mainly because the cultures were very different, and officers had become de-skilled in what the other Division did. Add to that the fact that a lot of officers didn't want to do what the other Division did. In the time that the work had been separated staff had been recruited to do the specialist role of whichever Division they were recruited into. So you can imagine just what a difficult task it was to convince everyone it was for the best. Some of the Communication events where Matt Sheridan; the AC for Anti-Smuggling; and I were trying to get our messages across to large groups of up to a hundred officers, reminded me of the Christians in the Coliseum. Matt and I being the Christians. I can still see my old friend Cliff Davis, an Anti-Smuggling SO, in fact one of the best, absolutely scarlet with rage over some point or other that he was trying to make. I thought he was going to burst. However I must say although it was difficult and Matt and I had many thorny issues to settle, I thoroughly enjoyed it. I understood the staffs and managers concerns and fears but I never felt they were insurmountable. I was always happy addressing large groups, I actually enjoyed the hurly burly of these large events, and I suppose it helped that I really believed in what we were trying to achieve. The end of RASC was worth blood sweat and tears.

Paul Stephenson, one of my Surveyors at the time and Tim Doran, DC, were the principle members of the "change team", with Glen doing a lot of the roster and figure work in the background. It was massive; over five hundred officers had to be given basic skills or had to be re-trained. The management structure was changed, yet again, every single team that worked in the Terminals had to be re-assigned. Matt and I had to work very closely as it was the "change teams" job to say what was going to happen, but it was up to us to make it happen. We were the ones grasping the nettles. We were the ones dealing with the appeals and the accusations and the potential Grievances. I think it's an indication of how transparently fair the processes were that only one official Grievance was made. And it wasn't upheld.

For the PSD Surveyors the change was considerable. It meant that they would now be incorporated in the Alpha One roster. Alpha One was the radio call sign for the Control Surveyor; this person had control of all the resources on duty for a given shift. He had all the information that needed to be addressed and he knew which high risk flights were due during his spell in charge. It was the one good thing that came out of RASC. As I was still on TP it didn't affect me immediately, but when I reverted to Surveyor I found the Alpha One role the most exhilarating and satisfying management work. It also had one major advantage over all the others. At the end of your shift you handed over and walked away; bliss. As AC you never walked away.

**

I carried on for a few more months after the merger and then suddenly after months of rumours in 2001 we had a new AC. Stella Jarvis an Essex girl; being from Essex myself I'm allowed to say that; who had been in Cargo, had returned from maternity leave and decided to move into the lion's den. Stella had a ferocious reputation that had preceded her. The story was told that on her first day as AC in Cargo she was being shown around and an officer was sitting at a desk upon which a telephone was ringing and ringing. Because it wasn't the officer's telephone he was ignoring it. Stella let this go on for a couple of minutes and then went over to the officer and said.

"You've got a choice. Either pick up that ******* telephone or pick up your P45 on your way out."

The telephone was duly picked up. I have to say that despite her reputation I found Stella to be one of the most kind hearted and caring people it was my pleasure to work with and for. But before I had the chance to work with her I was off again. It had been decided that as I'd been acting as AC for so long to make the transfer easier, after we'd had the official handover, I would disappear for a month to Malta. This was to give Stella a chance to get her feet under the table without the skeleton at the feast, that's me, blighting her every move. I think whoever made that decision underestimated both of us. But perhaps it was made with the best of intentions.

**

The job in Malta was to review the entire Customs and Excise department in Malta and make recommendations to get it ready to join the EU. Of course as it was such a mammoth task we had an enormous team. Yes true to form, there were two of us, me and Mal Riley from Manchester Airport. Mal, a laid back Manchester United supporter, was the perfect person to have to work with on what was a very intensive and sensitive piece of work. The systems in place in Malta were a nightmare. The only thing that vaguely resembled an effective Customs service was the uniform. And they had copied that from us.

It was a very intense month. The man in charge of the whole initiative was my ex training colleague in Russia, Pete Sokhi. There was literally no section that met the standards required for the EU. There were massive administration Divisions put in place purely to maintain fair distribution of unnecessary overtime. There were systems of clearance of commercial goods where officers operated alone and were therefore not only susceptible to bribery, and threats, it appeared to be almost compulsory. For approximately three hundred staff there were more than thirty messengers, despite the fact that the telephone network was more than adequate and e-mail was available for middle and senior managers. I worked out a way that the thirty could be reduced to five, it wasn't a difficult piece of work, and it took me all of five minutes. When I broached the subject there were just a lot of knowing smiles and much shaking of heads. What I didn't realise was that the messengers jobs were all sinecures and were linked to the distribution of the "little brown envelopes" on a Friday lunchtime. There were so many jobs that were done for no reason. When either Mal or I asked why they did them we were told, "Because we can". We never did really understand what that meant. Despite what was an absolute quagmire of overstaffing, poor management, poor control systems, lack of motivation, and just about anything else that would stop the Customs being effective, the report Mal and I produced was a piece of work that I will always be proud of. And the reason I'm so proud of it is that unbelievably Mal and I managed to cut through this quagmire and come up with a set of achievable recommendations that would have brought the Maltese Customs Division into the Twenty First century. On top of that we returned later and produced an implementation plan that set out exactly how they could put it into place.

Mal and I got on famously. We enjoyed the work, we enjoyed the hospitality, John Mifsud the soon to be head of Customs in Malta made sure our every need was met, and we enjoyed the Maltese cuisine. We had a few shocks along the way. One of which was when we found out that a local team that had tried to do what we were doing had had their cars and homes bombed. We hadn't realised how Sicilian the Maltese were. After we discovered this I moved out of the private apartment I was renting and into the Hilton. I figured bombing the Hilton would be a bit extreme. I must say I loved the time I spent there. Malta is charming island, the people are friendly, except the bombers that is, the climate is welcoming. The Spurs Supporters Club, of which the Head Messenger was the President, sold draught beer but didn't show any football. whereas the Manchester United club showed football from everywhere in the world; as long as United were playing; but only had bottled beer. It wasn't my idea of a pleasant evening, drinking bottled beer, watching

United play with the commentary in Icelandic, and the locals chanting "chumpions, chumpions, every time a United player was within a whisker of the opposition's goal. But I had to humour Mal, without his fix of United, he would have withered on the vine.

It was hard work, despite what my friend Ray Thorpe always thought about "jollies abroad", but it was very, very rewarding, and I don't mean financially.

**

On my return to Heathrow Stella was now in full flow and I was in charge of District One with about fifty staff. I was also on the Alpha One roster, and in addition I had responsibility for all complaints. I was lucky here because my old friend and colleague from T3, Derek Riley was available to take on these annoying diversions. Derek was particularly good at this work especially after we persuaded to dump his typewriter that had the letter e missing.

But there I was on the Alpha One roster. It was tremendous role. The rest of the Alpha One team were the ultimate in professionalism. My old friend Chak was there, Ray Thorpe or "Victor" as he was known was on it along with Malcolm Clark, Roger Puckey, Max Macson and others. You just never knew what would be thrown at you. We not only had information coming from all over the world, we also worked very closely with the security services and the police. When I started we were experiencing a surge in "swallowers". We were getting so many that on occasion we literally had nowhere to put them. They had to be in a secure area, they had to be watched continually by two officers, they obviously had to have access to appropriate toilet facilities. The first time I experienced this "where shall I put them scenario" I decided to double them up. It was my very first shift as Alpha One. Just about everybody was against the idea. The Custody Officers were quoting health and safety, chain of evidence, human rights, just about every reason you could think of not to do it. And the officers and Senior Officers, well they just didn't like it because it was different and we'd never done it before. But as I explained the alternative was to instruct the teams on duty to stop finding drugs until we had room for them. And I was not prepared to do that, and they wouldn't have liked it if I had. Fortunately Max was around at the time showing me the ropes, so I had the support of at least one person who could see the sense in what I was proposing. The strange thing is nobody had their health and safety put in danger, no chains of evidence were compromised, and no prisoner appealed that their human rights were being violated, and as is the way with these things in a short time it became common practice when demand made it necessary. I found in my career that many "holy cows" weren't actually holy at all when you stuck the knife in.

Some of the situations I had to deal with just weren't covered by the books of guidance. On one occasion I had information that the body of a well known Jamaican drug syndicate member was coming back from Ghana in a wooden box. He had been killed in a motor bike accident and his associates were bringing him back for burial. This was unusual to say the least. Druggies weren't normally that sensitive, especially as the dead man wasn't even from the UK. The information also said that they were in "the mood to party". I was convinced there had to be more to it. The problem I had was," what were our powers in respect of dead bodies"? Of course in a situation like this when you need some legal advice, its Sunday morning so there's no Solicitor available to consult with. Also I had the problem of who to give this lovely bit of information to. I didn't know what state the body was in, so I didn't know what they would be looking at when the lid was taken off. The team that met the flight was led by an old mate of mine, Bob Lake, he was an excellent SO who took his work very seriously. He volunteered on behalf of his team. What was in my favour was that it was very unlikely that there would be any friends or relatives to appeal against us inspecting the coffin and the body within it. So a local Funeral Director was contacted, the coffin was transferred to their premises and the lid was taken off. the net result?: nothing at all. There were no drugs in the coffin. The body was intact. So unless the corpse had had the foresight to swallow a lot of drugs before he went and killed himself on his motorbike we were pretty sure there was nothing there. So we were left with the conclusion that some drug gangs do actually have feelings, or they just like any excuse for a party; amazing.

Then one Saturday evening my old friend Wicksy from my Terminal Four days, who was working on a Divisional Information Team gave me some information that there was going to be a major cigarette run. Eight men had gone to Spain a week ago with no checked in baggage and were each returning with two suitcases. Now as each suitcase could potentially contain 10,000 cigarettes I was looking at a possible importation of 160,000 cigarettes. I mustered every officer I had available, I also brought in the police. We had had instances of cigarette gangs literally just charging through the controls. Not at Heathrow but at Dover and Pegwell Bay. The result was a very embarrassed Malcolm Nelson as a group of eight very drunk golfers made their way through the controls, each carrying a bag of golf clubs and a suitcase. It was a zero cigarette situation, for whatever reason the outward passenger list hadn't recorded the baggage that they had checked in on the way out. That little glitch in the system did in fact cost me a bottle of Scotch with which I made my apologies to the Police Inspector in charge that evening.

Sadly the last crises I had to deal with was when we had two deaths in custody. We had two confirmed swallowers in our secure unit. They were Brazilians, which was unusual, and they were carrying cocaine internally. Sadly for them the packaging was unravelling and the drugs were seeping into their digestive systems. The paramedics were called as soon as the officers became aware that they were distressed. The paramedics could not have arrived any quicker but unfortunately it wasn't quick enough, one actually died in the Custody Suite and one died later in hospital. The officers were quite traumatised and what made things worse was that the police had to investigate because they were sudden deaths. Everybody involved had to give statements and be questioned under caution. A very sad incident for all involved, including Chak who had all the paperwork to deal with the following morning, but especially for the officers guarding the swallowers. One minute they were looking after two people who they were now on first name terms with. The next they were trying to save their lives. Dreadful.

On a day to day basis the most common decision we had to make was to EMIT or not. EMIT being the urine testing of suspected swallowers. A typical real life example went as follows.

On the 2nd of February 2002 George Garrett, Officer, apprehended Erroll Lynford Smith. Mr Smith was travelling from Kingston, Jamaica, on flight JM001. Mr Garrett requested permission to carry out a urine test on Mr Smith for the following reasons:-

No good reason for travel.

Price of ticket was the equivalent of nine weeks earnings for Mr Smith.

Second visit to this country in the last three months.

The address he gave where he was visiting included a Post Code that does not exist.

Arrested at 12.25, EMIT agreed at 13.14.

Rights denied until EMIT and possible x-ray completed.

Result of EMIT positive.

Mr Smith eventually produced a large number of packages containing cocaine, and spent about five years in one of Her Majesty's Prisons.

This was run of the mill. Rights to contact anyone were denied until after any possible x-rays were taken. We might have to remove him to Hillingdon Hospital for the x-rays and we didn't want him tipping off his mates and them lying in wait to retrieve their friend with his packages.

**

So apart from Alpha One I was actually just running a District of my own. It was complicated District with lots of bits and pieces attached to it. The Firearms team, the Merchandise in Baggage team, in fact all the bits and pieces nobody else wanted, as well as fifty staff on the main roster. I was also running Practical Management workshops for new promotees. Despite all of this, after the time as AC the workload was comfortable. Stella was the AC and she and I had a very good working arrangement. We both knew how to get the best out of each other. She recognised when I was "managing up" and accepted that I only did it when necessary. And I recognised when she was talking good sense but not getting it across too well because she just needed to let off steam. I also recognised that she wasn't one of those managers who do things just to look good to their own manager. If she was proposing something it was because she thought it would work for the good of all concerned. Of course it was too comfortable, just when I thought I could see the last two or three years in this rewarding but not too arduous role there was a shuffle around at the top, John Whyte came in as Collector, Tim

Doran went and Stella was given the temporary Deputy Collector job. This meant there was a vacancy at Assistant Collector level and I was asked to act up again. I didn't know it at the time but this was to be my last move.

Although I was only temporary I was the missing link. The resources for Passenger Services work nationally were continually being cut down. Since the days of Geoff Newman the Heathrow AC with control of Passenger Services had always been responsible for how they were allocated nationally. There were all sorts of anomalies and "understandings" that went towards the final allocation. Smoking mirrors, Matt Sheridan would call them. Geoff had been the master of smoking mirrors, Tony Walker had carried it on and then Stella had the job of trying to unpick just exactly how the resources were allocated. And in between these three there was me. I was the missing link. It was the closest thing to rocket science that I ever had to grapple with. Some of the "understandings" weren't for public consumption so there was nothing written down on the official allocations. But they had to be carried forward from year to year otherwise it just didn't make any sense. I can remember Stella and I were almost in tears as we tried to piece the jigsaw together.

**

On May the 18th 2003, at the age of eighty nine, mum finally gave in to the grim reaper. She had been unwell for some time and had been living in a Nursing Home in Chelmsford, close to Valerie, and our niece Sarah. She was in and out of hospital with a number of minor ailments and eventually the body couldn't take any more.

The death certificate said the cause of death was "old age", which is a nice way to go if your time is up. We knew she was on a downward spiral when she lost her appetite for her gin and tonic. It was strange how during the last couple of years when her memory was going a bit she didn't always recognise me at first. But when I took Daisy she always remembered her straightaway. Or was she just trying to make me feel guilty for not visiting her a bit more often! Claire who by now was a qualified psychiatric nurse assured me it was the former. But I'll never be really sure; she knew how to make a point when she wanted to.

**

During this last chapter in my career I was able to implement one of the things I was most proud of. When RASC was first implemented the Training Team; which was a team of practical trainers who took trainees after they had completed their centrally delivered theory training, and prepared them for the real world; was removed. It was felt they didn't provide value for money. However without a Training Team it was a constant gripe from the Surveyors and the SOs that they were getting personnel who still needed training after they arrived in the Teams. And more importantly the fact that some of them would never be suitable to be Customs Officers. The trouble was once we had them, removing them by using the staff reporting system was lengthy, it took a matter of years, and was unreliable. It depended on the SO being prepared to take a lot of time and suffer a lot of grief, and naturally there were SO's who would, and SO's who wouldn't. As a consequence it was also inconsistent. My proposal to re-introduce the Training Team, with Alan Morris as the SO, was accepted as a good idea. But when I brought in a pass or fail element to it, much as managers generally welcomed the idea, nobody thought it would happen. I'm pleased to say that they were wrong. I had to go right out on a limb when it came to sending staff back whence they'd come. Fortunately for me, because the practical training was so good, it didn't happen very often. But when it did it was a real battle. The problem being that within the Civil Service it is deemed that if you are a Band 5 in one Department this means you are suitable to be a Band 5 in any other Department. This palpably isn't true. A Band 5 who is good at pushing bits of paper around in the Home Office won't necessarily be able to cope with the confrontation and stress a Band 5 in Detection has to deal with, and vice versa. I don't know of anywhere else in the Civil Service where this pass or fail element happens. I just hope my successor is as diligent in making sure this continues. If nothing else it sent out the message that the work we performed was, and is different from the rest of the Civil Service, not harder, not better, but different. It also told the officers that we "the Management" were not prepared to see them saddled with people who were only there to boost their overtime or their pensions.

Change was constant. I was now working on a group of the ten major airports in the EU trying to standardise the way we worked. I realised how difficult this was going to be when the Italian representative admitted that they had no formal training for their officers. They just paired them up with whoever was available. I seemed to be forever on a flight travelling from one EU Capital to another. John Whyte the Collector actually let me work on for a couple of months after my retirement to finish a benchmarking exercise that was intended to be the blue print for future EU Customs. It was good and constructive piece of work but without the ownership and direction it needs I doubt if it will ever come to be fully implemented; which is sad.

I was also working with Kerry Spendiff who had transferred in to gain operational experience. She was actually acting down, that is she was normally the equivalent of a DC but while she was at Heathrow she filled an AC position. Between us Stella, who was our manager, Kerrie, and I formed a very happy and effective management team. I think this was because none of us took ourselves too seriously. Kerry was very petite and had a cheery disposition that disguised a will of iron. I remember the first joint management meeting we held together. There was a lot of flak flying in my direction because I was increasing the size of the Alpha One roster. Nobody was losing any money and everybody was gaining more time to manage their Districts. Unfortunately as usual, old Bullhead hadn't taken enough time consulting. I had asked for suggestions and then I had bounced my own idea off of a couple of the group. Not receiving any objections I had steamed ahead with the implementation. I had then informed the group by e-mail. Every one of them thought I should have waited until they had all found the time to give me their opinions. They were undoubtedly right, and I duly apologised for the poor communications. However despite the fact that nobody had any real business related objections they wouldn't stop going on about it. Deep down the main objection was that they enjoyed doing Alpha One, and who can blame them, and under my proposal they would be doing less of them. Anyway I was obviously inclined to let them have their say, having been already found guilty of not allowing this to happen. However Kerry had had enough.

"That's it; you've had your say. You've had your apology. Nobody has an objection that makes any sense. We're moving on. What's the next item on the Agenda?" She said. Stunned silence, but move on we did.

There was also the occasion when we were filling two Surveyor posts. There was a displaced Surveyor available to fill one of the posts and normally this would be done automatically. There were however big questions about this persons suitability to carry out the Alpha One role. It was therefore decided to run a promotion exercise for both posts and the displaced Surveyor would compete with those looking for promotion. It should have been easy for a substantive Surveyor to meet the criteria. But this person didn't. Kerry, who was the Chairman of the Promotion Panel, offered the two posts to two promotees. She was going right out on a limb. The TUS were up in arms and the displaced Surveyor appealed to HQ. But Kerry stuck to her guns and refused to accept the person. It was like the trainees. If they're not fit to do the work then we won't take them whatever the Grade.

Then Alby Kiy re-appeared. Having worked all over the place since our days at London Port he ended working for Matt Sheridan as the Surveyor in charge of the Regional Task Force. As I said previously I was re-arranging the Alpha One roster at the time and I decided to increase the number of Surveyors. Alby was just the right person to be included in it. It was really good to see him around the place. It wasn't very often because he now lived at Ingatestone in Essex, and when he'd finished his Alpha One shift he had a long journey home. But now and again he would meet with Matt who had her office just down the corridor from me. Since we had last worked together on the Harpy Mobile, he had acquired a wife, Andy (short for Andrea), and a son and daughter, Robert and Gillian, but he was still the same Alby. Which is a shame but you can't have everything can you.

In March 2004 the then Chancellor, Gordon Brown, announced the merger of HM Customs and Excise, with Inland Revenue, to form a new Department, Her Majesty's Revenue and Customs (HMRC). Implementation date was April 2005. Life became manic. During this period I was assessed by a group doing a time and motion study of Senior Managers in the Civil Service. The idea was that I was observed for a whole day and I gave a sort of running commentary of what was going. I always started at 7 o'clock. At 8 o'clock the young lady observing me informed me that I had already carried the number of "actions" she would normally observe during a whole eight hour day. By actions, she meant taken a decision, delegated a bit of work, sent an instruction, communicated information to a person or persons. According to her I was working approximately eight times harder than was normal, and I wasn't the only one on our corridor that this applied to. Matt was always in sharp at seven along with me. And she was always there when I left at about 16.45.No wonder I and my colleagues were always feeling tired. It was all becoming a bit silly. The in tray was always so full and the deadlines became tighter and tighter, you could never do anything to your complete satisfaction. It was mayhem.

**

Almost at the same time Carol and I were invited to go and have tea with the Queen. It was a great day. The tea was served in bone china, the sandwiches had had their crusts removed, and the Queen was resplendent in a light green outfit which we agreed we had seen her wear before. Prince Charles was there and the Duke of Edinburgh; and about three thousand other people who had also been invited to tea. However the highlight of the day was a cameo performance by my Carol who was looking an absolute picture in an outfit bought especially for the occasion. Nothing previously worn for Mrs Nelson when she goes out for tea. I had been off filling up our plates with more salmon and cucumber sandwiches and when I returned Carol was looking rather quizzical.

"You know", she said, "I can never make up my mind if that's Carol Barnes or Jan Leeming". I looked at the person she was indicating and it was Jennie Bond the Royal reporter for the BBC.

"Actually it's Jennie Bond", said I.

Carol walked away laughing and laughing. Eventually she managed to tell me what had happened. Apparently she had been sitting next to Jennie Bond and her mum when she said to her;

"You know I'm never sure if you're Carol Barnes of Jan Leeming".

"No, a lot of people have that problem", said Jennie. Then she just carried on talking to her mum. Carol was still unsure who she was when I came along and enlightened her. I think that was probably one-nil to Ms Bond.

**

I'm often asked what was the most difficult situation I had to face as an AC. One situation stands out above all others and it wasn't work related. A young Officer, John Ferri, had returned from a holiday in Las Vegas. He was suffering with a viral infection and I was informed that he had actually been admitted to hospital. This was a bit unusual but John was a big guy with some respiratory problems so it wasn't a complete surprise. I then went on holiday. On the day I returned there was the normal mountain of mail, the normal hundreds, yes hundreds, of e-mails, and post-its all over the place. This despite the fact that someone had been sitting in for me during my two weeks away.

It was 07.10 and the phone rang. This was unusual. The reason I started at 07.00 was that I could get a lot of work done before the phone started ringing. The caller introduced themselves. It was Dorothy Watson the SO in charge of the Firearms team.

"Big John didn't make it", she said. I will never forget those five or six words.

John had slipped into unconsciousness and had never recovered. It was unbelievable. He was a young man with his whole life ahead of him. It was tragic.

It was to be a Service Funeral. Pall bearers in full uniform under the direction of Les Scriver, all carried out with military precision. I as John's AC would read the Eulogy on behalf of HM Customs and Excise. The service was held in St Ethelberts, Slough. John came from a large Italian family. Hundreds of Officers wanted to attend. The church, a very large church, was packed and some people had to stand outside. When I reached the pulpit and turned to deliver the Eulogy I was totally unprepared for what greeted me. John's mum and aunt had thrown themselves prostrate over the coffin and the whole of the front rows were totally consumed with grief. They were inconsolable. I have never seen so much human unhappiness in my entire working life and I hope I never do again. It was without doubt the most moving and unnerving moment in my career.

**

Back to the mayhem. My luck within my career held out to the end. Just when I was wondering how I could survive in this madhouse, suddenly from nowhere an early retirement package was on the table. It was too good an opportunity to miss.

**

8. Bowing out gracefully

During my last 5 years I spent a lot of time acting up on Temporary Promotion as Assistant Collector although I never quite managed to make it permanent. In all I acted up as AC, some people said quite unkindly that I had acted up my whole career, for over four years. I battled my way through several reorganisations and eventually became involved with the merger with HM Inland Revenue to form the new Her Majesties Revenue and Customs. I was having serious problems seeing how the two Departments would merge. The cultures were so different. HM Customs and Excise could only exist with by delegation and lashings of empowerment Whereas HM Inland Revenue didn't value either of these, its managers appeared to be shackled by its own management structure. One meeting I attended exemplified this. I met with three of my future colleagues to discuss the thorny problem of where to deposit Tax Returns if people were leaving the country and needed to make their Tax Return before they returned to this country. The Inland Revenue gave a commitment that people would always be able to deposit a Return at one of their offices. Consequently they felt that if we were all one Department we would be failing the public if they were unable to deposit their Returns at our offices. The main area they were worried about was passengers on their way out of the country. If they couldn't deposit their Returns they could be liable for charges while they were away. I told them how we would manage this intricate problem. Our officers would accept the returns and send them to a Central point. We would have a Helpline telephone number just in case there problems with the Return. It wasn't going to be difficult. Firstly I was asked how I could be sure this would happen throughout the UK. Quite simply John Whyte, my Collector had responsibility for Outward Baggage Control Points at Ports and Airports, and he delegated this to me as the Assistant Collector responsible. And I knew he would accept my recommendation. I also knew that it would be as simple as sending an e-mail to various responsible Surveyors throughout the Regions. If there were any issues that were show stoppers they would let me know. Pretty simple, but obviously too simple for the Inland Revenue. The three people, all substantively at Assistant Collector level, had to take it back to their bosses. The three bosses then had to meet and come to a collective decision. The meeting I attended was in May 2005. When I retired on 30 September that year I was still waiting for a decision. I have since been informed that since my retirement the system I proposed has been accepted and successfully implemented.

Then a piece of bureaucratic nonsense convinced me that my time was up, and that the Department I had known and loved for nearly 40 years was indeed gone. I was informed that my title was to be changed from Assistant Collector to Assistant Head of Region. Collector was a title that had survived since 1290 when it was first introduced by Edward the 1st, and a faceless individual who probably didn't understand its true meaning, had removed it at the stroke of a pen because it didn't quite fit with HMRC. No consultation, nothing. Although only a change of title, it was symbolic of the greater change.

HM Customs with its history, its excitement, its amazing characters, and its dynamism was gone forever. The Department that had nurtured the likes of Geoffrey Chaucer, Thomas Payne, and Rabbie Burns, and which had its beginnings as far back as 742 when Ethelbald King of Mercia introduced taxes, was gone.

And on 30 September 2005 so was I.

**

Ken Joy, Paul Dhand, and Alby taking it easy on board my lovely Silent Might

Last of the Summer Wine. From left to right, Ken Joy (Still fuming about the Rev R), Nick Fisher, author, Chak and Alby

From left to right Glen and Pauline Sankar, Charlotte, Stella, Chak, Alby and his wife Andrea, Keith and his partner Deana. This at my "surprise" 60th birthday party arranged by Claire, and paid for by Carol.

9. And afterwards.

Well amazingly the world didn't stop turning the day I left Customs. Not for me, not for them. In fact for a short while I was back and forth to the airport and to other European airports finishing off the EU Benchmarking project that I was involved in. Then I was contracted back on to a Review Team to try and solve the Red Channel problem, as I said previously I was the missing link and there simply wasn't anyone available to join it all up.

When I retired I was asked what would I do with all my time? Play golf, go up and down the Thames on my boat; a 34 foot motor cruiser by the name of Silent Might; and walk my dog, was my reply. How wrong I was. It all started off alright, except that I was forever getting under Carol's feet as she was still running her Travel business from home. Then in July 2007 Carol had a bad accident getting off of the boat. We were at Bray Marina and she was disembarking for the very last time; we were trading her in for a different boat; that's Silent Might we were trading in, not Carol; when she slipped and fell. No she hadn't had a drink. That's probably why it happened. She broke her left arm in three places just below the shoulder. She broke bones in her right foot and tore the ligaments in her right ankle. She was confined to a wheelchair for some months. The prognosis was that she would never be able to throw a rope again; the left arm would never be fully operative. Silent Might was sold with the idea that if she did recover enough we would buy another boat. It's strange but when we bought a boat our friends all placed bets on who would be the first to fall in, not the last. In fact I was the first, down at Henley, followed very quickly by Carol at midnight in the Marina. That time she had had a drink or two and I had to pull her out by the hair. But it wasn't only us who missed going on the boat. A certain Surveyor, who I won't name for political reasons, felt the Team Building events held on Silent Might were the best ever. And so did those members of his team who were still capable of speech by the end of them.

Then just as Carol was recovering I was told I needed a hip replacement, then the other hip, and then my right shoulder. The net result of this has been, no boating, no golf, and for a time very limited Daisy walking. For me the upside of these handicaps has been that I am unable to do any DIY. Carol always maintained that the only reason we moved house so often was because I hated decorating.

However during these disasters I was starting to put into practice something that Carol and I had discussed over the years. I became a public speaker and an after dinner speaker. To use the modern phraseology, I "re-invented" myself. The idea had originated when I was delivering a talk to BAA Security personnel when they were on their introduction training. After one particularly lively Q&A session one of their trainers enjoyed it so much he suggested that I should take up public speaking for a living. Then one day out of the blue Carol suggested the same thing and later suggested I should I try to lecture on cruises. Then while I was still mulling it over a friend of ours asked me if I would give a talk to a club she belonged to. The rest as they say is history. I now deliver 60 to 70 talks a year, and lecture on as many cruises as they will let me. My topic; "Forty Years Catching Smugglers". And I love it.

It's strange, although I've been away from it all for nearly five years you can never completely switch off. As they say you can take the man out of Customs but you can't take Customs out of the man. Last year on holiday we met a really nice couple and their two children. When we arrived they had been there ten days and had four days to go. When we left they were still there. First there was this reason, then that reason, then something else. They were always getting a flight the day after tomorrow. To me they were obviously waiting for something. They were keeping their children out of school. They weren't super rich. What could they be waiting for that would make them delay their return? We were in the Caribbean so there are a few alarm bells there. The same old thing "something wasn't quite right". In the end we flew back and they were still there. I couldn't help myself I called Glen Sankar and he passed it on to Gatwick where they were supposedly flying back to. I never heard if they were met. Perhaps they're still there.

Actually it's not just the humans who can't switch off. Lesley Husher; mentioned previously; adopted one of our retired drugs dogs. The first time her husband took it to their local inn the dog was all over one of the regulars. He had a quick word with the gentleman in question and this chap, who apparently had a small piece of cannabis in his jacket pocket, exited stage left. A week or so later the same thing happened again. This time the landlord barred him, the man that is not the dog, from the pub.

**

Forty years eh? Well 39 years and 7 months. And all because Walter George Nelson read the Daily Telegraph.

THE END

Glossary

AC	Assistant Collector
APO	Assistant Preventive Officer
AS	Anti-Smuggling
Assistant Officer	The equivalent of an APO prior to the Re-organisation of 1971/2
BA	British Airways
BAA	British Airports Authority. The owners of Heathrow Airport.
Bag full	Slang for a bag or suitcase that had nothing in it except drugs.
BEA	British European Airways
Ben Boat	A shipping line where every boat was named after a Scottish Mountain. Hence Ben Boat.
Blue Book	The ships record made out on a ships arrival from Foreign.
BOAC	British Overseas Airways Corporation.
Boarding.	Term used at Heathrow to indicate the work of clearing aircraft and their crew.
Boatswain	Pronounced Bosun. Senior hand in charge of all deck and maintenance on board.
Brightstar.	A type of torch. Especially for use on tankers because they are gas proof.

C104	Written declaration by a passenger when goods are in dispute.
C142	Crew declaration.
Carton	A pack of 200 cigarettes.
Caution.	The warning given to offenders prior to interview or on arrest.
Charter Mark	An accreditation awarded by the Cabinet Office to Government Departments that are deemed to have given excellent service
Christmas Tree	A ship with lots of easy seizures just waiting to be found.
Chaser/Chase the lady	A card game played extensively throughout London Port.
Ciggies	Cigarettes.
Charlotteberg.	A German brandy.
City boats	Ships belonging to the City Ellerman Line. All named after Cities.
Coke	Cocaine. Class A drug.
Codes	The Customs Codes or books of instruction and guidance.
Collector.	The head of a Customs region, previously called a Collection.

Compromise Penalty	An on the spot fine instead of going before a Magistrate
Cough	Admission of guilt.
Compromise Penalty.	The alternative offered to offenders in lieu of going before a Magistrate.
CPO	Chief Preventive Officer equivalent to HEO and SO.
CRO	Criminal Records Office. Abbreviation used to indicate person had been in jail.
Cutters	The Customs ships that spent their whole time patrolling the coasts of the UK.
DC	Deputy Collector
Definitions Book.	During my study for PO. The book I used to record definitions.
Deep rummage	Not easy, not in the cabins requiring a lot of hard work.
Detached Duty	When working away from the Port or Airport where you normally worked.
Donkeyman room.	A greaser who worked in the engine
Double Bottom Tanks	Oil tanks that are placed between the two hulls at the bottom of a ship.
DSO	Duty Senior Officer.
EMIT	Enzyme Multiplied Immunoassy Test

Fundador.	Spanish brandy.
Geest truck.	A very large trolley capable of carrying up to 30 suitcases.
Grievance	An official complaint where a member of staff felt they had been treated unfairly by a member of management.
Gunwales	Pronounced Gunnels. The upper edge of the side of a vessel.
Guv	Team leader.
Head Shop	A shop that sells drugs paraphernalia. Especially in the USA.
HEO	Higher Executive Officer, same as Senior Officer.
HQ	Headquarters.
Jacobs ladder	A ships ladder made of rope with wooden rungs.
Job	Seizure of goods, and offence.
Knocking Off	Situation where undeclared goods have been found and the offender is being dealt with i.e. offered the option.
Knuckle.	The point outside of a lock where ships tie up waiting to enter the lock.
KSF	King Size Filter
Light.	In respect of cargo ships the term indicates they have no cargo on board.

Little Red Book.	The thoughts of Chairman Mao and for many years their political bible.
Minder.	Slang for a person accompanying a drug smuggler but who has no drugs themselves.
Muggo	The docker's tea break.
M/v	Motor vessel
Networking	Using contacts to find out what's going on in other parts of the organisation.
Notice No 2	The notice that explained the Passenger Allowances
OAP	Old Aged pensioner.
Officer	The equivalent to a Preventive Officer after the Re-organisation of 1971/2
officer	Generic term used when referring Officers and Assistant Officers.
OGD's	A derogatory term to indicate officers who had come into Customs from Other Government Departments.
Openers.	A term used at the London Overseas mail Office to denote those packages that had been selected to be opened.
Other Goods Allowance.	The allowance for items other then the specific allowances.
Pea souper	Very thick fog.
Plastics.	OGD's.

Pink raffle tickets	The offender's copy of the R&R was pink. Hence "pink raffle ticket"
PO	Preventive Officer
Post it	A small piece of paper with a sticky edge used for short messages and reminders.
PRC	Peoples Republic of China.
PSD	Passsenger Services Division at Heathrow.
Restoration.	The money paid by an offender to reclaim seized goods.
Roads	Mooring site for ships before they came alongside or entered the dock.
R&R	Receipt and Receipt. The document issued when an offender elects to pay a compromise penalty.
Rubbed down.	Slang term for a body search without asking the person to remove all clothing.
Sear Instructions	Detailed instructions that applied to a particular office.
Seizure.	An offence situation.
Seizure King.	An Officer who was particularly good at making seizures.

Sandfly	A UK resident who spent the majority of their working lives working in the Middle East mainly in the oil fields.
Smoking mirrors.	A tern that indicates something isn't exactly what it appears to be.
SO	Senior Officer. The equivalent of a Higher Executive Officer or Chief Preventive Officer.
Sol y Sombre.	A Spanish Drink made up of brandy and anise.
SS	Steam Ship
Stag	To stag a ship; to lie in wait and watch to catch anyone coming off with excess or prohibited goods.
Swallower.	A person who has swallowed drugs in order to smuggle them into the UK.
T&DU	Training and Development Unit
Timber Deck Cargo	Cargoes of timber on the open deck.
The option	The alternative of paying a Compromise Penalty or going before a Magistrate.
Topsides.	Upper and open decks.
TP	Temporary Promotion
TUS	Trade Union
Waterguard	The uniform branch of HM Customs. Formed in 1809 and disbanded in 1971

| Wray and Nephew | Jamaican rum, normally white. |
| Zephyr | A large Ford car. No longer produced. |

ISBN#98-1-905553-67-9